DEACCESSIONED

D1072644

CATASTROPHE

CATASTROPHE

AN INVESTIGATION INTO
THE ORIGINS OF THE
MODERN WORLD

DAVID KEYS

BALLANTINE BOOKS · NEW YORK

A Ballantine Book
Published by The Ballantine Publishing Group

Copyright © 1999 by David Keys

All rights reserved under International and Pan-American
Copyright Conventions. Published in the United States by
The Ballantine Publishing Group, a division of Random House, Inc., New York.
Ballantine and colophon are registered trademarks of Random House, Inc.

Originally published in Great Britain by Century Books, Random House UK Ltd., in 1999.

www.randomhouse.com/BB/

Library of Congress Cataloging-in-Publication Data
Keys, David.
Catastrophe / David Keys.—1st ed.
p.   cm.
ISBN 0-345-40876-4 (alk. paper)
1. Climatic changes—History.   2. Human beings—Effect of environment on—History.
3. Natural disasters—History.   4. Weather—Effect of volcanic eruptions on.
5. Asteroids—Collisions with Earth.   I. Title.
QC981.8.C5K45   1999
551.6′09′02—dc21   99-14357
CIP

Text design by Ann Gold

Manufactured in the United States of America

First American Edition: February 2000

10   9   8   7   6   5   4   3

TO GRAÇA, MICHAEL,
AND CAMILE

CONTENTS

AIMS AND CAVEATS

The aim of this book is to help change people's view of the past—and of the future. Although human inventions, achievements, and actions are obviously key factors in determining the course of human history, the forces of nature and other mechanisms beyond the control of individual human beings, or even states, play an even greater role, both directly and indirectly, by conditioning the circumstances that induce, produce, or permit individual or collective human actions.

Determinist views of history have been out of favor now for several decades, and this book should rightly be seen as an attempt to reinstate respect for the basic concept of determinism—though not for the often simplistic nature of much past deterministic thinking.

In this book I will attempt to describe a process that could perhaps be labeled "evolved determinism." My research does suggest that a force of nature ultimately lay behind much of the change experienced by the world in the sixth and seventh centuries A.D. But it also shows that key aspects of change, while ultimately triggered by a force of nature, were finally delivered through a plethora of consequent ecological, political, epidemiological, economic, religious, demographic, and other mechanisms that interacted with each other for up to a hundred event-filled years before producing final, irreversible change.

Moreover, toward the end of this book I suggest what triggered the sixth-century climatic catastrophe. I am reasonably sure of my conclusions as to the type of event that set all the climatological and historical

dominoes falling. But, as you will see, I have also chanced my arm at pinpointing the event geographically. That is a more difficult task—and only
future geological and ice-core research will reveal whether all the circumstantial evidence I have gathered was indeed pointing toward the right
culprit.

Although the main title of this book is *Catastrophe*, that chiefly refers
to the natural trigger mechanism that set off the collapse of so many
dominoes and, through the medium of those dominoes, effected permanent historical change. This book does not attempt to deny in any way the
range of other factors which, over many centuries, helped in the downfall
of the ancient world. But I do believe that the final decisive factor in its
demise was the mid-sixth-century natural catastrophe described in this
book. And I do believe that that catastrophe was the only worldwide
common element involved in that demise. It is because of that fact that I
believe one can talk of semi-integrated world history even in the sixth and
seventh centuries A.D. The political repercussions of commonly caused
events in places as far apart as Mongolia and East Africa did interact with
each other to shape history: and civilizations in both the Old World and
the New were changed forever by a common catastrophe.

In many areas, these changes laid the geopolitical foundations of our
modern world. That's why I prefer—in geopolitical terms (not economic
or even cultural ones)—to use the term protomodern rather than early-
medieval when describing the sixth- and seventh-century emergence of
the post-ancient world. Moreover, I believe the evidence in, and the perspective argued for within, this book suggests that one can talk of a
sixth/seventh-century protomodern geopolitical genesis in many different
parts of the world—not just in Europe and the Middle East.

In order to help change people's view of history, I have tried to write
this book in as accessible a manner as possible. I have tried hard to make
sure that the data and other information on which I have based my arguments are as accurate and up-to-date as possible. Indeed, to ensure this, I
sought the help and advice of more than fifty academic specialists and
authorities in more than twenty different disciplines in a dozen countries.

I believe that the case for a mid-sixth-century worldwide climatic catastrophe is incontrovertible. And I think that, without doubt, the catastrophe was the major worldwide factor in finally bringing the ancient
world to a close, and helping to lay the geopolitical foundations of our
modern one. The mechanisms are clearest in Europe, the Middle East,
Africa, and Asia. In Mesoamerica, where archaeology rather than history

has to provide the bulk of the evidence, the argument is strong, but has by definition to be more circumstantial. And in South America, where there is no sixth/seventh-century written history at all, one is reliant on the relatively inexact dating and often hotly debated interpretation of purely archaeological evidence. Nevertheless I believe that even there, the evidence for a climatic catastrophe is incontrovertible and it is only the suggested mechanisms of change that remain reasonable proposals rather than totally proven theses.

Lastly, I believe that my book is not simply about the past and its influence on the present, but also, hopefully, illuminates the whole question of the influence of the natural environment in human history. This is particularly relevant now, as global warming threatens to destabilize our climate to an extent that has not occurred since the climatic crisis of the sixth century. Three-quarters of this book is about the repercussions of that Dark Age disaster—and it should serve to alert us to the sheer scale of the geopolitical and other changes that can flow from climatic catastrophe. History is usually seen predominantly as a discipline of the humanities. This book will help demonstrate that it also belongs to the realms of the natural and social sciences.

ACCENT NOTE
Accents have not been used in words that have been transliterated from non-Latin scripts.

ACKNOWLEDGMENTS

It took four years to research and write this book. Because it covers so many different disciplines—everything from epidemiology and astrophysics to volcanology and archaeology—I sought the often-detailed advice of dozens of academic specialists.

I am grateful to all of them for their depth of knowledge—and for their patience. I thank them for all the advice they gave me, most of which I accepted, and ask them to forgive me for the small number of instances in which, bemused by contrasting strands of counsel, I occasionally opted for one interpretation rather than another.

I am particularly indebted to Byzantinists Michael Whitby, Peter Llewellyn, Peter Sarris, Anna Leone, and Stephen Hill; Islamicists Hugh Kennedy and Patricia Crone; Yemen specialists Christian Robin, Ueli Brunner, and Iwona Gajda; Turkic specialist Peter Golden; Jewish history specialist Norman Golb; African archaeology specialist Mark Horton; Far East and/or Southeast Asia specialists Andreas Janousch, Scott Pearce, Richard Stephenson, Simon Kaner, Stanley Weinstein, Joan Piggott, Jonathan Best, Nancy Florida, Willem van der Molen, Roy E. Jordaan, and Eric Zürcher; Indian specialist Michael Mitchiner; historians, archaeologists, and others specializing in western Europe and/or the British Isles, Ian Wood, David King, John Hines, Barbara Yorke, Roger White, Ewan Campbell, Charles Thomas, Heinrich Härke, Daniel McCarthy, and Donnchadh O'Corrain; Arthurian literature specialist Elspeth Kennedy; Pre-Columbianists David Browne, Frank Meddens, Claude Chapdelaine, Bill

Isbell, Alan Kolata, Paul Goldstein, John Topic, Steve Bourget, Linda Manzanilla, Michael Spence, George Cowgill, Esther Pasztory, Izumi Shimada, Simon Martin, Michael Moseley, AnnCorinne Fretter, Bob Birmingham, and Rebecca Storey; Dendrochronologists Mike Baillie, Keith Briffa, Jeffrey Dean, Pepe Boninsegna, and Ricardo Villalba; lake sediment specialists Alex Chepstow-Lusty and Mark Brenner; volcanologists Ken Wohletz, Alain Gourgaud, Clive Oppenheimer, Tom Simkin, and Jerry Sukhyar; epidemiologists Ken Gage and Susan Young; ice-core specialists Claus Hammer, Henrik Clausen, and Lonnie Thompson; astronomer Alan Fitzsimmons; locust experts Nick Jago and Jane Rosenberg; geneticist David Goldstein; zoologist Frank Wheeler; grazing ecologist John Milne; late Roman ivory experts Tony Cutler and David Whitehouse; and low-frequency atmospheric sound transmission specialist Rod Whitaker.

I apologize to anyone I have inadvertently left off this list; and I must also point out that the responsibility for the views expressed in this book is of course mine alone.

I would also like to acknowledge the four academics who first realized that there had been a climatic disaster in the mid–sixth century—Richard Stothers and Michael Rampino, who published some of the Roman historical evidence in a paper in the *Journal of Geophysical Research* 88 in 1983; Kevin Pang, whose work on the Chinese records of the catastrophe was reported in *Science News* 127 in 1985; and Mike Baillie, who first noticed the tree ring evidence for the disaster and published it in *Nature* 332 in March 1988, and—together with the Roman and Chinese historical evidence—in *Archaeology Ireland* in summer 1988. Indeed I first heard about the climatic events of the mid–sixth century at a lecture given by Mike Baillie at an archaeology conference in Bradford in April 1994.

I want also to give special thanks to my agent Bill Hamilton; to Barbara Basham, who did so much of the typing; Julian Saul, who drew most of the diagrams and maps; meteorological library assistant Barbara deCrausaz; Kate Brundrett, who did additional work on many of the graphics; Andrew Rafferty, who took the photograph used to produce the cover; my publisher, Mark Booth; my managing editor, Liz Rowlinson; my copy editor, Roderick Brown; the cover designer, Arvin Budhu; the proofreader, Jane Selley; the indexer, Ann Hall; the typesetter, Peter Brealey; copyright clearance assistant Paul Rodger; and my wife, Graça, for doing the massive quantity of administrative work generated by the writing and researching of the book and for helping to research and produce many of the maps. But above all I want to thank Graça and our two children, Michael and Camile, for their unbounded patience and tolerance over these past four years—and my late parents and grandmother, whose influence over the decades helped me develop and sustain an appreciation of our world and its story.

Last but not least, I would like to thank a rural Victorian whom I never met but who first created my interest in human history—the anonymous man, woman, or child who, a century or so ago, in a field west of London, dropped a humble penny—a coin that I found when I was a child and which triggered my fascination with the vanished past and how it has created the present and will help create the future.

David Keys
March 1999

LIST OF ILLUSTRATIONS

CATASTROPHE

INTRODUCTION: FIFTEEN CENTURIES AGO, SOMETHING HAPPENED

In A.D. 535–536 mankind was hit by one of the greatest natural disasters ever to occur. It blotted out much of the light and heat of the sun for eighteen months, and the climate of the entire planet began to spin out of control. The result, direct or indirect, was climatic chaos, famine, migration, war, and massive political change on virtually every continent.

As the engine for extraordinary intraregional change in four great areas of the world—Afro-Eurasia (from Mongolia to Britain, from Scandinavia to southern Africa), the Far East (China, Korea, Japan), Mesoamerica (Mexico/Central America), and South America—the disaster altered world history dramatically and permanently.

The hundred-year period after it occurred is the heart of history's so-called Dark Ages, which formed the painful and often violent interface between the ancient and protomodern worlds. That period witnessed the final end of the supercities of the ancient world; the end of ancient Persia; the transmutation of the Roman Empire into the Byzantine Empire; the end of ancient South Arabian civilization; the end of Catholicism's greatest rival, Arian Christianity; the collapse of the greatest ancient civilization in the New World, the metropolis state of Teotihuacan; the fall from power of the great Maya city of Tikal; and the fall of the enigmatic Nasca civilization of South America.

But it was also the hundred-year period that witnessed the birth, or in some cases the conception, of Islam, France, Spain, England, Ireland,

3

Japan, Korea, Indonesia, Cambodia, and the power of the Turks. It also produced a united China and the first great South American empires, the forerunners of the Incas.

Until now, these geographically widely dispersed tragedies and new beginnings—occurring well before the Old and New Worlds knew of each other—have been viewed by historians as largely separate events. Now, for the first time—as a result of the research done for this book—the origins of our modern world can be seen as an integrated whole, linked by a common causal factor.

This climatic disaster half destroyed the Roman Empire, unleashing hordes of central Asian barbarians against the empire's northern borders, triggering geopolitical processes that created Arab pressures on its southern flank, and causing a series of killer epidemics that drastically reduced its population.

In Arabia and the Mediterranean world as a whole, an apocalyptic zeitgeist, which at base was the result of the shift in climate, led to the emergence of Islam.

In western Europe, the climatic catastrophe and its epidemiological aftereffects destabilized the demographic and political status quo and led to the birth of at least four major nations.

In western Asia, the disaster triggered the rise of the Turks—a process that eventually led to an expansion of Turkic influence everywhere from India to eastern Europe and ultimately to the emergence of the Ottoman Empire.

The same worldwide climatic chaos also destabilized economies and political systems in many areas of the Far East, opening up the way for the reunification of China, the birth of a united Korea, and the emergence of Japan as an embryonic nation-state.

In the New World, a popular revolution was triggered that destroyed the greatest of all ancient American civilizations, the Mexican empire of Teotihuacan. That collapse freed up the Mesoamerican world and led to the rapid growth, and consequent collapse, of much of Maya civilization. In Peru, power shifted from the arid lowlands to the wetter, mountainous Andes, which paved the way, centuries later, for the rise of pre-Columbian America's largest empire.

The mystery climatic disaster of 535–536 resynchronized world history.

The contemporary Roman historian Procopius wrote of the climate changes as "a most dread portent." In describing the climate in that year, Procopius wrote that "the sun gave forth its light without brightness like the moon during this whole year." Other accounts of the event say that the sun became "dim" or "dark" for up to eighteen months. Its light shone "like a feeble shadow," and people were terrified that the sun would never shine properly again. In some parts of the empire, there were agricultural failures and famines.

In Britain, the period 535–555 saw the worst weather that century. In Mesopotamia there were heavy falls of snow and "distress among men." In Arabia there was famine followed by flooding.

In China in 536 there was drought and famine, and "yellow dust rained down like snow." The following year, the crops were ruined again—this time by snow in the middle of August. In Japan, the emperor issued an unprecedented edict, saying that "yellow gold and ten thousand strings of cash [money] cannot cure hunger" and that wealth was of no use if a man was "starving of cold." In Korea, 535 and 536 were the worst years of that century in climatic terms, with massive storms and flooding followed by drought.

In the Americas, the pattern was similar. Starting in the 530s, a horrific thirty-two-year-long drought devastated parts of South America. In North America, an analysis of ancient tree-ring evidence from what is now the western region of the United States has shown that some trees there virtually stopped growing in the years 536 and 542–543, and that things did not return to normal until some twenty-three years later, in 559. Similar tree-ring evidence from Scandinavia and western Europe also reveals a huge reduction in tree growth in the years 536–542, not recovering fully until the 550s.

Up until now, there has been no explanation for such extraordinary climatic deterioration. Certainly the dimming of the sun (without doubt caused by some sort of atmospheric pollution) and the sudden worldwide nature of this deterioration point toward a massive explosion in which millions of tons of dust and naturally occurring chemicals were hurled into the atmosphere.

But what was the nature of that explosion?

I believe that I have discovered what happened so many centuries ago—and, toward the end of this book, I make my case for proving exactly what this staggering disaster was. Before you reach that portion of the book, however, you will see, in substantial detail, the effect that event had on the entire world that existed then—and how an ancient tragedy shaped the world in which we live today.

In doing the research for this book, I have developed a greatly increased respect for the forces of nature and their power to change history. That respect, as well as the new perspective it engenders, has changed my view of the very nature of history, which must be understood in holistic terms and which really functions as an integrated, planetwide phenomenon.

If I have done my job well, what you are about to read is an analysis of the mechanisms and repercussions of catastrophe, a hitherto unknown explanation of our history, and a chilling warning for the future.

PART ONE
THE PLAGUE

1

THE WINEPRESS OF
THE WRATH OF GOD

"With some people it began in the head, made the eyes bloody and the face swollen, descended to the throat and then removed them from Mankind. With others, there was a flowing of the bowels. Some came out in buboes [pus-filled swellings] which gave rise to great fevers, and they would die two or three days later with their minds in the same state as those who had suffered nothing and with their bodies still robust. Others lost their senses before dying. Malignant pustules erupted and did away with them. Sometimes people were afflicted once or twice and then recovered, only to fall victim a third time and then succumb."[1]

Thus wrote the sixth-century church historian Evagrius, describing the gruesome symptoms of the bubonic plague, which devastated the Roman Empire and much of the wider world between the middle of the sixth century and the latter part of the seventh.

The first area of the empire to be hit by plague was Egypt. The town where it first appeared was the Mediterranean port of Pelusium—traditionally the point of entry for Egypt's enemies for over a thousand years. Persians, Syrians, Romans, and Greeks—even Alexander the Great himself—had invaded Egypt through it. But this time the enemy was not proudly clad in armor. It was invisible, carried ashore on the backs of scuttling rats. It had arrived in Pelusium from the south via the Red Sea and the Roman equivalent of the Suez Canal—a waterway built by the emperor Trajan more than four centuries earlier to help link the Indian Ocean with the Mediterranean.

After devastating Pelusium, the disease quickly spread to Alexandria, then on to Constantinople and the empire as a whole. Up to a third of the empire's population died in the first massive outbreak, and in the capital, more than 50 percent of the inhabitants are thought to have perished.[2]

"God's wrath turned into, as it were, a wine-press and pitilessly trampled and squeezed the inhabitants [of many cities] like fine grapes," wrote another eyewitness of the catastrophe, the hagiographer and historian John of Ephesus, in a moving and vivid account of the horror unleashed by the epidemic.

There were "homes, large and small, beautiful and desirable, which suddenly became tombs for the inhabitants and in which servants and masters at the same time suddenly fell [dead], mingling their rottenness together in their bedrooms."[3]

Everywhere one looked were "corpses which split open and rotted on the streets with nobody to bury [them]." There were those "who perished falling in the streets to become a terrible and shocking spectacle for those who saw them, as their bellies were swollen and their mouths wide open, throwing up pus like torrents, their eyes inflamed and their hands stretched out upward, and [over] the corpses, rotting and lying in corners and streets and in the porches of courtyards and in the churches." There were "ships in the midst of the sea whose sailors were suddenly attacked by [God's] wrath and [the ships] became tombs adrift on the waves."

John tried to flee from the plague, but no matter where he went, the epidemic caught up with him. In the end, there was nowhere else to run to. On his journeys, after trying in vain to find a safe haven, he witnessed the ferocity with which the plague devastated the countryside just as much as the cities.

"Day by day, we too—like everybody—knocked at the gate of the tomb [literally, "on death's door"]. If it was evening, we thought that death would come upon us in the night, and again if morning had broken, our face was turned the whole day towards the tomb [i.e., "toward thoughts of death"]."

On the journey "we saw desolate and groaning villages and corpses spread out on the earth; staging posts on the roads full of darkness and solitude filling with fright everyone who happened to enter and leave them." And "cattle abandoned and roaming scattered over the mountains with nobody to gather them."

He saw fields "abundant in grain which was becoming white and stood erect" yet had no one "to reap or gather it in." And he observed "flocks of sheep, goats, oxen and pigs which had become like wild animals, having forgotten [life in] a cultivated land and the human voice which used to lead them."

In Constantinople, John recorded in considerable detail the scale of the catastrophe. "When this scourge weighed heavy upon this city, first it eagerly began [to assault] the class of the poor, who lay in the streets.

"It happened that 5,000 and 7,000, or even 12,000 and as many as 16,000 of them departed [this world] in a single day. Since thus far it was [only] the beginning, men [i.e., government officials] were standing by the harbours, at the cross-roads and at the [city] gates counting the dead.

"Thus the [people of Constantinople] reached the point of disappearing, only a few remaining, whereas [of] those only who had died on the streets—if anybody wants us to name their number, for in fact they were counted—over 300,000 were taken off the streets. Those [officials] who counted having reached [the number of] 230,000 and seeing that [the dead] were innumerable, gave up [reckoning] and from then on [the corpses] were brought out without being counted."

The authorities quickly ran out of burial places. "The city stank with corpses as there were neither litters nor diggers, and corpses were heaped up in the streets." Some victims would take days to die. Others became ill and died within minutes.

"In some cases, as people were looking on each other and talking, they [began to] totter and fell either in the streets or at home. It might happen that a person was sitting at work on his craft, holding his tools in his hands and working and he would totter to the side and his soul would escape.

"It might happen that [a person] went out to market to buy necessities and while he was standing and talking or counting his change, suddenly the end would overcome the buyer here and the seller there, the merchandise remaining in the middle with the payment for it, without there being either buyer or seller to pick it up.

"And in all ways, everything was brought to nought, was destroyed and turned into sorrow alone and funeral lamentations. The entire city then came to a standstill as if it had perished, so that its food supply stopped."

At first, when burial space ran out, the dead were buried at sea. Vast numbers of corpses were taken to the seashore. "There, boats were filled with them and during each sailing, they were thrown overboard and the ships returned to take other [corpses].

"Standing on the seashore one could see litters colliding with each other and coming back to carry and to throw upon the earth two or three [corpses] to go back again and to bring [further corpses]. Others carried [the corpses] on boards and carrying-poles, bringing and piling [them] up one upon another. For other corpses, since they had rotted and putrefied, matting was sewn together. People bore them on carrying-poles and coming [to the shore] threw them [down] with pus running out of them."

Thousands of corpses "piled up on the entire seashore, like flotsam on great rivers, and the pus flowed, discharging itself down into the sea." Even with the ships busy dumping their macabre cargoes at sea, it was proving impossible to clear the backlog of dead bodies.

The emperor, Justinian, therefore decided on a new corpse-disposal strategy—the creation of giant mass graves, each capable of accommodating seventy thousand individuals. The high official who was given the gruesome task of organizing the scheme was one of the emperor's *referendarii* (top civil servants), a man by the name of Theodore. The emperor "gave him instructions to take and spend as much gold as should be necessary."

Theodore arranged for the mass graves to be dug on a hill, immediately north of the city, on the other side of the Golden Horn waterway. "He took along many people, [and] gave them much gold" to dig the pits and start burying the dead. "He placed there [some] men who brought down and turned over [the corpses], piled them up and pressed the layers one upon another as a man might heap up hay in a stack.

"Also [Theodore] placed by the pits men holding gold and encouraging the workmen and the common people with gifts to carry and to bring up [corpses], giving five, six and even seven and ten dinars for each load. While men stood below [in the pits], deep as in an abyss, and others above, the latter dragged and threw down [the corpses], like stones being thrown from a sling, and the former grabbed and threw them one on top of another, arranging the rows in alternate directions.

"Because of scarcity [of room] both men and women were trodden upon, young people and children were pressed together, trodden upon by feet and trampled like spoiled grapes. Then again from above [other corpses] were thrown head downwards and went down and split asunder beneath, noble men and women, old men and women, youths and virgins, young girls and babies.

"Whole peoples and kingdoms, territories and regions and power-ful cities were seized [by the plague]. Thus, when I [John of Ephesus], a wretch, wanted to include these matters in a record of history, my thoughts were seized many times by stupor, and for many reasons I planned to omit it, firstly because all mouths and tongues are insufficient to relate it, and moreover, because even if there could be found such that would record [at least] a little from among the multitude [of matters], what use would it be, when the entire world was tottering and reaching its dissolution and the length of generations was cut short? And for whom would he who wrote be writing?

"[But] then I thought that it was right that, through our writings, we should inform our successors and transmit to them [at least] a little from among the multitude [of matters] concerning [God's] chastisement [of us]. Perhaps [during] the remainder of world [history] which will come after us, they will fear and shake because of the terrible scourge with which we were lashed through our transgressions and become wiser through the chastisement of us wretches and be saved from [God's] wrath here [in this world] and from future torment."

John was describing the epidemic of 541–543—the first visitation of the plague. But the full social and political impact of the disease lay in its re-morseless habit of returning to claim the lives of those it had previously spared.

The church historian Evagrius lived through four great plague epi-demics and lost most of his family to them. In the year 593, at the age of fifty-eight, he wrote down his memories in a very personal lamentation.

"I believe no part of the human race to have been unafflicted by the disease," for it occurred in some cities "to such an extent that they were rendered empty of almost all their inhabitants." Evagrius regarded it as his responsibility to describe these events, as he was present at the begin-ning of the spread of the bubonic plague, and was struck by it while still a schoolboy.

"And during the course of the various visitations, I lost to the disease many of my children and my wife and much of the rest of my kin . . . For now, as I write this, I am 58 years old and it is not quite two years since the fourth outbreak of plague struck Antioch and I lost my daughter and the son born to her in addition to those [I lost] earlier.

"The means by which one contracted this disease were diverse and beyond telling. For some perished just through association and living together, others by physical contact, or by being in the same house, or even [through contact in] the market-place. Some people had escaped infected cities and themselves remained well, but passed on the disease to those who were not sick. There were those who remained entirely unaffected, even though they lived with many of the afflicted, in fact coming into contact not only with many sufferers but also with the dead. Others positively embraced death on account of the total loss of their children and family, and for this reason went cheek-by-jowl with the sick, but still were not struck down, as if the disease resisted their will."

Many historians have tended to see the plague pandemic that devastated so much of the world in the sixth and seventh centuries as consisting of a series of distinct outbreaks. Some church historians and others who were alive at the time even saw it that way, but they were often looking at the catastrophe from the vantage point of the large cities where they lived—places such as Constantinople, Antioch, and Alexandria.

In reality, both the major plague epidemics and the less extensive outbreaks should be regarded as one integrated event, albeit a very long one, which lasted for between 180 and 210 years. Rather than looking at the records of simply the most prolific contemporary historians, it is vital to trawl through a wider number of sources to find even the smallest reference to plague.

Historians have found that there were *dozens* of outbreaks over the years from 541 to 717, and perhaps even as late as 745.[4] And those are just the epidemics and outbreaks that are recorded. From c. A.D. 600 onward, there appears to be a reduction in the frequency of plague outbreaks in the Roman Empire, but this may simply be a function of the paucity of sources from the seventh century. Indeed, probably only a small percentage of the outbreaks were ever recorded, and of those records that were made, only an even smaller percentage have survived to the present day. These records are best for the eastern Mediterranean region and for western Europe; the pandemic also affected, though not initially, China and Persia. Yemen was almost certainly hit by some time in the 540s. And then there are vast areas—such as Africa or central Europe—that no doubt were affected but for which virtually no written records exist.

The plague passed from rat to human, sometimes from human to human, hardly pausing on its unpredictable journeys. Everywhere it rampaged, it must have substantially reduced population levels, thus creating

THE DARK AGE PLAGUE: A CHRONOLOGY

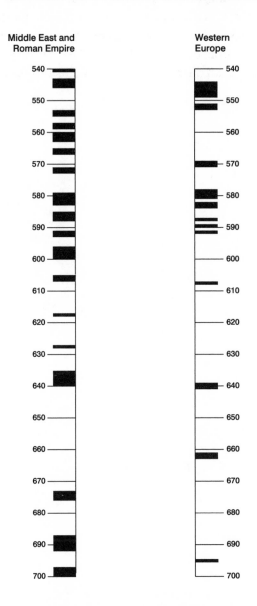

Middle East and Roman Empire

Western Europe

The horizontal black marks indicate those years or groups of years in which plague is recorded as having raged in some part of the Roman Empire, Middle East, or Western Europe.

vast tracts of abandoned agricultural land.[5] Sometimes it would spread to myriad towns[6] and villages in a single year, while on other occasions it would bide its time, skulking in a few quiet or remote localities, only to burst forth from these nameless havens of death a few years later. Indeed, it is likely that at no time between 541 and c. 750 was the plague ever entirely absent from the Mediterranean region and its various hinterlands.

2

THE ORIGINS OF
THE PLAGUE

Twenty-five days' sailing time down the east coast of Africa, one arrives at a "metropolis" called Rhapta.[1] This information, recorded by the second-century A.D. Greek geographer Ptolemy, is the last-known contemporary reference to a now long-lost African city that once flourished somewhere along the coastline of what is now Kenya and Tanzania.[2]

The only other reference—in a first-century A.D. pilots' manual called *The Periplus of the Erythraean Sea*—says Rhapta was a source for "great quantities of ivory and tortoiseshell" and was inhabited by "very big bodied men."[3] The metropolis was located on a river "not far from the sea"[4] and was also involved in the export of "rhinoceros horn, and a little nautilus shell" and the importation of glass beads and iron goods, especially "axes, knives and small awls."[5]

According to *The Periplus*, written around A.D. 40, the place was at least nominally under the control of Arab merchants from Yemen. It appears that these merchants intermarried with local women, gave gifts of wine and grain to the local chiefs, and had royal Yemeni approval to exact tribute from the area.

From *The Periplus* and Ptolemy, it is clear that Rhapta was the most remote—and the largest—of four ancient East African trading ports, from north to south: Opone (now known as Ras Hafun, in Somalia), Essina and Toniki (both near modern Barawa in Somalia), and Rhapta itself.

Opone—spectacularly sited on what is essentially an island linked to the coast by a thirty-mile-long sandbar—may have had several hundred inhabitants, covered up to five acres, and appears to have been abandoned some time in the mid–sixth century A.D. The latest pottery found by archaeologists on the site dates from the fifth or early sixth century. Up till that time, it seems to have acted as a transshipment point for Mediterranean, African, and Indian trade goods.

The other three ports, Essina, Toniki, and Rhapta, have never been archaeologically detected—probably because, like Opone, they never made it into the medieval period. Certainly an examination of the twenty-two pre-eleventh-century settlement and trading sites on the East African coast that have been archaeologically investigated shows that nineteen started functioning only between the seventh and ninth centuries A.D., two may possibly have started up before the sixth century, and only one definitely came into existence before the sixth. That strongly suggests severe settlement discontinuity in the sixth century. What is more, throughout East Africa, the pottery type abruptly changes at exactly the same time. Before the sixth century it is all early Iron Age (Kwale ware), while after the sixth century it is all late Iron Age (Tana ware). There was also a move in some areas at the same time from a concentration on agriculture to a more pastoral economy.[6]

The sixth century was a great watershed in East African history—a period of very rapid change and probably decline, in which the key ports simply ceased to exist and the agricultural economy shrank. The culprit was almost certainly plague—the same epidemic that devastated Europe and the Near East in that same fateful century.[7] Indeed, it was most likely from an ancient East African wild-animal reservoir of plague that the disease broke out to infect so much of the late antique world.

Historically, there have been several major natural plague reservoirs in which the disease circulated harmlessly among specific high-immunity wild animals. These areas—the Himalayas, Central/East Africa, and the central Asian steppes—have been the ultimate sources for the plague epidemics that have hit Europe and elsewhere over the centuries.[8]

Evidence that the sixth-century pandemic originated in Africa rather than Asia is very clear.[9] First of all, the major Asian high-population region, China, did not become infected until half a century after the Mediterranean region had suffered its first visitation. Indeed, China was infected from the Mediterranean region via the Middle East. Certainly the major Middle Eastern power, Persia, was infected only after the disease had hit the Roman Empire. The Persians apparently contracted it from

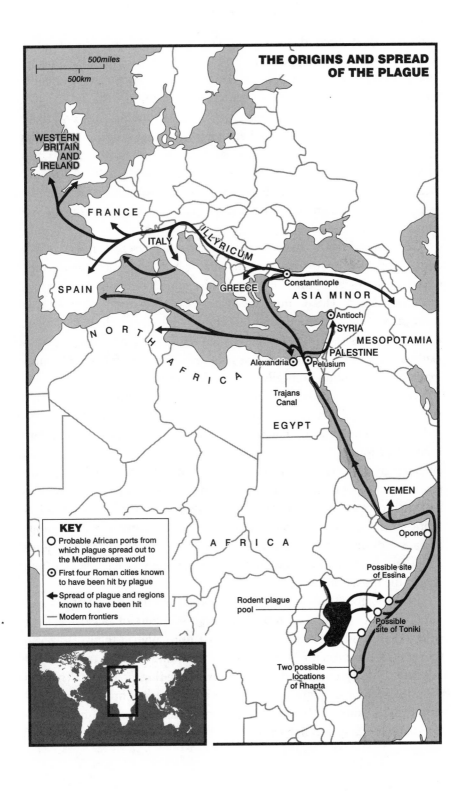

THE ORIGINS AND SPREAD
OF THE PLAGUE

500miles
500km

WESTERN
BRITAIN
AND
IRELAND

FRANCE

ITALY

ILLYRICUM

SPAIN

GREECE

Constantinople

ASIA MINOR

Antioch

SYRIA

MESOPOTAMIA

PALESTINE

NORTH

AFRICA

Alexandria

Pelusium

Trajans
Canal

EGYPT

YEMEN

Opone

AFRICA

Possible site
of Essina

Rodent plague
pool

Possible
site of Toniki

Two possible
locations
of Rhapta

KEY

○ Probable African ports from
which plague spread out to
the Mediterranean world

◉ First four Roman cities known
to have been hit by plague

◄— Spread of plague and regions
known to have been hit

— Modern frontiers

Roman soldiers. Second, there is no evidence of plague being endemic on the central Asian steppes prior to the later medieval period. Third, a major contemporary source, the Syrian-born historian Evagrius, actually recorded that the epidemic came from Africa ("Aethiopea").

As already described, the first town in the Mediterranean world to be hit was the port of Pelusium, where, after transiting the Roman world's equivalent of the Suez Canal, cargo originating in the Red Sea area and in Africa was unloaded for transshipment to the rest of the Roman world. What's more, Yemen—halfway between East Africa and the Mediterranean— seems to have been an early victim of the plague, being hit by the disease sometime in the 540s.[10]

But why did the plague break out of its animal reservoir in East Africa at that particular time?[11] The answer is prosaic in the extreme—the weather.

Modern research on surviving wild-animal reservoirs of plague— monitored by the U.S. Centers for Disease Control—has concluded that most plague outbreaks are caused by sudden and severe climatic change. Massively excessive rainfall is the most likely cause of plague spread, especially if it follows a drought, although a severe drought followed by normal weather could theoretically also spark an outbreak.

When there is excessive rainfall, vegetation growth increases. Thus there is more food available for herbivorous animals and insects, and rodents—including those that are carriers of the plague bacterium but are themselves immune to it—therefore breed more. Their larger numbers enable a greater survival rate vis-à-vis the slower-breeding predators who feed off the rodents, and a rodent breeding explosion occurs. In order to find their own foraging territory, the cumulative range of the rodents has to increase, and a virtual bow wave of these plague-carrying wild animals spreads inexorably outward over a period of months. Soon the creatures come into contact with other normally plague-free rodents, which then spread the disease to humans.

In the slightly less likely, though theoretically feasible, drought scenario, lack of rainfall and food kills huge numbers of plague-carrying wild rodents and the larger predators that normally eat them. However, the minute the drought is over, the fast-breeding rodents recover their numbers quickly compared to the slower-breeding predators. There is then, for a few years, a great imbalance between hunter and hunted in favor of the hunted. A breeding explosion takes place and the plague-infested rodents spread like wildfire.

However, the most dramatic scenario of all is one in which a severe drought is followed by significantly increased rainfall. That, or something very much like it, is almost certainly what took place in East Africa during the worldwide climatic chaos of the 530s.

While weather was without doubt the motor that drove the spread of plague in East Africa, the key vector was the humble flea. Although the rodents were immune to plague, the fleas that lived on them were not. Fleas die of plague—but it's actually the process of dying itself that helps them spread the disease.

As a flea becomes ill, and under specific climatic conditions, part of its gut becomes blocked by a mixture of multiplying plague bacteria and clotted blood.[12] The flea then begins to starve, and becomes so ravenous that it will jump onto virtually anything that moves, irrespective of whether it is its normal host species or not. Of course, the flea's hunger will not be satisfied, because its gut is blocked. So it will move rapidly from host to host, biting each one—and consequently spreading plague—in an impossible mission to quell its hunger.[13] The disease itself thus produces the very mechanism for its own spread.

The species in East Africa that were probably the reservoirs for the disease were gerbils and multimammate mice. The sandy-colored gerbil normally has two litters (totaling ten offspring) per year. Gerbils are very territorial, and an individual will travel two to three miles per season in search of an area it can control as its own exclusive territory. Thus in optimal food conditions, when gerbil numbers increased, the need of each gerbil to find its own territory would have resulted in a wave of plague-carrying individuals spreading outward at substantial speed.

The multimammate mouse—a dark brown rodent about the size of a golden hamster—lives in colonies consisting of up to fifty individuals. Their gestation time is twenty-three days, and they have two litters per year. Normally they have only five offspring per litter, but when there is optimal food availability, the number can treble to fifteen. A pair can produce over a thousand descendants in a year. Today they are still a principal wild host of plague in Africa.

It is likely that the gerbils and multimammate mice then passed the disease to a ratlike creature in the genus *Arvicanthus*. The latter would not have been immune to plague, but in appropriate climatic conditions would have outbred even the multimammate mouse: In wet weather it can achieve densities of up to a hundred per acre, and it and its offspring

FROM GERBIL TO DISASTER
How the plague traveled to Europe

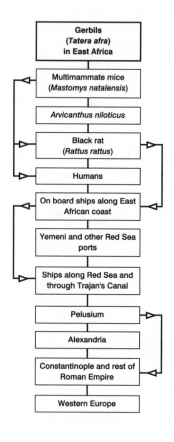

can produce thousands of new individuals per year. Neither the multi-mammate mouse nor *Arvicanthus* is averse to invading human settlements, and would therefore have come into direct contact with nonimmune *Rattus rattus*—the black rat, a species that specializes in infesting human environments, including farms, storehouses, houses, villages, towns, markets, ports, and ships.

In good climatic conditions, one pair of black rats (also known as house rats and ship rats) can produce thousands of descendants each year, especially if their slower-breeding predators are rarer than normal (due to, say, a recent drought). The species is aggressive, highly adaptive, and able to eat virtually anything—insects, seeds, meat, bones, fruit, even each other!

Once the starving fleas had jumped in their billions from gerbil and multimammate to *Arvicanthus* and on to the black rat, it would have been only a matter of days, even hours, before the first humans started contracting the plague.[14]

Transported by ships from port to port, *Rattus rattus* carried the plague bacterium from community to community. The archaeological evidence suggests that as the disease rolled northward up the Red Sea to Egypt, in its wake a whole way of life collapsed in East Africa and probably in southern Africa as well. The metropolis of Rhapta was inhabited by early Iron Age Bantu people, and the other ports of Opone, Essina, and Toniki were probably inhabited by late Neolithic Cushites, or possibly early Iron Age Bantu people.[15] At the time of the plague, as already noted, these ports seem to have virtually disappeared. Apart from Opone, their precise locations are not even known.

Inland, Bantu agriculture seems to have declined, and the Bantu appear to have rapidly and increasingly adopted from the Cushites both the latter's cattle-based pastoral economy and their particular style of pottery. In the seventh century (i.e., after the plague had started), this cattle-based pastoral tradition began to spread south and supplant cereal growing all over southern Africa.

Two questions remain, however. How did the plague give an advantage to pastoralism (a livestock-based economy) over agriculture (a crop-based economy)? The answer lies in the number of rats and other plague-carrying rodents attracted to the two different economic systems. Food crops—whether in fields or in storage—attract rats. Food sources on four legs—in this case, cattle—do not. It was this difference that appears to have given pastoralism an advantage over agriculture at this critical time.

The second question is, what were ships carrying between East Africa and the Roman Empire? Ivory was one of the most valuable commodities needed by the empire. Demand for magnificent ivory chairs, exquisite ivory children's toys for the rich, ivory writing tablets, religious relic boxes, and countless other ivory works of art had generated a trading system that no doubt stretched deep into Africa. Well before the sixth century, the elephants of Eritrea, on the Red Sea—used in antiquity as beasts of war— had all been hunted to extinction. So East Africa (modern Kenya and Tanzania) became virtually the only source for the vast quantities of ivory the Roman Empire desired.

Up until the plague and its destruction of the East African ports, the Roman Empire imported up to 50 tons of ivory every year from East Africa. This level of ivory trade necessitated the killing of up to five thousand elephants a year. In terms of cash, the merchandise was worth up to 220,000 gold *solidi* (equivalent to around $400 million today) to the Arab and Greek merchants who controlled the trade.[16]

In East Africa, the trade sustained not only a series of ports but also a series of coastal chieftaincies, which must have exercised disproportionate amounts of local power through the trade goods and imported weaponry at their disposal. After the plague had substantially reduced the population and destroyed the ports, the ivory trade virtually ceased.

Between the year 400 and the eve of the plague (c. 540), of the estimated 400,000 major ivory artworks made, some 120 survive; from the period 540 to 700, only 6 survive. The surviving figures are so strikingly different that they show, without doubt, that after the mid–sixth century very little ivory was coming into the empire. The golden age of ivory artistry had been terminated by the plague.

A century later, Mediterranean and European population levels had declined significantly, with Constantinople shrinking from a city of half a million to one of fewer than a hundred thousand inhabitants. Meanwhile, the mid-sixth-century climatic crisis and its consequences had been generating other mechanisms through which parts of Europe and Asia were to be transformed. The remote steppe of Mongolia was to become the unlikely source of change.

PART TWO

THE BARBARIAN TIDE

3

DISASTER ON
THE STEPPES

I n A.D. 557 or 558 a fierce Asiatic people called the Avars arrived on the
eastern fringes of Europe from Mongolia. Twenty years later, they had
conquered significant parts of the eastern half of the European continent and had humbled the Roman Empire by invading the Balkans, including Greece itself, either directly or by proxy through their vassals. They
became a major element in the drawn-out process in which the empire
gradually lost so much of its territory and its strength, and through which
European and Middle Eastern history was fundamentally changed. But
what caused the Avar migration has always been something of a mystery.

All that history records is that by A.D. 545, after 150 years of being the
ruling ethnic group in Mongolia, Avar power was challenged by another
Mongolian people—the early Turks. It is quite clear from the historical
sources that the Avars had inexplicably become weaker in relation to their
vassals, the Turks, and by 552 the Turks had turned the tables on their
Avar overlords and taken over Mongolia.[1] Many of those Avars who had
not been slaughtered by the victorious Turks trekked west into exile,
toward Europe.

To gain insight into the probable causes of this tribal revolution, let
us look first at other similar changes on the Mongolian steppes, and at
particular aspects of steppe ecology. Drought and famine on the steppes
were what had finally precipitated the end of the Hun empire in the
mid–second century A.D. at the hands of the Avars' ancestors, who had inhabited the semimountainous terrain of eastern Mongolia and western

Manchuria. And it is drought and famine that seem to have brought about the collapse of the now little-known Uighur empire around A.D. 840.[2] That famine weakened the once-powerful Uighurs through starvation and accompanying internecine strife, and made them sitting targets for subjugation by ferocious Kyrgyz tribesmen from the forests of the hillier adjacent regions.[3]

Tree-ring, ice-core, historical, and archaeological evidence from around the world shows that there were major climatic problems in the 530s. More specifically, the records of the nearest literate civilization, north China, reveal that severe drought did kill many Chinese in A.D. 537 and 538. It's highly improbable that the drought and famine stopped politely at the Great Wall of China; it must be assumed, with a considerable degree of confidence, that Mongolia too was hit by the disaster. Indeed, tree-ring evidence from Siberia—on the other side of Mongolia—reveals that in the years 535–545 the region suffered the worst climatic conditions in a 1,900-year period.[4]

The catastrophe would have affected both the Avar and Turkic inhabitants of Mongolia, but the Turks would almost certainly have been less affected than their Avar masters. Although some Turkic tribes lived on the flat steppe, many inhabited the partly forested hills and mountains immediately to the north. The grass-covered steppe was (and still is) much more sensitive to drought than the forested uplands. Grass, with its short roots, cannot flourish in temporarily waterless conditions, whereas trees and even forest undergrowth, with much deeper roots, can tap into damper ground hidden well below the surface. Additionally, any clouds that were around would have tended to shed their rain when they arrived at the mountains. Even in drought conditions, mountainous areas normally receive more precipitation than adjacent plains.

The Turkic economy was also much more varied than that of the Avars. The Turks had, for instance, an involvement with hunting and gathering, with mining and metalworking, and almost certainly with goats, sheep, horses, and above all cattle.[5] The Avar economy, on the other hand, revolved predominantly around raiding, sheep, and horses. To the Avars, the horse was everything—a source of meat, milk, cheese, yogurt, and even alcohol (the sweet fermented mares' milk called *koumis*). Moreover, the horse was the vital ingredient in Avar military power. It was what had made their ethnic group top dog in the Mongolian region for 150 years.

And yet the horse was also the Avars' Achilles' heel. Due to important

differences in their digestive systems, horses often find it much more difficult to survive drought than cattle do. Horses fail to digest—and therefore
they excrete—up to 75 percent of the protein they eat. By contrast, cattle
excrete as little as 25 percent of the protein they consume. Thus, when all
there was to eat was dried-out, low-protein grass, cattle had a marked advantage over horses.

The high-protein wastage rate that horses suffer from is a result of the
design of their digestive system. Both cows and horses have what are essentially fermentation vats inside them to convert plant protein into a us-
able source of energy. But the horse's fermentation vat is less useful
because it is located at a point where the food that passes through has already been digested. By contrast, the cow's fermentation vat is located at a
point where the food has not yet been digested.

In the cow, most plant protein is broken down by bacterial action inside the organ known as the rumen. It is the only way in which the bulk
of the plant protein can be utilized, because much of it is locked up in the
cell walls of the plant. The freshly broken-down protein then passes into
the cow's duodenum, where it is broken down further into amino acids.
These in turn pass into the small intestine, where they are absorbed into
the bloodstream and used to make muscle, produce milk, repair damaged
tissue, and nourish fetuses. The horse, however, has its fermentation vat
located in its hind gut—well after the food has already passed through
the duodenum and the small intestine. The horse therefore does not produce large quantities of amino acids and does not absorb large quantities
of protein through its intestine walls. Instead, the plant protein it eats is
broken down by bacterial action in an almost totally useless location, and
all the animal succeeds in doing is depositing extremely nitrogen-rich ex-
crement. This is good for the soil, but not of much short-term benefit to
the horse.

In normal climatic conditions, plant protein is so plentiful that neither horses nor cows need to retain all the protein they eat. But in
drought conditions, when plant protein is rarer, while living grass contains around 15 percent protein, dead grass has only 4 percent; this
makes a high protein absorption rate key to survival. The cow's much
more efficient protein extraction system succeeds in retaining three times
the amount of protein as the comparatively useless horse system.

Although horses are obviously of greater military use than cattle, their
poorer survival ability in times of prolonged drought or severe winters
put their Avar owners at a terrible disadvantage vis-à-vis the Turks. Even

one hard winter coupled with an ultradry summer could kill large numbers of Avar horses.[6] Two or three successive bad years could create terrible suffering. In the drought of the late 530s, mares would have been
unable to suckle their young, and what should have been the next generation would have died off. A few months later, the starving adult animals
would have started to die. Robbed of their sources of milk, cheese, and
yogurt, the Avars would have had to eat the carcasses of their dead horses.

As hard winters and drought continued into the second and third
years of the catastrophe, families would have begun to starve to death.
Unable to find their own food, unable to barter food from others (horses
had been their wealth), unable to raid effectively, unable to defend themselves adequately without healthy horses, the Avars' time had run out. Although the worst of the drought was probably over by the mid-540s, the
economic and geopolitical damage had been done.

First the Turks snubbed the now much-weakened Avars, their official
overlords, by establishing direct diplomatic links with the imperial government of northern China in 545. Then, in 551, the Turks virtually saved
the Avars from destruction by rebel tribes. And in the following year, the
Turks pushed for political equality with their Avar masters by demanding
that the Avar ruler give the Turkic *kagan* (king) one of his daughters as
a wife. The proud Avar leader refused, and the Turks used his refusal as a
pretext for overthrowing Avar rule.

Thousands of Avars were slaughtered or enslaved. Their leader,
Anagui,[7] committed suicide, presumably to avoid the humiliation and
ritual execution that would have befallen him if he had been captured by
the Turks. The Turks believed that as kings were divinely appointed individuals, their blood must never be allowed to touch the earth, so had they
found him alive, he would have been strangled with a silk cord.

Lesser members of the royal clan, however, were almost certainly captured. It is known that some captives were retained (or sold) as slaves.[8]
Some—especially the more important—would have been executed in
traditional steppe fashion, their bodies ripped asunder between two
young trees. Those Avars who survived fled into exile and began a three-
thousand-mile trek westward toward Europe.[9]

There are no eyewitness descriptions of the great journey to the west,
but the archaeological and historical record pertaining to later steppe mi-
grations provides a reasonable indication of what it must have been like.
Thousands of men, women, and children made the journey—mostly on
horseback. The entire caravan would have been more than a mile long.

Each family's possessions, including their round felt tents (known as yurts), would have been carried on large covered wagons pulled by oxen. The caravan may also have included large numbers of spare horses and flocks of sheep.[10]

The most likely route the Avars took from Mongolia to Europe was a relatively northerly one, avoiding the Dzungaria and other central Asian deserts. After following the course of the Irtysh River for some six hundred miles, the Avar refugee caravan would then have cut across what is now northern Kazakhstan, skirting the northern shores of the Caspian Sea into the fertile grasslands to the north of the Caucasus Mountains. Here they encountered and conquered a local tribal group called the Kutrigurs. Their numbers were also swollen by a kindred people—a partially proto-Mongolian and partially Hunnic group called the Hepthalites, or White Huns.

The Avar horde, now with many of its Kutrigur Hun vassals and Hepthalite allies, then proceeded northwest into what is now the Ukraine, where they conquered the Ukranian Slavs (the Antes). Next, the constantly expanding Avar folk migration (now including some Slav as well as Kutrigur and other contingents) rolled on. They then paused to demand land (unsuccessfully) from the Roman imperial authorities. Having failed at this stage to gain entry to the empire, they moved west around the northern tip of the Carpathian Mountains into what is now Hungary, where they subjugated the local population, the Gepids. (See Chapter 4.)

By 568 the Avars had created a new empire, every bit as impressive as the one they had ruled in Mongolia sixteen years and three thousand miles away. It consisted of eastern Hungary, western Romania, Slovenia, Moravia, Bohemia, eastern Germany, and the western Ukraine. It covered approximately a million square miles, from what is now Germany in the west to the river Volga in the east, from the Baltic in the north to the frontier of the Roman Empire in the south.

Perhaps the most historically significant of the Avars' vassals were the Slavs, who themselves were relative newcomers to much of eastern Europe. Together, these two barbarian peoples helped transform the world.

4

THE AVAR
DIMENSION

"They are treacherous, foul, untrustworthy and possessed by an insatiable desire for riches." These "scoundrels" are "very experienced in military matters" and "prefer to prevail over their enemies not so much by force as by deceit, surprise attacks and the cutting of supply lines."

Thus wrote the Roman emperor Maurice, in the late sixth century, in a detailed army manual describing in precise and far from complimentary terms the hordes of Mongolian Avars who had migrated across Asia and begun to cause major problems for his empire.[1]

The same climatic problems that had triggered the chain of events leading to the arrival of the Avars appear to have already led to increased pressure on the Roman Empire by the Slavs. And, as described in Chapter 1, since 541 there had been several major outbreaks of bubonic plague, which cumulatively had reduced the empire's population substantially.

Maurice was in many ways a highly competent ruler. Yet the combination of the Avars, the Slavs, and other problems, all ultimately triggered by the climatic events of the 530s, eventually led to a people's revolution that changed Roman and world history forever. How did the empire lose control?

In 536–537 the climatic problems that were affecting so many other parts of the world seem also to have hit the Slavs, an agricultural people who lived in Poland and the western half of the Ukraine and who had, since the 520s, also settled in parts of Romania.

It is known from imperial edicts that in 537 the food situation was dire in the neighboring Roman provinces—Moesia Secunda (northeast Bulgaria) and Scythia (southeast Romania)—and the agricultural problems without doubt extended over the border into Slav territory.

The situation was so bad that in 536 or 537 the Slavs poured over the Danube frontier and were reported by the Roman historian Procopius as having "plundered the adjoining country and enslaved a very great number of Romans."

It is almost impossible to believe that the only direction the Slavs took was into Roman territory. Hunger and the search for food would have forced them to expand into any adjacent area in which native resistance was weak. It is more than likely, therefore, that it was at this juncture that the Slavs started also to expand westward, up the Danube and through the strategic Iron Gate Pass, into what is now Slovenia.

From the Roman Empire's point of view, the years 536 and 537 marked the beginning of major Slav invasions of imperial territory. The episode seems to have ushered in a period of increased Slav political instability and aggression. Around 545—as the empire was recovering from the first bout of the plague—another invasion was launched by the Slavs.

"At about this time," wrote Procopius, "an army of Slavs crossed the River Danube and spread desolation throughout the whole of Illyricum [now the former Yugoslavia] as far as Epidamnus [Durres in Albania], killing or enslaving all who came in their way, young and old alike, and plundering their property."

Then, in 550, the Slavs poured over the frontier yet again, this time capturing a Roman commander and seizing a major Roman town. The captured commander—a man called Asbadus, who had been one of the emperor's personal bodyguards—was first tortured by the Slavs (who removed strips of skin from his back) and was then burned alive.[2] The Slavs rampaged throughout Illyria and Thrace so violently that "the whole land came to be everywhere filled with unburied corpses."

Procopius wrote in lurid detail of just how barbaric the invaders were: "Now they killed their victims, not with sword nor spear, nor in any other accustomed manner, but by planting very firmly in the earth stakes which they had made exceedingly sharp, and seating the poor wretches upon these with great violence, driving the point of the stake between the buttocks and forcing it up into the intestines.

"These barbarians also had a way of planting four thick stakes very deep in the ground, and after binding the feet and hands of the captives to those stakes, they would then assiduously beat them over the head with clubs, killing them like dogs or snakes or any other animal."[3]

Procopius also describes how, in what seems to have been some sort of sacrificial rite, some prisoners—together with cattle and sheep—were locked inside huts that were then torched.

Finally, the Slavs attacked the town of Topirus (modern Corlu in European Turkey) and slaughtered all the male inhabitants. Procopius recorded how the barbarians overwhelmed the town's defenders "by the multitude of their missiles and forced them to abandon the battlements, whereupon they [the Slavs] placed ladders against the fortifications and so captured the city by storm.

"Then they slew all the men immediately, to the number of 15,000, took all the valuables as plunder and reduced the children and women to slavery."

In A.D. 558–559 a fresh Slav invasion was launched. But on this occasion the causes, nature, and scale of the attack were quite different. It was the first occasion on which the Avars' migration from Mongolia began to have an effect—albeit an indirect one—on the Roman Empire.

As we saw in Chapter 3, a barbarian people, the Kutrigur Huns, who had lived in southeastern Ukraine, had been attacked and pushed west in the mid-550s by the hordes of refugee Avars who had been forced out of Mongolia following the climatic disasters of the 530s. These Kutrigur Huns then came into contact with the Slavs and, under Kutrigur leadership and pressure, the two groups staged a massive invasion of the empire.

The Kutrigurs and Slavs split into three groups. One invaded Greece and got as far as the famous Pass of Thermopylae—the same strategic bottleneck where the Persians had been held at bay a thousand years earlier. A second headed toward another strategic thoroughfare—the narrow straits of the Dardanelles, the least guarded of the crossing points to Asia Minor. And the third headed for Constantinople, the administrative heart of the empire itself. There was much destruction in the countryside, but the towns and cities—including Constaninople—held out and survived this particular barbarian tide.

The indirect cause of the mayhem of 558–559, the Avars, now began to arrive on the doorstep of the empire themselves. In the early 560s they started demanding land from the Roman government, were refused, and entered Hungary.

The arrival of the Avars in the Ukraine a few years earlier had dislodged the Kutrigurs, with appalling results for the empire. Now the Avars' own arrival in central Europe was to bring total destabilization to the continent and disaster to the empire.

First the Avars allied themselves with the Lombards, a Germanic people living in what is now the Czech and Slovak republics. On behalf of the Lombards, they attacked and completely destroyed the kingdom of the Gepids (modern eastern Hungary), which the Lombards hoped to get their hands on. But the Avars had no intention of handing over the newly acquired territory. Instead, they kept it for themselves and threatened to turn on their erstwhile allies.

Seeing what had befallen the Gepids, the Lombards fled west and invaded Roman-ruled Italy. There then followed a protracted war in which the Lombard refugees succeeded, over a period of some twenty-five years, in taking over the far north of Italy, most of Tuscany, and 75 percent of southern Italy. This new Lombard dimension changed Italian history forever.

Equally significant for subsequent European history were the repercussions that flowed from the tragic destruction of the Gepids. The Avars were not, in economic or social terms, the same as the Slav and other European barbarian peoples whose territories they invaded. They were nomad warrior pastoralists with experience of and an aptitude for empire building. They became a ruthless ruling elite—and where their swords cleared the way, their subject peoples, mainly Slavs, flowed in. Some of what had been Gepid land became populated by Slavs, and in the late 560s and 570s, under Avar encouragement, protection, and pressure, the Slavs moved into Moravia, Bohemia, and Germany as far west as the river Elbe.

Although the Avars themselves have long vanished into the mists of history, it is to them that the modern world owes much of the ethnic and political geography of modern eastern Europe. They were, to a large extent, a violent and catalytic phenomenon—a sort of bulldozer that often forced those in front to move on (to become someone else's tormentors) and enabled those to its rear to benefit as allied subject colonists of new lands.

The Avars' objective was to operate a massive protection racket of sorts. The Roman Empire was to be their milk cow, and (from c. 580 onward) the Slavs were to be the major instrument through which the racket would be made to work.

This heist went on for almost fifty years and netted the Avars at least seventy thousand pounds of gold (equivalent to around $11 billion in modern terms). It began in 572 when the Avars forced the Romans to start paying 80,000 gold *solidi* per year in so-called peace payments. Three years previously, the Avars had launched an unsuccessful attack on the Roman city of Sirmium (Sremska Mitrovica in modern Serbia), but in 571 the future emperor Tiberius had been defeated in an important battle in what is now northern Serbia, and the following year the Avars began demanding these payments in exchange for not invading the empire.

But in 578 the Avars were on the offensive once more, and again Sirmium was their target. If they were to extract an increased amount of gold from the Romans, it was essential that the strategically vital city be snatched from Roman control, for whoever controlled Sirmium controlled the route between the western and eastern parts of the empire. Roman control meant that Avar military use of the vital river Sava could be blocked or at least controlled and that Roman forces could use Sirmium as a base for penetrating Avar territory north of the river.

So it was that in 578 the Avars, under their ruler, the all-powerful *kagan* Baian, started one of the great sieges in European history. First, using captured Roman engineers, they cut the city off from the rest of the world by building two pontoon bridges across the river—one upstream of Sirmium, the other downstream. With the river firmly in Avar hands, an imperial relief expedition failed to break through. After two years of siege, the city was racked by starvation and disease. The desperate plight of its people was symbolized by a piece of graffiti found by archaeologists 1,300 years later. An unknown citizen had scrawled a message to God and posterity in ungrammatical Greek on a wall in the stricken town. "Lord Christ, help the city," he wrote, "and smite the Avars and watch over the land of the Romans and the writer. Amen."

Certainly from that day forth the "land of the Romans" was indeed in dire need of help. Sirmium was surrendered to the besieging barbarians, and as part of the surrender terms, the Roman authorities were allowed to evacuate the city's surviving inhabitants.

With strategic Sirmium safely in their hands, the Avars demanded a 25 percent increase in the peace payments, to 100,000 gold *solidi* per year. Instead, the Roman emperor, a military man named Maurice, tried to fob the *kagan* off with a pet elephant and a solid gold bed. The *kagan*, who was nobody's fool, sent them back and told the emperor he'd prefer cash—regularly.

Maurice, who was notorious even among his own troops for being somewhat careful with his money, said no. The Avar *kagan* was furious and promptly launched a new invasion. After seizing the neighboring city of

Singidunum (now Belgrade), at the junction of the Sava and the Danube, the Avars swept eastward along the southern bank of the Danube and spent the winter of 583–584 on Roman territory on the Black Sea coast.

Within a few months, Maurice had capitulated to the *kagan*'s demands. The 25 percent increase was duly paid, and the Avar warriors were withdrawn back to Avar territory in present-day Serbia and Hungary.

But the *kagan* had several more aces up his military sleeve. Within just a few months, the Slavs living on Avar-controlled land invaded Roman territory—no doubt with Avar encouragement—and attacked the great city of Hadrianopolis (modern Edirne), just over a hundred miles west of Constantinople.

Having turned the screw tighter, the *kagan* seems then to have made yet more financial demands on the emperor—and was once again turned down. In the seventh-century book *The Miracles of St. Demetrius*, the author, Archbishop John of Thessalonica, described how "the chief of the Avars, having sent an embassy to the Emperor Maurice which met with a rebuff, then looked for means to inflict the greatest possible damage on him."[4]

The damage was done by a huge army of Avars and Slavs sent by the *kagan* into Greece. Parts of Corinth and the lower city of Athens were sacked. From Corinth, the canopy of the church was carried off. In Athens, archaeologists have found evidence of the destruction of the great marketplace.[5]

The barbarian forces even tried to capture Thessalonica. On 22 September 586 a huge horde approached the city. "This was the greatest army that has ever been seen in our time," wrote the author of *The Miracles of St. Demetrius*. "It was estimated at more than 100,000 men and drank the rivers and wells dry and turned the land into desert.

"There was great terror in the city which, for its sins, saw now for the first time, and so close too, an army of barbarians, something never before seen by anyone except those who had been on active service far away. All faces were glum and dejected."

The city had already been weakened and partially depopulated by a bout of plague that had raged there and in some other areas of the empire in 585 and the first half of 586. And yet the Avar attack failed. Thessalonica's salvation was put down to the personal supernatural intervention of the city's patron saint, St. Demetrius.

Further Avar attacks took place in 587, when the Thracian countryside was ravaged and looted, and in 588, when the barbarians actually reached the Sea of Marmara, fifty miles to the west of Constantinople. Once again, yet more peace payments induced the Avars to withdraw.

The Avar threat was still very real when, after signing a peace treaty with Persia in 591, Emperor Maurice moved large numbers of troops to the Avar front.[6] Under Avar pressure and encouragement, Slav tribes began, around 600, to expand from what is now Serbia into the Istrian Peninsula and down the Dalmatian coast of the Adriatic. So by the start of the seventh century, thanks largely to the key role played by the Avars and to the effects of the plague, there was now a potential Avar/Slav threat all the way along the seven-hundred-mile Balkan frontier, and the Roman Empire was facing economic and military disaster.

PART THREE

DESTABILIZING THE EMPIRE

5

REVOLUTION

"In this terrible tragedy, the emperor demonstrated his courage for, when a nurse tried to substitute her own child for one of his, he would not allow it but pointed out his own child.[1] And, some report, milk flowed with the blood as the boy was killed so that all who saw it wept bitterly. And so at last the emperor, having shown himself above the law of nature, exchanged life for death. From that time on, vast disasters and many calamities continued to afflict the Roman Empire."[2]

That is how the eighth- and ninth-century Greek historian Theophanes described a particularly poignant episode in the tragic execution of much of the imperial family during a popular yet bloody revolution that engulfed Constantinople in November 602. It was an event of pivotal importance in the history not only of the Roman Empire but of the world as a whole.

In a sense, its consequences still reverberate today, for it weakened the empire at a critical time and led directly to the de-Romanization of most of the Balkans, the loss of 70 percent of the empire, and, perhaps most significant, the rise of Islam.

But how did the mighty Roman Empire come to be humbled by a populist revolution?

As we have seen, for some thirty years the empire had been milked of vast quantities of gold, up to thirty thousand pounds of it—the protection money paid to the Avars. In addition, successive bouts of plague and war had reduced the empire's population—and thereby its tax base—by up to a third.

Emperor Maurice's solution was to try to make the army more productive, but at the same time not just to pay it less but to replace cash payments with payments in kind—usually of military equipment. Then he changed the war-booty apportionment system in such a way that the imperial government got a much larger slice and the soldiers a smaller one. None of this sat well with the army rank and file. Nor were they pleased with the emperor's refusal to pay ransom money to the barbarians for the return of colleagues who had been captured.

One officer, speaking out against the imperial government, said the emperor's "avarice produces nothing good and honest, but it is the mother of all troubles."[3] Furthermore, it was said that Maurice sent money to the clergy throughout the empire "in order to gain their prayers, so that he might make atonement in this world rather than the next."[4]

The last straw came when the emperor ordered the army to cross the Danube and spend the winter in barbarian territory. It refused to move, and in mid-November 602 it mutinied and chose as its leader an outspoken centurion by the name of Phocas—a ruthless soldier who was destined to become emperor within less than a fortnight.

Having concluded—correctly—that Phocas was "a lover of blood and slaughter," Maurice took the precaution of mobilizing Constantinople's home guard. He also staged a day of chariot races and other circus games in a last, desperate bid to prevent the population from being influenced by the mutiny, but the ploy backfired. At the games, one of the capital's political factions—the so-called Greens[5]—shouted to the emperor that if he wanted to avoid bloodshed, he should sack his finance minister.[6]

Theophanes wrote that at this juncture, the people "could not bear the rule of Maurice any longer" and invited the emperor's eldest son, Theodosius, to become emperor, or, if he was unwilling, his father-in-law, Germanus. Maurice then tried to have Theodosius flogged and Germanus arrested. But the people protected them and rose in revolt, shouting, "Let any who love you, Maurice, be flayed alive."

As the Greens and others demonstrated in the streets, and the mansion of a prominent government official went up in flames, the home guard deserted their positions on the city walls.

"Throughout the night the people swarmed around, shouting obscene slogans and filthy insults against the emperor and hurled insults and even made fun of the Patriarch," noted Theophanes. At midnight, Maurice at last realized his position was untenable. After shedding "his official insignia and dress, and clad as a private citizen, he boarded a warship at midnight with his wife, children and [his most trusted official] Constantine [Lardys] and sought safety by fleeing."[7]

Germanus tried to bribe the Greens into making him emperor, but they turned him down. Instead, they left the city and joined forces with the mutineers' leader, Phocas. Phocas immediately convened a conference to decide who should be emperor and was himself nominated by the Greens and others. He was then crowned by the Patriarch of Constantinople in the great church of St. John the Baptist, just outside the metropolis, and entered the capital two days later in the imperial chariot.

The following week a reign of terror began. Phocas decided to eliminate the former imperial family completely, so "he sent soldiers with orders to kill Maurice and his family.

"His five boys," wrote Theophanes, "were first killed before the emperor's own eyes, thereby first punishing the emperor through the murder of his children.[8] Maurice bore the tragedy with firmness of mind, continuously invoking God, the presider over all things, and saying reflectively over and over again: 'Just art thou, O Lord, and just are thy judgements.' " Then the former emperor himself was executed.

Phocas issued orders that the heads of Maurice and his sons be put on public display. According to Theophanes, "The citizens all went out of the city to witness this show while the heads rotted."

Maurice's wife and daughters were not executed at this time but were placed in a convent.[9] Other supporters of the former government were systematically rounded up and murdered. The former praetorian prefect, Constantine Lardys, and Maurice's eldest son, Theodosius, were executed at the Diadromos (probably a stadium),[10] while the army's commander in chief, the patrician Comentiolus, "was slain on the far side of the Golden Horn [waterway], by the Church of St. Conon, by the shore, and his body was eaten by the dogs."[11]

The following year the empire began to feel the repercussions of revolution. Both internally and externally, the destabilization caused by the mutiny and the fall of Maurice began to make itself felt. In Constantinople, riots broke out. The new authorities, ruthless as they were, lost control, and a large section of the city was burned to the ground by disaffected citizens. The leader of the Greens, who had helped bring Phocas to power, was himself killed in the mayhem.

Externally, the relationship between the Roman Empire and its archrival, the Persian Empire, was fatally undermined. The Persian ruler, Chosroes II, had enjoyed an extremely cordial relationship with Maurice (to whom he owed both his life and his throne).[12] He was very angry when he heard that his friend had been murdered, and refused pointblank even to receive ambassadors from the new Roman government.[13]

The mutiny and revolution not only resulted in civil unrest but also split the army itself in places. In the east, an experienced Roman general, Narses—who had in the past been much feared by the Persians—rebelled against Phocas, took control of the city of Edessa (now Urfa in southeastern Turkey), and "wrote to King Chosroes begging him to assemble his army and invade Roman territory."[14]

In direct response to the destabilization of the Roman imperium, the Persians swooped like vultures on the stricken empire in late 603. At the first encounter the Roman commander, Germanus, was fatally wounded, and Phocas withdrew troops from the Avar frontier to the new Persian one. At the first major battle—at the river Arzamon (near Mardin in southeastern Turkey) in early 604—the imperial forces were utterly crushed.

Theophanes wrote that the Persian king "drew up his elephants like a camp and gave battle, winning a great victory and capturing very many Romans, whom he beheaded." The Roman general Leontius escaped the Persians but was arrested on Phocas' orders and brought in chains to Constantinople. The rebel Narses was then finally apprehended, and publicly burned to death in the capital.

Order was also breaking down in Antioch, Palestine, and Egypt, the sources of at least a third of the empire's tax revenues. In Antioch people were cut down by troops as they assembled in the city's major church, and according to the historian John of Nikiu, the slaughter continued until the soldiers "filled every building with blood." The Antioch unrest was finally suppressed by a Roman general who had the rebels strangled, burned, drowned, or "fed to wild beasts."

In Egypt, anti-Phocas rebels attacked the local Roman governor and "put him and his followers to the sword"; five Egyptian cities fell to the rebels.[15] And by late 603 or 604, although Phocas had paid out a fortune in peace payments to the Avars, their vassals, the Slavs, could not resist invading the empire once Roman troops had been withdrawn to fight the Persians. One frequent target for the Slavs appears to have been Thessalonica, which is known to have been unsuccessfully attacked in October 604 by an army of around five thousand Slavs, whose war cries the citizens' "ears were well accustomed" to hearing.[16] A true dark age had begun to descend on the "Eternal Empire."

The following year, 605, was no improvement on its predecessor. More blood flowed in Constantinople, and the Persians overran all of Roman Mesopotamia. The new praetorian prefect, a man by the name of Theodosius, who had succeeded to the job when the previous incumbent was executed, was in turn put to death, as were six other prominent officials. All were beheaded except one, who "had his tongue cut out and was spread-eagled on a stretcher and dragged about [the city] for a show" before being "taken down to the shore where his eyes were removed and he was thrown into a small boat and burnt."[17]

Whether drink, madness, or merely the intoxicating effect of total power was to blame for Phocas' conduct is not known. It was probably a mixture of all three. In 606, for instance, at his daughter's wedding, he became insanely jealous of the bride and bridegroom and started making preparations to have his own supporters executed for praising the newlyweds too enthusiastically. And in 607 and 608, after uncovering evidence of dishonesty, he ordered the killing of dozens of leading political and administrative figures—including the late Emperor Maurice's wife, Constantina, and their three daughters, whom he had executed outside the city gate in the same ditch in which Maurice had been dispatched.

The other victims that year were either burned alive after having their hands and feet cut off, strangled, or simply beheaded. Entire families were wiped out, notably any relatives of Maurice and the former general, Comentiolus, whom Phocas had disliked even before the mutiny.

While Constantinople reeked of fear and of spilled patrician blood, the Persians seized the Roman Empire's Armenian and eastern Anatolian provinces and began to threaten its very heartland. However, at last, Phocas' power began to ebb away. Revolt started to erupt all over the empire. There was civil unrest in Constantinople; many citizens were killed or thrown into prison. The Greens, formerly Phocas' supporters, accused him of drunken lunacy. "You have drunk again from the goblet, you are losing your senses again," they shouted.[18] But the increasingly paranoid emperor responded by "chopping off the limbs of many of them and hanging them in the middle of the [city's chariot-racing] stadium." Others he beheaded or "tied in sacks and threw into the open sea."

At this point civil war broke out in earnest. In the capital, the Greens rioted, burned the city administrative offices, and opened up the prisons. In Antioch the Jewish population also staged a revolt and seized the local Christian patriarch, stuffing his severed testicles into his mouth and dragging him, still alive, through the city before killing him. The homes of the rich were then burned to the ground. In the great north African city of Carthage, the son of the region's leading politician—a young man called Heraclius—set sail with a fleet of ships bound ultimately for Constantinople. His aim was to remove Phocas and become emperor himself.

Meanwhile, numerous other plots were hatched against the emperor and yet more people were arrested and executed. Phocas, it seems, had grown bored with conventional beheadings, so he ordered one leading official to be used for archery target practice in the stadium and then had him suspended alive from a flagstaff at the emperor's favorite barracks.

At last Heraclius' fleet reached Constantinople, and Phocas' reign came to an abrupt and fitting end. The Greens and others seized him and burned him alive. But while internally the nightmare was over, externally the empire's problems were only just beginning.

6

"THE CUP OF BITTERNESS"

Although the empire's internal bloodletting had largely come to an end with the accession of Heraclius, the process by which it was to lose 70 percent of its territory within thirty years continued apace. The destabilization of the empire's relationship with the Persians and barbarians alike, which had followed the mutiny of 602, had done its damage. Pandora's box had been opened, and the utmost efforts of even such a determined and stubborn ruler as Heraclius could not put the lid back on.

Theophanes, describing the chaotic state into which the empire had slipped, wrote that "Heraclius, on becoming emperor, found the whole Roman state in a terrible condition.

"For the Barbarians [the Avars and Slavs] had made Europe a desert, while the Persians had given over all Asia to ravaging and had led whole cities into captivity and had constantly swallowed up whole Roman armies.

"On seeing this, the emperor had grave doubts about what to do. For the army had entirely disintegrated. Of all the officers who had rebelled with Phocas against Maurice and were still alive, he found, on enquiry, only two still remaining with the legions."

In the northwestern part of the empire, the Slavs smashed through Roman forces in the Istrian Peninsula and attacked all the major Roman towns of the Adriatic coast. Within three years most of the cities, some of the most prosperous in Europe, lay in ruins. The majority of the citizens had fled, their towns—Salona, Scardona, Narona, Risinium, Doclea, and Epidaurum—reduced to smoldering hulks.

Refugees either emigrated to Italy or poured into a few key defensible sites along the coast. The inhabitants of Epidaurum made their way to the coast and founded a new city, Ragusium (modern Dubrovnik). The refugees, determined to stand their ground in their new home, built a massive circuit of defensive walls, and survived. A few miles away the people of Risinium were probably responsible for the founding of Cattaro (modern Kotor in Montenegro). And 140 miles to the north, the people of Salona fled to the nearby coastal town of Split, where they converted the mausoleum of the third-century emperor Diocletian into a cathedral.[1] However, the much-venerated relics of Salona's martyrs were spirited off to Rome as the Slavs closed in. Split, which had declined in the fifth and sixth centuries, was rebuilt by the refugees and became an important town. (Five hundred years later it was to play a vital role in helping to create the medieval Croatian state.)

All three places of refuge had one major thing in common: their access to water. Unlike the inland towns the refugees had fled from, Dubrovnik and Split were directly on the sea, while Kotor was on a fjord-like inlet. If necessary, all three could receive supplies from the sea, so barbarian land sieges would have been uncomfortable and inconvenient but not fatal.

Meanwhile, other Slav tribes—"an immense horde of Drogubites, Sagudates, Belegezites, Baiounetes and Berzetes"—descended on Greece and even attacked the Greek islands and parts of Anatolia (now Turkey).[2] It was at this time—roughly 610–620—that Greece underwent fundamental change at the hands of the barbarians. The largely Mediterranean ethnic makeup of Classical and Roman Greece was altered irreversibly as tens of thousands of Slav warriors invaded the area and then settled their families throughout the country.

An analysis of the surviving place names in Greece reveals that virtually every area of the country had substantial Slav communities from this time onward; indeed, several regions must have had majority Slav populations. Place-name research carried out in the 1930s by a German called Vasmer showed that even in this century around two thousand Slav place names survived throughout Greece.[3] Seven hundred and thirty of them were found in northern Greece; a further 509 were in central Greece, 429 in the Peloponnese, and 382 in the rest of southern Greece.[4]

It was at this period that the Slavs appear to have started making use of seagoing boats for their military operations, raiding the Cyclades and the islands off Thessaly. What's more, much of this maritime expansion seems to have been carried out through the skilled use of nothing more sophisticated than large dugout canoes. "They had discovered how to make boats dug out from a single tree trunk," explained the author of *The Miracles of St. Demetrius*. Modern analysis of place-name evidence confirms that they reached the islands, though to sail to some they must surely have had larger boats, perhaps captured ones.[5]

As we have seen, the Slavs poured out from the Avar empire, so their expansion has to be seen as having not simply the Avars' blessing but also their encouragement and possibly even participation. In 615 the Slavs had even given a share of their plunder to the *kagan*, a fact that suggests they were acting as Avar surrogates. Moreover, they told the *kagan* that if he wanted more loot, he should actually provide Avar troops for the next attack.[6] From late 617 or early 618, specifically Avar forces (rather than their surrogates) swept into Roman territory and came within a few miles of Constantinople. The *kagan*'s plan seems to have been to first plunder and then extract protection money. In 623 the Avars broke a temporary truce and made an unexpected attack on Heraclius.

"The emperor was panic-stricken by this unforeseen event and fled back to the city," Theophanes wrote. "The Barbarian captured all the emperor's equipment and anything else he could seize, and then withdrew." The towns of Thrace were all plundered.

By 626 Avar pressure for protection money was increasing, and they were threatening Constantinople itself. Another surprise attack brought them to the walls of the capital.

"His forces reached the Golden Gate, taking everything they could find outside the walls and in the suburbs, men and animals, as plunder," wrote the anonymous author of the *Chronicon Paschale*.

"They forced their way into the holy Church of Saints Cosmas and Damien in Blachernae, and into the Church of the Holy Archangel the other side of the city in the suburb of Promotus. They not only took the chalices and other church plate but also broke up the altars of the churches. They then removed everything, including their prisoners, across the Danube and there was no resistance."

Meanwhile in Asia, the Persian War—which had begun following Phocas' revolution—continued to humble the empire. In 611 the Persians occupied Cappadocia and Antioch, and by 613 they had seized Damascus.

The following year the Roman imperial system was dealt a double blow, one with both territorial and religious dimensions, when the Persian army captured Christianity's most sacred city, Jerusalem.

With the loss of Jerusalem, the morale of the empire was irreparably damaged. Psychologically it was perhaps the single greatest blow of the Persian War. The Persian army slaughtered thousands of Jerusalem's Christians and (according to the cleric Antiochus Strategus) took thousands more as captives to Mesopotamia, where "by the waters of Babylon" they "sat down and wept."[7]

Yet more Christians perished from heat and overcrowding in a makeshift prison established by the Persians, and age-old religious, ethnic, and cultural conflict reemerged between Jews and Christians, resulting in further Christian deaths. What's more, the Persians seized and took back to Mesopotamia Christendom's most holy relic, fragments of a wooden cross believed by the faithful to be the very one on which Christ had died.[8]

From this point on, a dangerous spirit of defeatism seems to have taken root in the Roman Empire. Certainly the blame for the loss of Jerusalem was heaped not on the "evil Persians," who were the "hated of God," but on God himself, who had used the Persian army "as a rod of chastisement and as a medicine of rebuke" against the Romans.[9]

What was happening to the empire was beginning to be seen as God's will. Describing the scene as the Persian army moved in for the kill, Antiochus revealed the depths of Roman fatalism, which had by now reached almost apocalyptic levels.

"And as we knew not God nor observed His commandments, God delivered us into the hands of our enemies. The Lord has given over this Holy City to the enemy," he wrote.

"The Persians perceived that God had forsaken the Christians and that they had no helper," so with "increased wrath" they began to build in a circuit around the city great wooden towers "on which they placed catapults.

"The struggle lasted 20 days, shooting their catapults with such force that on the 21st day they broke down the city wall. At this, the evil enemy entered the city in great fury, like angry wild beasts and enraged serpents.

"The men defending the walls fled to hide in caverns, conduits and cisterns to save themselves; and the people fled in crowds to the churches and their altars and there they were slaughtered.

"For the enemy entered in great wrath, gnashing their teeth in violent fury; like evil beasts they roared, like lions they bellowed, like ferocious serpents they hissed, and slew all they found.

"Like mad dogs they tore with their teeth the flesh of the faithful, respecting no one, neither man nor woman, neither young nor old, neither child nor baby, neither priest nor monk, neither virgin nor widow.

"They destroyed persons of every age, slaughtering them like animals, cut them to pieces, mowed many down like cabbages, so that every individual had to drain the full cup of bitterness."

After the city had fallen, Antiochus Strategus went on to describe what a group of fleeing Jerusalemites saw as they looked back at their city: "Once more, they raised up their eyes and gazed upon Jerusalem and its holy churches.

"A flame as from a furnace reached up to the clouds as it burnt.

"Then they fell to sobbing and lamenting loudly and all together. Some smote themselves on their face, others rubbed their faces in the dust, others strewed ashes on their heads, others tore their hair when they beheld the [Church of the] Holy Resurrection on fire. [The Church of] Sion [enveloped] in smoke and flames, and Jerusalem devastated."

Soon the whole of Egypt and Libya as well as the Levant was in Persian hands, and in 616 a Persian army arrived on the eastern bank of the Bosphorus, less than a mile of water away from Constantinople.

Would the capital suffer the same fate as Jerusalem? Again the Romans saw what they believed to be their impending doom as the will of God—a punishment from on high for the conduct of their empire, especially for the sins of Phocas' revolution. A group of Roman magnates sent a letter across the Bosphorus to the Persian king in which they virtually trembled with guilt and fear.

"Attacked by you as a reward for our sins, the affairs of the Romans have reached this sorry state of weakness," they wrote.[10]

They abjectly begged that "your most great majesty, your most peace-loving majesty"—referred to by the Romans in less awkward times as "the Hated of God"—might make peace "by the Grace of God" as soon as possible. "We also beseech your gentleness that you hold our most pious Emperor Heraclius as a true son of yours, for he is ready in all things to concede to Your Serenity due reverence and duty.

"For if you do this, you will acquire a double glory, first for fortitude in war and then for granting peace.

"We ourselves would enjoy your never-to-be-forgotten gift of tranquillity, and it would be an occasion for us to offer daily prayers for your life. As long as the Roman Empire lasts, your beneficence would never fall into oblivion among its recipients," the magnates groveled.

The empire had indeed become humble in its desperation. The currency was on the verge of collapse, and soon the loss of territory also began to reduce food supplies for Constantinople. In 618 government bread distribution was stopped. Three-quarters of the empire had been lost: The Levant, Syria, Egypt, Libya, and most of Anatolia had fallen to Persia, while much of Thrace, Greece, and Italy had been overrun by Avar, Slav, and (in Italy) Lombard barbarians. With the Avar and Persian armies preparing for the kill, the virtually bankrupt Roman government, holed up in Constantinople, appealed to the Church in 622 to hand over its gold and silver treasures, its church plate and altar fixtures, to pay for the empire's preservation. Something in the region of 200,000 pounds of gold (worth in modern terms around $32 billion) was collected, ostensibly to raise a new army against the Persians.

However, within a few months the Avars, who had no doubt heard of the emperor's newfound "wealth," forced the Romans to double their protection payments to 200,000 gold *solidi* per year.

By 626 Constantinople was completely surrounded. The situation appeared hopeless. The Avars and their Slav vassals were just outside the city to the west, while just across the Bosphorus to the east was the Persian army. They were in contact with each other and acted in concert.

The Avar *kagan*—also "the Hated of God" as far as the Romans were concerned—even offered the people of the capital a deal whereby they would lose their worldly wealth yet save their lives.

"If any of you in the city wish to leave it, with only your shoes and shirt, then let us make a pact and treaty with my friend Shahbaraz [the Persian general]," the *kagan* told a delegation of citizens.[11] "If you cross over to him, he will do you no injury. Leave your city and your fortunes to me, for there is no other way for you to find safety, unless you turn yourselves into fish and escape by sea, or into birds and fly off through the air," he warned.

But 626 was to be a temporary turning point in the fortunes of the empire, for in the end the Avar attack failed and the Persians were beaten back.

Over the next four years, Emperor Heraclius managed to retake all the lost lands of western Asia and North Africa. But the cost in cash and manpower of this twenty-five-year-long war had been massive for both the Roman Empire and Persia.

For the former it was a Pyrrhic victory, but for the latter it was a prelude to final catastrophe. From the 540s onward, the mounting cumulative effect of plague and barbarian attacks had caused financial problems that in turn had led to mutiny and revolution. That pivotal event—Phocas' takeover—had furnished the Persians with the excuse to attack the empire at its weakest moment, and that very weakness had resulted in the length of the war and the empire's temporary loss of territory. The immediate result was that by the end of the war in 630, both sides were exhausted militarily and financially.

7

CHANGING THE EMPIRE:
THE CUMULATIVE IMPACT
OF THE PLAGUE AND
THE AVARS

T hough millions died from the plague, it would be an oversimplification to say that the disease alone brought the Roman Empire to death's door. Its role was more complicated than that.

As we have seen, plague deaths reduced the tax base, and to compensate, the imperial government increased the rate of taxation. Along with Avar protection money demands, this played a crucial role in creating the difficult financial circumstances that destabilized the army, the empire, and the geopolitical status quo in the revolutionary events of 602.

In the period 541–602 there had been dozens of plague outbreaks, including four major epidemics. The empire's population had shrunk by around a third, and its GNP had been reduced by at least 10 percent, possibly by as much as 15 percent.[1] By 602 it had therefore lost wealth equivalent to at least 30 million gold *solidi* due to plague. In addition to that, the empire had paid over the years a couple of million *solidi* in protection payments to the Avars, and over 5 million *solidi* had been lost as a result of Avar and Slav occupation of land in the Balkans.

Thus it was the cumulative effects of the plague and the Avars that led to the revolution of 602, the disintegration of the geopolitical status quo, and therefore the war with Persia. No doubt there would have been a war with the Persians at some point, but the particular circumstances of 602 determined its date, its nature, and in a way even its duration.

The Persian War cost the empire even more than the plague had directly. Over twenty or so years of warfare, the empire suffered total losses of an estimated 40 million gold *solidi* (equivalent today to around $80 billion). And the Avar advance in the west, which accompanied the Persian land seizures in the east, cost the empire a further 8 million or so gold *solidi*. Continuing losses from past plague in territories not taken over by Persians or Avars must have come to around 5 million *solidi*.

In the last fourteen years of the Persian War (616–630), Roman wealth loss reached truly catastrophic proportions, averaging 3.5 million gold *solidi* per year (mostly due to Persian land seizure)—a loss of 70 percent of the empire's annual imperial revenues.

Looked at in the long term, the ninety-year period 541–631 saw total losses of approximately 90 million gold *solidi*. The plague was directly responsible for more than a third of this. Losses in sources of wealth due to the Persian War (a war caused by partially plague-induced economic and political destabilization) came to an estimated 40 million. Military expenses in the Persian War totaled tens of millions of gold *solidi*. Avar protection-money payments came to about 5 million, while loss of wealth due to Avar/Slav land seizures totaled perhaps 13 million.

Plague had also led to the decline of urban markets, further undermining the rural economy. Rural and urban governmental infrastructure had been hit hard. Much of the government mail service and much of the highway road-station system—especially in Asia—had been closed down.[2] The cities' strategic role in defense had also been undermined by the partially plague-induced population reduction.[3] And the cities themselves, in their shrunken state, no doubt commanded less political authority vis-à-vis their hinterlands.

The loss of most of the Balkans to the Avars or to Avar vassals robbed the empire of one of its prime military recruitment grounds—and it is likely that plague often hit the military in their cramped barracks even more fiercely than the population as a whole.[4]

In terms of composition and organization, the army of the 630s was very different from what had existed in, say, the early sixth century. Then the empire was capable of fielding substantial mobile armies with combined strengths of up to a hundred thousand men, made up mainly of regular troops. In contrast, by the end of the Persian War in 630, financial stringency, loss of manpower resources (due partly to plague), and loss of key recruitment grounds had forced the empire into a position in which it was capable of fielding an army of only thirty thousand to forty thousand men, split between various commands.

* * *

And yet soon the empire's reduced resources and smaller military machine would be severely tested. Within five years of the end of the Persian War, a new military power was to erupt with almost volcanic intensity and suddenness from out of the sands of Arabia. Totally unexpected and extraordinarily successful, the new geopolitical force called itself Islam.[5] Within a generation it had destroyed the Persian Empire completely, reduced the Roman Empire's size by 50 percent, and established its own empire, which would soon stretch from the Atlantic to the borders of India.

Some early Arab historians even saw Islam's founder, Muhammad, as a sort of new Alexander the Great. And of course today, fourteen hundred years later, Islam is still having a major political and religious impact on the world.

Muhammad himself was very much a son of Arabia, but some of the factors that led to the foundation of the new faith, and most of the reasons for its phenomenal expansion, came from outside Arabia—from the Roman and wider worlds.

And although Muhammad was born in c. 575 and began his ministry only around 610, many of the vital external factors that influenced him and led to his success had their genesis in the climatic disaster of that vital earlier decade, the 530s.

PART FOUR

THE SWORD OF ISLAM

8

THE ORIGINS
OF ISLAM

"They [Mankind] were wicked so We sent on them the flood of Iram [the dam of Marib] and in exchange for their two [good] gardens [We] gave them two [bad] gardens bearing bitter fruit . . .

"This We awarded them because of their ingratitude . . .

"They wronged themselves . . . therefore We . . . scattered them abroad— a total scattering."[1]

Thus, according to the Koran, God spoke to his last and greatest prophet, Muhammad, sometime in the second decade of the seventh century A.D.

The flood and the subsequent scattering of the wrongdoers almost certainly refers to a known historical event—the breaking of the greatest dam of the ancient world, that of Marib in the arid interior of Yemen.

Up till the mid–sixth century, Yemen had been the most powerful native political force in the Arabian Peninsula. But with the destabilization of the world's climate in the second half of the 530s and the 540s, two disasters hit Yemen.

First, bubonic plague devastated the country—probably from 539 or 540 onward. Certainly the disease had arrived there by the 540s. And second, the agricultural economy of a key part of the country was substantially destroyed by the collapse of the Marib Dam.

This huge structure was not one of the seven wonders of the ancient world, but it probably should have been. It was one of the largest and most spectacular feats of civil engineering achieved by humanity in pre-modern times. The main dam was 53 feet high, 2,046 feet long, and at least 200 feet wide at the base. Its main job was to concentrate floodwaters so that they reached a particular height and could be channeled through 2 main sluices into a 3,700-foot-long canal and thence through 15 secondary sluices and 121 tertiary sluices into a massive irrigation system consisting of hundreds of miles of canals. In total, the complex irrigated twenty-four thousand acres and supported a population of between thirty thousand and fifty thousand people.

The city of Marib had been the capital of the powerful kingdom of Saba (sometimes said to be Sheba in the Bible) up till the late third century A.D. and then became a major center of the united kingdom of Saba and Himyar, after ancient Saba had become subject to the Himyarites.

The worldwide climatic disruption that started in A.D. 535 and lasted for up to thirty years was almost certainly responsible directly and indirectly for a series of floods and dam bursts that ultimately led to the deterioration and abandonment of the dam and the consequent collapse of agricultural production.

The deterioration of the Marib Dam complex, culminating in its final abandonment around A.D. 590, should be seen as a process spanning fifty to sixty years—a series of connected events rather than a single catastrophe. However, that process was initially triggered by the climatic chaos of the mid–sixth century, which seems to have produced not only drought but also occasional rainstorms of extreme severity. One of these freak deluges produced such massive quantities of water that, sometime in the 540s, the great Marib Dam gave way for the first time in a hundred years.

The event was recorded in a royal inscription, and a workforce from all over Yemen had to be raised to repair it, so serious was the damage. Archaeological work at the site suggests that the force of the flood was unprecedented. Certainly the authorities took unprecedented measures to try to stop it from happening again. For the first time ever, large blocks of stone were used to reinforce the dam.

Severe floods harmed the complex in two quite distinct ways: They tended to weaken or break the dam itself, and they swept thousands of tons of silt into the reservoir basin that lay behind the dam. As the basin got filled up with alluvial sediment, the distance between the basin floor and the top of the dam decreased, and it became less and less useful as a reservoir.

Geomorphological investigations at the dam have revealed that in the ten years after the dam burst in the 540s, the rate of silt deposition increased dramatically. In one part of the basin sediment levels rose nearly thirty feet in a decade. Although the parts of the basin concerned are different and therefore not fully comparable, it is striking that in the hundred or so years between the breaking of the dam in c. 450 and its giving way in the 540s, only sixteen feet of silt were deposited.

In the 550s the dam seems to have broken again. This time the silting up of the basin was so severe that the entire design of the dam complex had to be rethought. Building the dam much higher would have been one way of overcoming the sedimentation problems, but it would have been very expensive. Instead, the authorities decided to abandon the major sluice system and most of their agricultural land, opting instead to use the reservoir to water previously uncultivated land to its north. At a stroke this reduced the amount of agricultural land and food production by around 50 percent.

After the 550s Marib was therefore probably no longer capable of feeding its population, and many clans within the oasis, as well as the nomadic groups that interacted with them, would have been forced to migrate or to drastically change their annual migration patterns, respectively.

Nevertheless, the scaled-down Marib Dam complex, now watering just the area north of the reservoir, continued in use. However, the drought conditions and intermittent storms of the 530s, 540s, and 550s had combined to damage not only the dam and the reservoir but also the ecology of the highland area from which the water swept down. Drought must have killed off much of the highland vegetation; as a result, erosion increased dramatically, and more and more silt was swept down into the Marib reservoir.

Even after the climatic chaos of the mid–sixth century had subsided, it would have taken several decades for the plant ecology to fully recover and the rate of erosion and alluvial deposition to slow. The geomorphological evidence shows that silt was still being washed down in above-average quantities for part or all of the period between 560 and 590.

Thus, when floods broke the dam yet again in c. 590, the great structure was abandoned, Marib's population fell to a fifth or a sixth of what it had been, and agricultural production at Marib declined to a mere shadow of its pre-530s level. The recently reduced population of Marib, and indeed the plague-hit population of Yemen, was simply not able to afford the increased cost of repairing the dam. Thus it was that one of the greatest engineering achievements of the ancient world passed into history.

According to both the Koran and other Arab sources, the deterioration and final abandonment of the Marib Dam did indeed force large
numbers of people to leave the Marib area in search of new lands.[3] Thus
it was that two tribes—the Banu Ghassan and the Azd—are said to have
migrated north to the Medina oasis in central Arabia.

At the same time, the climatic problems that started in the 530s were
forcing the pace of change in two other ways in the Arabian Peninsula.
First, the climate problems in central and northern Arabia—this time
probably drought—seemed to have caused agricultural failure and famine. In Mecca—the city in which, forty years later, Muhammad was to
be born—there appears to have been a serious famine, probably in the
mid- to late 530s. The Mecca famine was reported by several eighth- and
ninth-century Arab historians as having taken place in the lifetime of
Muhammad's great-grandfather Amr.

Although the earliest of the great Islamic historians, Ibn Ishaq, was
writing 150 years after the time of Amr, the famine probably was a real
historical event, as it seems to have occurred at around the time that similar famines were breaking out in many other areas of the world as a result
of the global climatic problems of the 530s.

The available textual evidence suggests that the famine was so bad
that, as one of the leaders of his people, Amr had to obtain wheat from
as far away as Syria, and that he fed them on a sort of broth made with
broken-up loaves. "Amr, who made bread-and-broth for his people—
a people in Mecca who suffered lean years," wrote a sixth- or seventh-
century poet, quoted by Ibn Ishaq.

Another sixth-century poet, Wahb ibn 'Abd Qusayy—quoted by the
ninth-century historian al-Tabari—reported how Amr saved his people
from the famine.

> [Amr] took upon himself the responsibility which no other mortal was
>   able to undertake.
> He brought them sacks from Syria, full of winnowed wheat,
> And gave the people of Mecca their fill of broken bread.
> Mixing the bread with fresh meat, the people were surrounded by
>   wooden bowls piled high whose contents were overflowing.[4]

Another Meccan poet quoted by al-Tabari, Matrud, wrote:

> Amr, who broke up bread for tharid [broth] for his people
> when the men of Mecca were drought-stricken and lean.[5]

Amr's efforts to counteract the famine seem to have—quite literally—made his name. Thenceforth he was known almost exclusively as Hashim (ostensibly after the word *hashama*, meaning "to crumble," in commemoration of his crumbling or breaking of the bread made from the wheat he brought from Syria).

Amr's role in saving his people earned his family increased status. He was referred to by the poet Matrud as "the Lofty One," and by others as one of "those who make mighty."

It is probable that Amr's high reputation, gained in the crucible of the 530s famine, helped to cement the social standing of his descendants—including ultimately his great-grandson Muhammad.

Another climatically triggered destabilizing factor in mid-sixth-century Arabia was the plague. Evidence from Ibn Ishaq, the Koran, and an inscription suggests that in the 540s Yemen and possibly other areas of the Arabian Peninsula were racked by the depredations of bubonic plague. The identification of the disease as plague is made more secure by the date, for the 540s is the exact period when one would have expected the plague to afflict Yemen, having arrived there en route from East Africa to the Mediterranean.

An early reference to what appears to have been plague in Yemen is from one of the earliest parts of the Koran itself. Viewing the plague as an affliction from on high, and the dark skin boils as "baked clay" dropped by God-sent "flying creatures," the Koran describes what befell an army from Yemen that was threatening Mecca around 550.

> Hast thou not seen how thy Lord dealt with the [enemy],
> Did He not bring their stratagem to naught.
> And send against them swarms of flying creatures
> Which pelted them with stones of baked clay.
> And made them like green crops devoured [by cattle].

Ibn Ishaq expanded on this by recording that as the army withdrew, "they were continually falling by the wayside, dying miserably by every water-hole."

> [The enemy leader] was smitten in his body, and as they took
>   him away his fingers fell off one by one.
> Where the fingers had been, there arose an evil sore exuding
>   pus and blood.
> They allege that as he died, his heart burst from his body.[6]

And lastly, an inscription discovered by archaeologists at Marib records that repair work on the dam there had to be delayed in the 540s because the workforce had been decimated by plague.

The collapse of the Marib Dam (and no doubt the destruction of countless other smaller irrigation systems) and the onslaught of the plague were two of the key factors that appear to have led to the demise of Yemeni power from the mid–sixth century onward. Yemen had been the principal indigenous power within Arabia for at least a thousand years. Indeed, its people had comprised half the population of the entire Arabian Peninsula, and its fall must have created a huge power vacuum there. Certainly within two generations the focus of geopolitical power within Arabia had shifted, with Muhammad's help, to the oasis of Medina, a central Arabian town dominated until then by Arabian Jewish tribes.

But it wasn't just a power vacuum that gave Muhammad the opportunity to flourish. Other factors were at work in shaping the environment from which Islam emerged.

The key factor that led to the emergence of Islam was almost certainly the unique political and theological situation existing in the wider world at the very time that Muhammad was developing his religious ideas.

The earliest parts of his religious philosophy were first formulated, committed to memory, and then written down, in the form of the early sections of the Koran, in the period A.D. 610–620—the very decade in which everybody, in Arabia and in the world at large, fully expected to witness the demise of the Roman Empire, the imperial system that had dominated the Mediterranean world for eight hundred years. It was as if the entire world political system was about to collapse—and many if not most people would have regarded that apparently imminent catastrophe not just in purely political and military terms but also in religious and cosmic terms.

Christian and Jewish communities both inside and outside the Roman Empire had long apocalyptic traditions in which the broad outline of human history was seen as a divinely preordained chronological structure that one day would end with the resurrection of the dead, the Day of Judgment, the dissolution of the mortal world, and its replacement by an everlasting Kingdom of God in which the righteous would live forever. According to both Jewish and Christian prophetic traditions, the end of the world would come in three distinct stages—the rule of the Devil and the barbarian invasions, the coming of the Messiah and the defeat of the

Devil, and the resurrection of the dead and the Last Judgment. The whole sequence was seen as God's plan for the denouement of human history.

Both Jews and Christians certainly saw the Persian War of 605–630 in more starkly cosmic terms than previous conflicts. And at the time, many would have viewed the apparently imminent collapse of the empire in 610–620 (precisely the time of the emergence of Muhammad) as heralding the coming of the Messiah and the end of the world. Indeed, when the Persians captured Jerusalem in 614, it was said that "the assembled angels," unwilling to "oppose the will of God," deserted the Holy City because the Almighty had given it to the enemy, Christian sin having "exceeded God's grace." A Christian prophecy purporting to have been written before the Persian War (but, in fact, written just after it) said that soon "the day without evening" would arrive for Mankind and "there will be an end to earthly power."[7]

That prophecy stated in more precise terms the apocalyptic views aired by the Christian John of Ephesus during a comparatively early stage of the Avar wars, which racked the Roman Empire between 570 and 626. He had written in c. 580 of the "devastation and slaughter which has occurred in our times" so that "for the knowledge of future generations, if indeed the world is to last longer," we may "expound and make known these things which Christ teaches, warns and shows to us about the time of the conclusion of the world."

Jewish opinion also saw the events of the time in cosmic terms— probably more so than at any time since the Jewish revolts against Rome in the first and second centuries A.D., the very period out of which Jesus Christ himself had emerged.

The so-called *Book of Zerubabel*, written by a rabbi of that name in Persian-ruled Babylon in the first quarter of the seventh century A.D., prophesied the coming of the Jewish Messiah (and his mother) and their defeat of the Christian Roman monster—an emperor/pope called Armilus, the son of Satan.[8] Furthermore, a Palestinian Jew called Jacob, who had been forcibly baptized by the Romans in Carthage, described the empire in typically apocalyptic terms as "the fourth beast," which was being "torn in pieces by the nations, [so] that the ten horns may prevail and Hermolaus Satan [the Devil] the Little Horn may come."[9]

The Jews viewed the apparently imminent collapse of the Roman Empire in the first quarter of the seventh century as evidence that the "beast" (the formerly pagan but now Christian empire) was doomed, that the Devil in the guise of the last Roman emperor or Christian pope would be killed by the coming Messiah. They saw the Persians (and a few years later, the Arabs) as the agents who would help destroy the "Roman beast." Violent and often Messianic Jewish revolutionary attitudes had been spreading and increasing in fervor throughout the second half of the sixth century and went into overdrive as the empire began to totter in the first quarter of the seventh. In Antioch in 608, Christian attempts at forced conversion, as the Persians threatened the city, triggered a major revolt in the Jewish quarter. At first the Jewish rebels were successful, and their community's archenemy, the city's powerful Christian patriarch, Anastasius, was captured, killed, and mutilated. But the revolt was soon put down, and the eight-hundred-year-old Antiochan Jewish community was almost totally extinguished.

At the fall of Jerusalem and the siege of Edessa (modern Urfa in Turkey), Jewish anti-Roman, anti-Christian participation was equally violent and determined. And after the birth of Islam, as the early Muslims began to humble the Roman Empire, Jewish communities—oppressed and waiting for Messianic deliverance—were overjoyed. Some Jews thought that Muhammad was obviously a prophet who had come to prepare the way for the Messiah.

"The *candidatus* [a Roman official] has been killed [by the Arabs] and we Jews had great joy. And they say that a prophet [Muhammad] has appeared [among the Arabs] and proclaims the coming of the [Messiah]," said the Jews of Sycaminum in Palestine in 634.[10]

Certainly Islam was a creed ideally suited to its time—a new religion that emerged directly out of the apocalyptic atmosphere of the period. The early surahs (chapters) of the Koran have an overwhelmingly apocalyptic flavor.[11] Muhammad, described as a messenger of God, is said to have come to warn mankind of what lies ahead at and beyond the Day of Judgment. In the Koran, seen by Muslims as the word of God, the expression *"yaum al-qiyama"* (the Day of Resurrection) occurs no fewer than seventy times, while an alternative word for that event, *al-sa'a* (the hour) occurs a further forty times. The last day and the Day of Judgment itself are cited forty-five and twenty-two times, respectively. Other expressions such as *"yaum al-hisab"* (the Day of Reckoning) also occur frequently.

In a historically vital surah of the Koran, dating from a year or two after the Persian seizure of Jerusalem as the Persians closed in on Constantinople, Muhammad was told by God that "the Romans have been defeated" and "know only some appearance of the life of the world and are heedless of the Hereafter."[12]

"Evil was the consequence of those who dealt in evil because they deny the revelations of Allah and made a mock of them," says the Koran a few verses later, referring to both the Romans and the Persians.[13] "And in the day when the hour riseth, the unrighteous will despair."

The destiny of nonbelievers and evildoers is quite clear throughout the Koran. They will be "assembled on the Day of Resurrection" and "their habitation shall be Hell"; whenever the fire abates, "we shall increase the flame." On the Day of Resurrection, "when the trumpet is blown," God shall "assemble the guilty white-eyed with terror."[14]

"He who turneth away from remembrance of Me [God], his life will be a narrow life and I shall bring him blind to the assembly on the Day of Resurrection," says the Koran.[15]

"Thus do We reward him who is prodigal and believeth not the revelation of his Lord and verily the doom of the Hereafter will be sterner and more lasting."[16]

The Koran never says exactly when the end of the world will come, but its imminence is hinted at in surah 7. "The Destined Hour [the Day of Judgment] is heavy in the heavens and the earth," says verse 187, echoing earlier non-Muslim apocalyptic texts in which metaphorically the pregnant (heavy) cosmos gives birth to the events of the last days.

Increased interest and belief in the end of the world—indeed, in its fairly imminent arrival—were to a large extent prerequisites for both the emergence and the spread of Islam.

It was—and, arguably, is again today—a religion ideally suited to the political and popular theological mood of the time. But although it is clear why Islam emerged and flourished, one key question demands an answer: How were these apocalyptic and monotheistic ideas—traditionally associated with the Jewish and Christian religions—transmitted to the deserts of Arabia?

Certainly both Judaism and Christianity had a strong presence in Arabia. There were Christian tribes and statelets on the northern fringes of Arabia, and there had been a Christian presence in the south (Yemen) as well. Jewish influence had also been widespread in Yemen and was most substantial in northwest Arabia, particularly in Medina—the very city (along with Mecca) in which Muhammad had family connections and which he used as his main power base following negotiations with the Medinans in 621.

Although the apocalyptic atmosphere of the early sixth-century Mediterranean and Middle Eastern world was probably the key element in the birth of Islam, it was only one of the factors that allowed the new religion to flourish.

The Persian War weakened the ability of both empires to exercise political influence in Arabia and helped accentuate the power vacuum that had been developing since the demise of Yemeni influence in the previous century. The war also reduced the two empires' ability to defend themselves against third parties, and this created new opportunities for Arab aggression in the form of raiding and territorial expansion.

This explosion of external opportunities was the key factor that initiated, then drove the pace of, political change internally within the Arabian Peninsula. Indeed, the seventh-century series of Arab raids into Roman territory started (in a small way) before Islam had begun to play any role in them at all. The first major Arab attack of the period took place in 612. "The Arabs raided Syria, destroyed towns and many houses and then withdrew," wrote the eighth-century Roman historian Theophanes, who was almost certainly quoting from a now-lost seventh-century source.

Islam as a fundamentally political as well as religious development was an organizational and ideological innovation, through which Arab society adapted to the new political and military realities and opportunities—a way in which the Arabs were able to more efficiently take advantage of the weakness of the Roman Empire and Persia. Muhammad's teachings created a situation in which it was not just expedient but also ideologically desirable to attack the two weakened superpowers.

"God says, 'My righteous servant shall inherit the earth'; now this is your inheritance and what your Lord has promised you," Muslim commanders told their troops on the eve of the conquest of the Persian Empire. In the event of a Muslim victory, the enemy's "property, their women, their children and their country will be yours."

The defeated Persian general was informed by the victorious Arab commander that God had "sent a prophet from among [the Arabs] and one of his promises was that we should conquer and overcome these lands."[17]

According to Muslim tradition, Muhammad informed both the Roman and Persian imperial authorities (probably via their frontier governors) of the teachings of Islam—but they took no notice. In fact, his envoy to the Romans was seized and executed. Both empires were no doubt seen by early Muslims as rejecting the word of God and so laying themselves open to conquest.

A chapter of the Koran known as "The Spoils of War" makes it abundantly clear how Islam would aid the process of victory. This text uses as its lesson the experiences of the children of Israel in their conflict with Egypt at the time of the exodus, prior to the conquest of the promised land. The way of the nonbelievers is like "the way of Pharaoh's folk . . . They disbelieved the revelations of Allah and Allah took [destroyed] them for their sins. Lo! Allah is strong, severe in punishment."[18]

The nonbeliever's way is "as the way of Pharaoh's folk; they denied the revelation of their Lord, so We destroyed them for their sins. And We drowned the folk of Pharaoh. All were evil-doers," says verse 54 of "The Spoils of War"—a surah dating from around the time of Islam's first great battle, that of Badr against the nonbelieving Meccans in 624. "Lo. The worst of beasts in Allah's sight are the ungrateful who will not believe."[19] The surah adds, "Oh Prophet! Exhort the believers to fight. If there be of you 20 steadfast, they shall overcome 200, and if there be of you a hundred steadfast, they shall overcome a thousand of those who disbelieve because the disbelievers are a people without intelligence."[20]

The ideology of Islam matched exactly what was required by the Medinans in order to conquer the Arabian Peninsula and then for the Arabs as a whole to exploit the exhausted and weakened state of the Roman and Persian empires.

The new ideology raised the normal antagonism felt toward an enemy to an altogether higher level. Instead of conquest and victory being seen in purely material and political terms, Islam allowed them also to be seen in terms of destiny and religious duty.

"When thy Lord inspired the angels, saying 'I am with you,' so make those who believe stand firm. I will throw fear into the hearts of those who disbelieve. Then smite [their] necks and smite of them each finger.

"That is because they opposed Allah and his Messenger [Muhammad]. Whosoever opposeth Allah and his Messenger [for him] lo, Allah is severe in punishment."[21]

"Oh ye who believe! When ye meet those who disbelieve in battle, turn not your backs to them," says a passage in "The Spoils of War" referring to the religious need for determination and courage.[22]

"Whosoever on that day turneth his back to them, unless manoeuvring for battle or intent to join a company, he truly hath incurred wrath from Allah, and his habitation will be Hell, a hapless journey's end."[23]

In a sense, even the killing in battle of a nonbelieving enemy was seen as the work of God.

"Ye [Muslims] slew them not, but Allah slew them. And thou [Muhammad] threwest not when thou didst throw, but Allah threw," says verse 17 of surah 8, written at the time of the Battle of Badr.

Even the taking of prisoners was divinely discouraged in some circumstances. "It is not for any prophet to have captives before he hath made slaughter in the land."[24]

Again there are parallels with what the Old Testament relates as the events surrounding the Jewish exodus from Egypt. In early ancient Israel, the concept of holy war existed, inasmuch as fighting for God was seen as a sacred activity. The Book of Joshua (chapter 6, verses 18–24) provides a gruesome example, the capture of Jericho, in which all living things— men, women, children, and animals—had to be put to death and all buildings and property had to be burned as an act of ritual destruction.

In Arabia in the 620s, Muhammad's ability to survive as a radical politico-religious leader depended on military success. In order to succeed, he had to keep expanding. He had to keep on delivering success to his followers—and to would-be followers.

"If we give allegiance to you and God gives you victory over your opponents, will we have authority after you?" one hopeful Arab tribal leader with an eye to the future is said to have asked Muhammad.[25]

Furthermore, Arab tribal society was very warlike and always had been: "How many a Lord and Mighty Chief have our horses trampled underfoot . . . we march forth to war," wrote a pre-Islamic poet, glorifying conflict.[26] "When I thrust in my sword it bends almost double. I kill my opponent with a sharp mashrafi[27] sword, and I yearn for death like a camel over-full with milk," wrote one of his Islamic successors.[28]

The conquest of nonbelievers was thus seen as a fundamentally good thing in terms of political survival, tribal tradition, and religious obligation. As one prominent historian of early Islam, Patricia Crone, put it, "Muhammad had to conquer, his followers liked to conquer and his deity told him to conquer."[29]

9

ISLAMIC
CONQUESTS

The Muslim advance was one of the most rapid in human history. Indeed, as we have seen, medieval Arab historians likened the swift progress of early Islam to the conquests of Alexander the Great a thousand years earlier. In one illuminated manuscript,[1] Alexander is seen as a sort of proto-Islamic precursor of Muhammad—and is pictured actually standing beside Islam's most holy place, the Kaba in Mecca.[2]

The first clash between Muslim and Roman forces (the Battle of Mu'ta) took place in 629 in the political and military vacuum that existed immediately after the Persian withdrawal (628) and the proper reestablishment of Roman rule. Although the Romans were victorious, their success did not stop four Roman-controlled Arab towns (Aqaba, Jarba, Adhruh, and Ma'an) from defecting a year later to the newly emerging Muslim power. In the Roman authorities' determination to prevent such civil defections, the governor of one of these towns, Ma'an, was promptly arrested and executed.

For a few years Islam bided its time and built up its army. Then in 633, the year after Muhammad died, Muslim forces invaded both the Persian and Roman empires and scored notable successes—at the Battle of the River of Blood, against Persia, and at the battles of Dathin, Ajnadayn, and Fahl, against the Romans. Islamic forces even temporarily captured Damascus and Hims.

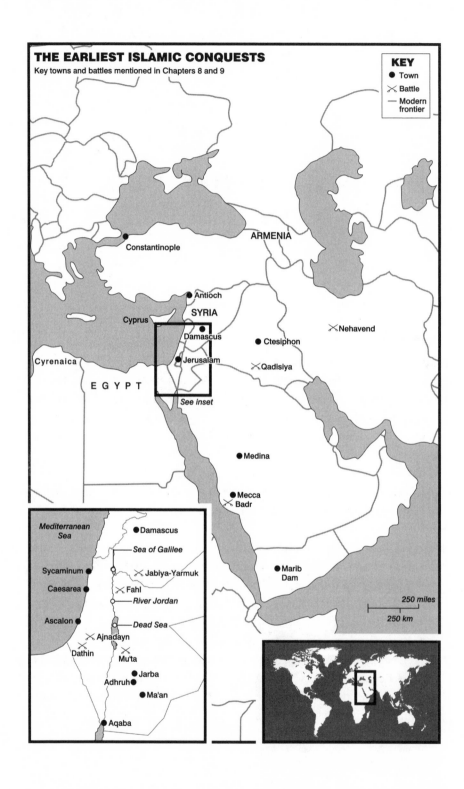

THE EARLIEST ISLAMIC CONQUESTS

Key towns and battles mentioned in Chapters 8 and 9

KEY
● Town
✕ Battle
— Modern frontier

Constantinople

ARMENIA

Antioch

SYRIA

Cyprus

Damascus

✕ Nehavend

● Ctesiphon

Cyrenaica

Jerusalem

✕ Qadisiya

E G Y P T

See inset

● Medina

● Mecca
✕ Badr

● Marib Dam

250 miles
250 km

Mediterranean Sea

● Damascus

Sea of Galilee

✕ Jabiya-Yarmuk

Sycaminum ●

✕ Fahl

Caesarea ●

River Jordan

Ascalon ●

Dead Sea

✕ Ajnadayn

Dathin ✕

✕ Mu'ta

● Jarba

Adhruh ●

● Ma'an

● Aqaba

Smarting from defeat, the emperor ordered a counterattack. Damascus came once again into Roman hands, but its local Roman chief administrator, Mansur, who was an ethnic Arab, refused to cooperate with the Roman military and withheld vital provisions.[3]

The Roman army, fifteen thousand to twenty thousand strong—its leadership divided between mutually suspicious generals—then collided with the Islamic forces eighty miles south of Damascus at Jabiya-Yarmuk.

The battle—or, more accurately, a series of clashes culminating in a large battle—lasted some one and a half months. Much of the local population, including important local Jewish communities, was either indifferent or hostile to the Roman cause. And as described above, the Roman forces were riven with discord.

In the end, it seems to have been a Muslim night attack, which took advantage of poor Roman discipline, command, and control, that turned the tide. In the dawn conflict that followed, the Romans were utterly annihilated. Thousands were killed in battle. Many of those who were not killed in the battle, their morale at rock bottom, simply sat down and tried to surrender, but they were slaughtered where they sat, for the Muslims were taking no prisoners. Those who escaped were pursued relentlessly. One group of fleeing soldiers was said to have been chased for five hundred miles!

Jabiya-Yarmuk ranks among the most important battles in world history. After the defeat, Roman power in the Middle East virtually collapsed, and most of Syria and Palestine fell to Islam almost immediately. Jerusalem was captured and would remain in Muslim hands for most of the subsequent thirteen and a half centuries. Gaza was stormed and its garrison members were executed by the Muslim army—then declared martyrs by the Church at the insistence of the emperor.[4]

Muslim soldiers swept to victory at the Battle of Qadisiya, not far from what is now the southern Iraqi town of Al Hammam. Most of what is now Iraq (then the western part of the Persian Empire) fell to Islam. The spectacular and bejeweled Persian capital, Ctesiphon (twenty miles southeast of modern Baghdad), was sacked and occupied.

In 639 more Roman towns (Caesarea and Ascalon) were captured, and in 640 the expanding Islamic armies invaded Egypt, Armenia, and the beleaguered Persian Empire's heartland, highland Persia itself. Persia fell at the Battle of Nehavend, known in Arab tradition as the "Victory of Victories."

Two years later, in 642, Islamic armies completed the conquest of

Egypt, thus robbing the Roman Empire of at least half its remaining wealth and its main source of grain. The Muslim conquerors then invaded and occupied Cyrenaica (modern Libya).

By 652 the Islamic empire had reached the borders of India. In 653 an Islamic navy seized Roman Cyprus, and by 670 the Roman capital, Constantinople, itself was under siege, though the Muslim army never broke through. Indeed, Muhammad's former standard-bearer—by then a rather aged warrior—died of illness in that abortive campaign and was buried outside the city walls.

In the west, Islamic armies pushed on, ending the Roman Empire's nine-hundred-year control of North Africa in a seven-year campaign between 698 and 705, and then invaded southern Europe, conquering most of Spain in 711 and penetrating deep (though temporarily) into France between 718 and 732.

Over subsequent centuries, Islam was to spread across the Sahara to West Africa, along the East African coast as far as Mozambique, and east to western China, India, Indonesia, and even the Philippines. Today it is one of the world's three largest religions, has five hundred million followers, and is a major player on the world geopolitical stage. Yet its emergence 1,400 years ago—like so many other aspects of the modern world—owed much to the political, economic, epidemiological, and religious factors that flowed from the climatic chaos of the mid–sixth century.

10

BEHIND THE
ROMAN COLLAPSE

The reasons for the partial disintegration of the Roman Empire in the seventh century were legion, but each of them stemmed from one or more of five sometimes interrelated historical problems: a chronic lack of cash; the Avar/Slav seizure of the Balkans; the Persian occupation; the plague; and religious dissension. Ultimately, those five problems had grown either directly or indirectly, wholly or partially, out of the climatic problems of a century earlier.

Some of the complex factors (specifically the plague and the Avars) that led to the empire's dire financial problems have been described in Chapter 7, but the way in which lack of cash translated into military disaster in the seventh century was equally complex and almost fatal.

First of all, the lack of funds significantly limited the size and nature of the Roman army. It was both cheaper and more convenient to recruit local Arab tribes to do at least some of the fighting against the Muslim insurgents. The reduced size of the Roman army meant that only small contingents could be allocated on a long-term basis to the Arabian frontier region. This forced the Roman military to opt for a mainly defensive strategy in which most units of troops were stationed inside walled towns—a practice that eroded their will and ability to fight and which, by its very nature, split Roman forces into a myriad of often uncoordinated fragments. Soon this defensive town-based strategy was incapable of denying the Islamic enemy access to the countryside. This, in turn, made

THE CONSEQUENCES OF A.D. 535: ISLAM, AVARS, PLAGUE, AND THE ROMAN EMPIRE

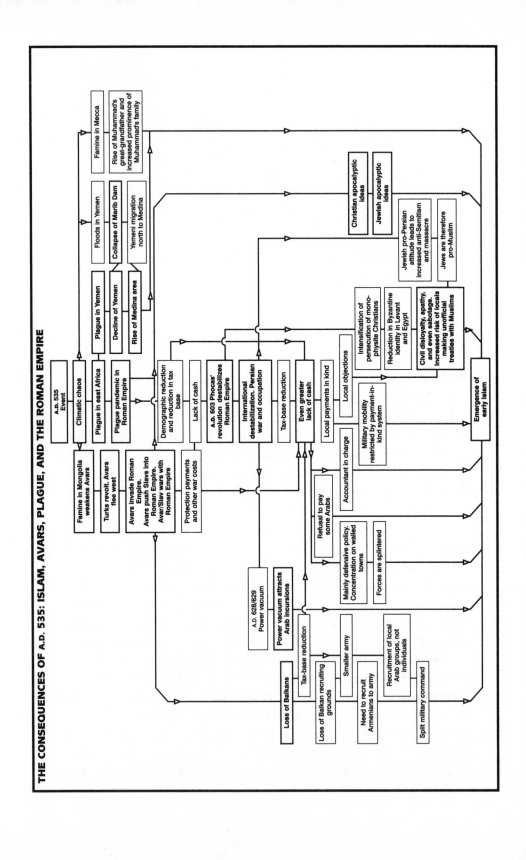

communications and coordination between the town-based military units even more difficult.

The empire's financial problems also produced distortion in the way its Arabian frontier army was run. With cash control probably uppermost in his mind, the emperor, Heraclius, appointed Theodore Trithurios, a pen-pushing accountant (a *sakellarios*, Greek for "treasurer"), to command this vital, if undermanned, military machine. Though it probably reassured the worried troops that they would at least get paid, the appointment almost certainly meant that budgetary and cash-flow considerations often took precedence over purely military ones.

Poor central funding also meant that food and other provisions had to be obtained from the local Syrian and Palestinian population. This was not a new idea, but the empire's financial stringency and the appointment of an accountant as senior commander probably led to this local "war tax" being extracted with unprecedented vigor from an area that had not experienced it for more than a generation.

The war-tax system also further restricted military mobility, because the army could not easily be moved too far from war-tax sources. And it certainly won no friends among the local population. Indeed, just prior to one vital battle (Jabiya-Yarmuk, in 636), the local chief civil administrator of Damascus, Mansur, actually refused to supply the army with provisions it had tried to requisition and then went on to launch a fake attack on a group of Roman soldiers in order to frighten them away, presumably so they could not enforce the war tax.

A second long-term imperial problem that affected the army was the Avar/Slav occupation of most of the Balkans, which had started in the second half of the sixth century and intensified in the first quarter of the seventh. This region had traditionally been one of the main sources of individual recruits to the Roman army. Now that source was no longer available, and the imperial government had to seek other options.

As more forces were required in the Arab frontier region, the authorities recruited more local Arabs and thousands of Armenians. But de facto control of both the Arab and Armenian contingents rested with their leaders, Arab tribal chieftains and Armenian warlords. At the disastrous Battle of Jabiya-Yarmuk, for example, the Armenian general, Vahan, and the overall regional commander, the accountant Trithurios, distrusted each other, and the third military boss, a local monarch called Jabala, may well have been distrustful of both his colleagues.

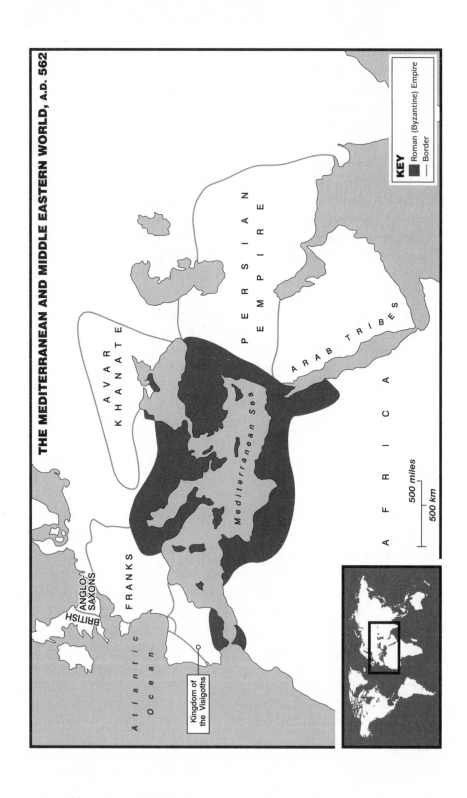

THE MEDITERRANEAN AND MIDDLE EASTERN WORLD, A.D. 562

KEY
■ Roman (Byzantine) Empire
— Border

BRITISH
ANGLO-
SAXONS

FRANKS

Atlantic
Ocean

Kingdom of
the Visigoths

AVAR
KHANATE

PERSIAN
EMPIRE

ARAB TRIBES

Mediterranean Sea

A F R I C A

500 miles
500 km

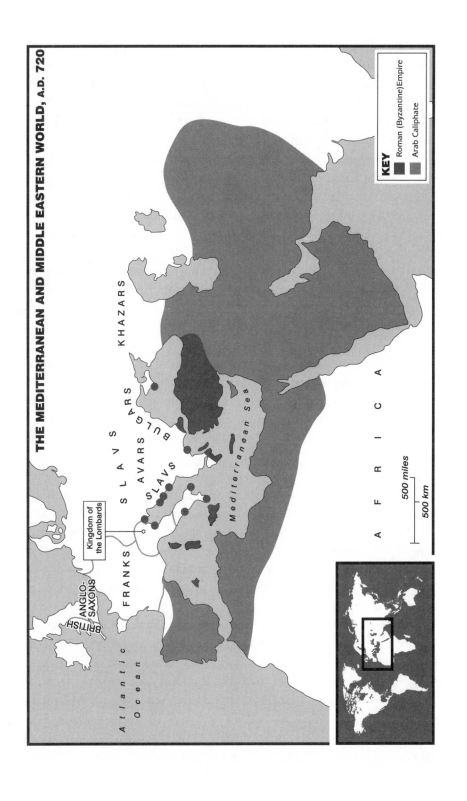

THE MEDITERRANEAN AND MIDDLE EASTERN WORLD, A.D. 720

BRITISH

ANGLO-
SAXONS

FRANKS

Kingdom of
the Lombards

Atlantic
Ocean

S L A V S

A V A R S

S L A V S

B U L G A R S

KHAZARS

Mediterranean Sea

A F R I C A

500 miles

500 km

KEY

Roman (Byzantine) Empire

Arab Caliphate

There was also conflict within the large Armenian contingent. On the eve of the Battle of Jabiya-Yarmuk, a senior officer on the Armenian right flank refused to obey his superior's orders.[1] A hint of further discord is provided by an Arab source who claimed, somewhat unbelievably, that a top Armenian officer converted to Islam just before the battle.[2] A further indication of turmoil within the Armenian force on the eve of this vital battle is the equally bizarre report that there was an attempted mutiny designed to put General Vahan on the imperial throne in place of Emperor Heraclius. The details of these stories are probably wrong, but they are almost certainly indicative of severe discord within the Roman ranks.

It was not only the nature and effectiveness of the army that was determined to a significant extent by financial considerations. The morale of some Arab forces in the Roman military machine was no doubt also affected, in a more direct way. There was at least one occasion on which the Roman authorities at the local level simply refused to pay allied Arab troops their wages.

The third background problem to generate a host of negative factors was the Persian occupation itself. Persian forces withdrew from Roman territory after occupying it for fifteen to twenty years. But the Roman authorities took many months to reoccupy all the areas, and even after they had done so, Roman troops were unfamiliar with the territory and the local politics.

In 628 and 629, when the Persian withdrawal treaty had been signed and there was a temporary military and administrative vacuum, Islam was beginning to penetrate the extreme eastern part of the Roman Empire, the area just to the east of the Dead Sea. Indeed, a Muslim was murdered by Christians in the town of Umm al-Rasas (thirty miles south of modern Amman) in 628, and the first battle between the empire and Islam took place thirty-five miles farther south at Mu'ta in 629, as mentioned in the previous chapter.

Another consequence of the Persian occupation was a real increase in Roman anti-Semitism. The Jews, long oppressed by the Christian imperial authorities, had been delighted when Persia seized much of the Roman Empire in the first quarter of the seventh century. The Jews had seen the Persians as liberators, and the Romans had seen the Jews as anti-Christian traitors.

The Roman-Persian conflict totally destabilized thirty-five years of calm, though admittedly cool, relationships between Christians and Jews in the Middle East. When the Roman Empire turned the tables on the Persian foe, it was the Jews who paid the price. In 630, under pressure from local Christians and their priests, Emperor Heraclius ordered the massacre of Jews in the Jerusalem and Galilee areas. There was even a celebratory liturgy and a fast arranged by the Church authorities to expiate the act of massacre.[3] The emperor also ordered a series of forced baptisms.

It's true that the Muslims had treated the Jews of far-off Medina badly in A.D. 626. But the degree of Jewish enmity toward the Roman state was far deeper; the massacres of 630 were more recent and geographically nearer. So Jewish communities were, on the whole, pro-Muslim and anti-Roman. When a high-ranking Roman officer—probably a friend of the emperor—was killed by Muslims at the Battle of Dathin in 634, the Jewish community in Palestine was overjoyed, according to a near-contemporary account. As noted earlier, some even thought Muhammad might be the harbinger of the Messiah, the one who would herald their liberation from Roman oppression.[4]

Given these sentiments, the Roman military would therefore not have been delighted that the two towns nearest the site of the battle at Jabiya-Yarmuk, Nawa and Adhri'at, were largely Jewish, and may well have been willing, if clandestine, sources of help for the Muslims.

The Persian occupation must also have played a role in further reducing the already patchy sense of Roman identity felt by the disparate peoples of Palestine, Syria, and Egypt. Although the occupation had lasted only fifteen to twenty years, that was long enough for an entire new generation of citizens to have grown up with minimal recollection of Roman rule.

The region's sense of Roman identity, strong in the second to fifth centuries, had begun to deteriorate in the sixth with the Roman suppression of a popular local variant of Christianity, the so-called monophysite heresy, which taught that Jesus was not both fully divine and fully human (as the Catholics believe) but was instead fully and exclusively divine. The heresy became the majority religion in Roman-ruled Upper Mesopotamia, Syria, and Egypt.

Persecution of the monophysites was intermittent, but when the domestic and international political situation was destabilized by Phocas' revolution in 603 (described in Chapter 5), the empire's religious balance also collapsed. Phocas—an enthusiastic Catholic—presided over the ferocious harassment of the monophysite heartland in the Middle East. This unleashed a tide of anti-Roman feeling and promoted local separatist nationalism, most notably in Egypt. Syria and Upper Mesopotamia (or at least the monophysite majority there) began to increasingly identify themselves as more Arab than Roman. In Egypt, for example, there was a new pride in the ancient pharaonic past, and the story was proudly told of the monophysite bishop who, fleeing from the Persians, hid in the magnificent tomb of a dead pharaoh. The ghost of the pharaoh started to haunt the unfortunate bishop, but the ever-diligent cleric decided in the end to baptize the long-dead ruler. The tale illustrates the growing sense of nationalistic oneness with the glorious Egyptian past and, conversely, the decline in identity with the late Roman Empire's Greek soul.

Both the resurgence of antimonophysite persecution at the beginning of the century and the Persian occupation that almost immediately followed it eroded the Middle Eastern population's loyalty to the empire. And these factors, combined with the unpopular local war tax, produced a lethal cocktail of civil disloyalty, apathy, collaborationist ideas, and even anti-Roman sabotage.

As outlined at the beginning of this chapter, the Roman disintegration at the hands of Islam had five original interrelated causes: chronic lack of cash; the Avar/Slav seizure of the Balkans; religious dissension; the Persian occupation; and the plague. All five were the direct or indirect consequences of the climatic problems of the mid–sixth century. And just as the Avar hordes had moved west following the climatic destabilization of Mongolia, another central Asian people, the Turks, were to make their mark on the world as a direct result of that same chaos.

PART FIVE

THE TURKIC DIMENSION

11

THE TURKISH
TIME BOMB

J ust as the climatically induced political changes on the Mongolian
steppe had helped to reshape Eastern European and Middle Eastern
history through the agency of the defeated Avars, so it was that those
same changes, this time through the good offices of the victors, the Turks,
led ultimately to huge changes in the Balkans, North Africa, and the Middle East, and even in India and in the Jewish world.

However, whereas the Avar-associated changes took only 150 years to
unfold (see Chapters 3 and 4), equally dramatic changes in the Turkic
world took nearly a thousand years to do so. How did a climatically induced political and ethnic revolution in sixth-century Mongolia end up a
thousand or more years later affecting so much of humanity from Bohemia to Bangladesh?

The sequence of events was complex, but the trigger that set it in
motion was almost certainly the climatic chaos of the 530s. As already described in Chapter 3, it was the differences in their respective vulnerability to drought that led to the mighty Avar empire being overturned by
the Avars' vassals, the Turks. Whereas the Avar leader committed suicide
and many of his people fled west, the victorious Turks set about creating
their own steppe empire. Within a decade, it stretched from the borders of
Korea to the Crimea. At its heart was a royal clan, an emperor (known as
the *kagan*), a mysterious legend, and a sacred cave.

The royal clan of the Turks, the Ashina (literally, "noble lord") family,

traced its ancestry back through legend in typical totemic style to an animal, not a human. Their family origin myth tells the story of a young
child who was the sole survivor of a tribal massacre. All his family and
friends having been slaughtered, he alone escaped and hid in a nearby
cave. There he encountered a she-wolf and, like Romulus and Remus of
ancient Rome, was adopted and suckled by her. The pair became insepa-
rable, and when the child grew into a man, he had sex with the wolf,
which then gave birth to a son—the first Ashina.

The sacred cave—where, according to legend, the sole survivor of the
tribal holocaust was suckled by the wolf and where the first Ashina was
conceived—became the religious and ritual epicenter of the empire. Although the supreme deity of the Turks was Tengri, the sky god, it was the
cult of the wolf that was politically far more important. The cave—the exact location of which has now long been forgotten—lay somewhere in
the sacred core territory of the Turk nation, a sort of Turkic holy land, the
area of Mongolia known as Outuken Yish (literally, "forested mountain
of the Otuken").

According to ancient Chinese sources, the cave of the wolf ancestor was a place of sacrifice and ritual.[1] It was probably there that the
bizarre coronation rituals of the *kagan*s took place. Riding across the
steppe, their long black hair streaming out behind them, their giant mus-
taches rigid and stiff despite the relentless wind, thousands of Turk noble-
men and their families and retainers would have converged on the holy
ground. An aura of dust whipped up by countless horses' hooves and the
massive high wheels of heavily laden ox-drawn carts would have begun to
envelop the city of round felt tents that had begun to spring up around
the sacred cave.

When all had arrived, the new *kagan* was brought out, held aloft on a
large felt rug. He was spun around and thrown into the air nine times,
then placed on a horse that he had to ride in a circle nine times. Next he
was lifted off the horse, placed upon the ground, and half strangled with
a silken cord. As he gasped for air, his consciousness beginning to alter
and reduce, he had to answer one ritual royal question: "How long will
you reign?"[2]

The answer, uttered by the semiconscious *kagan*-elect, was seen as
having divine authority. The assembled multitude may well have seen the
reply as emanating from the spirit of the first Ashina or his wolf-mother
rather than merely from the mouth of their new monarch. His destiny

now mapped out, the silken noose was loosened and the new *kagan* was free to breathe again and rule for the allotted time.

Although the *kagan* was the overall ruler of the Turkic empire, he governed in conjunction with a powerful, though technically junior, partner known as the Yabghu. This co-ruler was responsible for governing the whole of the western half of the empire. The first Yabghu was the extraordinarily talented Ashina Turk general who first conquered the 2,500 miles of steppe between Mongolia and the Ukraine. His name was Ishtemi, and as the brother of the first *kagan*, Bumin, he had almost unchallenged political authority in the Turkic world.

Armed with bows and arrows, swords, lances, and even battle lassoes for pulling their opponents off their horses, the mounted hordes of Turk warriors penetrated every region of the steppes. The realm of the proto-Mongolian White Huns collapsed under Turk pressure, and on the southern fringes of the steppe, the great Iranian city-states of Bukhara, Samarkand, and Khwarazm surrendered to Ishtemi and his armies.

Ishtemi ruled as Yabghu for twenty-four years (552–576), and although he never became supreme *kagan*, he was for periods the only really permanent ruling personality within the empire, as his brother Bumin died in 553 and three of his sons succeeded him between that year and 573.

The empire continued (apart from a brief twenty-five-year interlude) for almost two centuries until the 740s, when the Ashina ruling clan was dislodged from power by a coalition of other Turks, including Uighurs (long-standing rivals of the Ashina), Qarluqs (whose leaders were actually of Ashina origin), and Oghuzis. The most powerful element, the Uighurs, then seized power, turned on their Qarluq allies, and proceeded to try to wipe them out. Those who remained alive fled west in 745 and had succeeded in taking over the western part of the empire by 766.

So far, the expansion and evolution of Turkic influence and power, first uncorked by the climatic catastrophe of the 530s, had been relatively conventional. But in the early and mid–tenth century, intermittent conflict between the Arab caliphate (the Islamic empire founded by Muhammad and ruled by his successors) and the Qarluq Turkic state resulted in large numbers of Qarluq and other Turkic prisoners being captured by the caliphate. The caliphate's strategy (operated on their behalf by their eastern governors, the Samanids) was above all to acquire slaves, as well as to discomfit and discourage potential Turkic aggressors.[3] The Turkic

prisoners were turned into slave-soldiers, most of whom were then converted from paganism to Islam and given their freedom on condition
they remained loyal to the caliphate.

But ultimately the policy backfired dramatically. For instead of buck-
ling down to a life of unquestioning obedience, the Turkic slave-soldiers
tried in 962 to help "fix" the Samanid succession. They failed, but proceeded nevertheless to set up their own Turkic slave-soldier state (that of
the Ghaznavids) in southern Afghanistan.

Within forty years the Arab caliph had formally given the slave-
soldier state's ruler, Mahmud, the title of sultan. Mahmud, the second
ruler in the Ghaznavid dynasty, proceeded to establish a substantial empire within and outside the caliphate. His territory stretched from eastern
Iran to what is now northern Pakistan, and it was Turkic involvement in
the latter area that was to launch the religious transformation of much of
the Indian subcontinent over subsequent centuries. From 1040 onward
military pressure from their enemies forced the Ghaznavids to concentrate their energies on northwest India. Prior to that date, they had pri-
marily been interested in raiding wealthy Hindu temples, but beginning
in the middle of the century, they increasingly established political control in such areas as Kashmir, Lahore, northern Sind, and Baluchistan.

It was this political control that first saw the substantial introduction
of Islam into India—a process that was to further accelerate under later
Turkic and then Mughal rulers in subsequent centuries and which ultimately led to the partition of India in 1947 and the creation of Pakistan.
If the Ghaznavid empire of the eleventh century had not established a
substantial Islamic bridgehead into India, thus altering the religious and
therefore geopolitical balance, it is doubtful whether later Muslims, culminating in the Mughals, would have been able to complete the job.

Just as the Qarluq Turks had fled from their erstwhile allies (the
Uighurs) in 745, their fellow rebels, the Oghuz Turks, also fled a generation later, in the 770s.[4] And just as the Qarluqs had had an impact on India, so the Oghuzis were destined to have an equal, if not greater, effect
on Europe and the Middle East. The Oghuzi refugees, fleeing for their
lives, arrived on the banks of the Aral Sea and rapidly created their own
Turkic state around the north, east, and west of that great inland expanse
of water. On the banks of the Syrdarya River, they then set about creating
a capital for themselves, Yangi Kent (literally, "new city").

Gradually one of the Oghuzi clans, the Seljuks, began to emerge as a

powerful element within the Oghuz Turkic state, and in 985 they converted to Islam, a move which enabled the clan to more "legitimately" attack its still-pagan fellow Oghuzis.

Soon the Seljuks had become the leading element among the Oghuz
Turks, a status that was confirmed in 1040 when they led the Oghuzis
into battle against their fellow Turks of the Ghaznavid dynasty and won.
This had the dual effect both of forcing the Ghaznavids to retreat and
concentrate on faraway India and of allowing the Seljuk clan to evolve
into a superpower, for when the official ruler of the Arab caliphate heard
of the Seljuks' success, he invited them into his territory—indeed, into his
capital, Baghdad—to ally with him against his enemies. Thus it was that
in 1055 the Seljuks and their Oghuz army annihilated the Iranian military warlords who had run the caliphate, irrespective of the caliph's
wishes, for the previous 110 years.[5]

The victory made the Seljuk Turkic clan virtual masters of the Islamic
world. Two extraordinary brothers, Toghrul and Chaghri, were made sul-
tans of the caliphate by the caliph himself. Soon the Oghuz were colliding with the eastern frontiers of the Roman Empire, and in 1071, at the
Battle of Manzikert in eastern Anatolia, Chaghri's son and heir, Alp Arslan
(literally, "brave lion"), shattered the Roman army.[6]

In a sense, the Battle of Manzikert marked the beginning of the end
for the Roman Empire, for by the late thirteenth century, another Oghuz
group was coming to prominence in the frontier country where the
caliphate and the empire met. Their leader was Osman, the founder of
the Ottoman dynasty, which was destined to create one of the world's
greatest empires.

Within fifty years the Ottomans had taken over most of Anatolia
(modern Turkey) and had been invited to participate in the internal affairs of the Roman Empire.[7] Soon they were in Europe, and they had
reached the Danube by the 1380s. More than 1,750 years of Roman imperial history finally came to an end with the fall of Constantinople in
1453 when the Ottoman sultan, Muhammad the Conqueror, claimed to
combine in his rule the imperial traditions of the Turkic steppe, the
caliphate, and the Roman Empire itself.

Over the next few centuries the Ottoman Empire conquered and
ruled all of southeast Europe, most of North Africa (including Egypt),
and most of the Middle East. In the late sixteenth century their armies
even reached the outskirts of Vienna. Today the Republic of Turkey, the

Turkish presence in Cyprus, and the sometimes embattled enclaves of
Bosnia and Kosovo as well as Albania are the living legacy of the Ottoman advance.

Perhaps an even more fundamental geopolitical legacy is the fault line
that divides the political and social culture of Europe between East and
West. For although the Ottoman Empire was one of the world's most glit-
tering political achievements between the fifteenth and seventeenth centuries, by around 1700 the state had become deeply conservative,
resistant to any and all innovation. Politically and economically, eastern
Europe bears the mark of up to 180 years of stiflingly conservative government experienced at precisely the time that western Europe was industri-
alizing and internationalizing.

Thus it was that, for good and for ill, the Turkish genius for empire
building and for adapting was liberated in the wake of the climatic catastrophe of the sixth century. And thus it was that the Turk tide rolled ever
westward (and southward) to shape so much of today's world.

THE CONSEQUENCES OF A.D. 535 FOR THE TURKIC WORLD

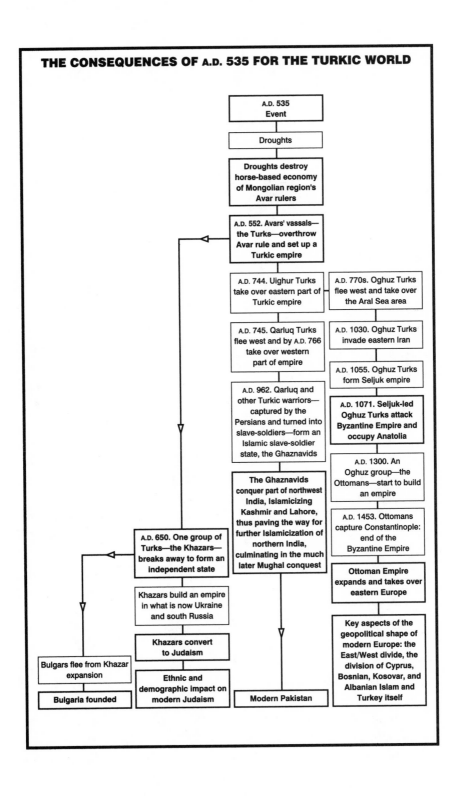

12

THE JEWISH
EMPIRE

"Dishonoured and humiliated in our dispersion, we have to listen in silence to those who say: 'Every nation has its own land and you [the Jews] alone possess not even a shadow of a country on this earth.' I feel the urge to know the truth, whether there is really a place on this earth where harassed Israel [the Jewish people] can rule itself, where it is subject to nobody."

Thus wrote the Jewish chief minister of Moorish Spain (the Umayyad caliphate, based in Cordoba) to the king of a faraway empire that, according to reports reaching Spain, was a Jewish state.

"If I were to know that this is indeed the case, I would not hesitate to forsake all honors, to resign my high office, to abandon my family, and to travel over mountains and plains, over land and water, until I arrived at the place where my Lord, the [Jewish] King rules."[1]

For hundreds of years after the Romans destroyed the Jewish Temple in A.D. 70, there had been no Jewish state, and the Jews had been scattered all over the known world. So when, in c. 955, the Jewish chief minister of Muslim Spain, Hasdai ibn Shaprut,[2] learned about the existence of a Jewish kingdom 1,500 miles east of Spain and 700 miles north of Jerusalem, in and to the east of what is now the Ukraine, he could hardly credit what he heard.[3]

What he did not know at the time, however, was that this Jewish empire had already been in existence for more than two hundred years. (So poor was information transmission and international political knowl-

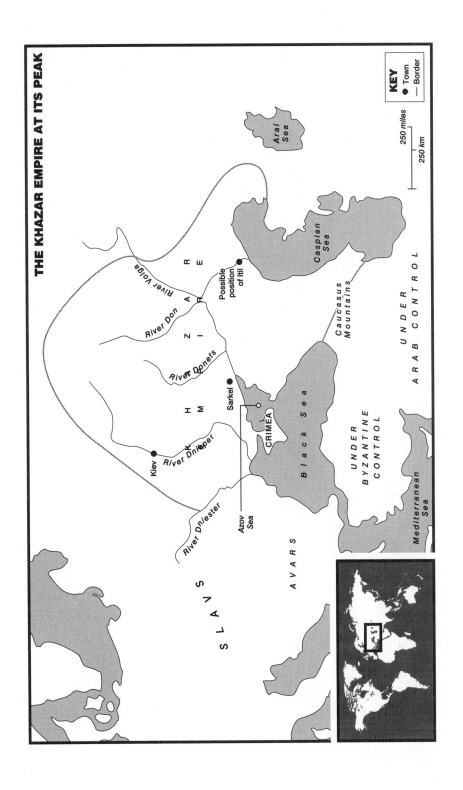

THE KHAZAR EMPIRE AT ITS PEAK

KEY
● Town
—— Border

250 miles
250 km

Aral Sea

Caspian Sea

Possible position of Itil

River Volga

River Don

River Donets

Sarkel

CRIMEA

Kiev

River Dnieper

River Dniester

Azov Sea

Black Sea

Caucasus Mountains

UNDER BYZANTINE CONTROL

UNDER ARAB CONTROL

Mediterranean Sea

SLAVS

AVARS

edge in medieval times that the Ukraine might as well have been on the dark side of the moon as far as Hasdai was concerned.) It had already played a vital role in world history and would ultimately do so again. But how had a Jewish empire come into existence on the Eurasian steppes, and what impact did it have on the international stage?

Following the climatic problems of the 530s, the Turks had overthrown Avar rule in Mongolia and had established their own great empire.[4] However, within just over a hundred years, one key element of that Turkic empire—a group probably related to its ruling clan—broke away to form a state of its own. This group, the Khazars, rapidly set about constructing an empire that stretched from central Asia to the borders of Poland. As the Khazar state grew stronger, it became a northern buffer between the Christian late Roman Empire and the Muslim empire of the Arab caliphate.[5]

Confronted with the two superpowers, the Khazars realized that neutrality became a political necessity. The pagan Khazars could well see that most of the "civilized" world followed one or the other of the politically powerful monotheistic creeds, Christianity or Islam. The Khazars felt it was desirable to place themselves on the same monotheistic theological (and therefore political) level as the two superpowers, but sensibly, they did not wish to take sides.

In practice, neutrality meant opting for a "common-denominator" religious affiliation, one that could not be seen as leaning in either a Christian or a Muslim direction. Judaism fitted the bill exactly. Despite some Christian antagonism toward Judaism, both the Christian church of the Roman Empire and the Muslim caliphate regarded it as a legitimate faith. Christians found less to disagree with in Judaism than in Islam—and, likewise, Islam found Judaism less offensive than the "man-god" ideas inherent in Christianity. Of the three faiths' holy scriptures, it was the Old Testament—the bedrock of Judaism—that was accepted as the word of God by Jews, Christians, and Muslims alike. For these reasons Judaism appealed politically to the Khazars, and they adopted it as their faith.

Surviving records suggest that, at least for the appearance of fairness, representatives of the three faiths were invited to the Khazar royal court to present their arguments.[6] There seems to have already been a strong Jewish influence there, for the Christian and Muslim representatives had to be sent for from abroad, whereas the Jewish representative was on the spot. It is possible that the Jewish presence in Khazaria even predated the

Khazar state and consisted of Crimean Jews and refugees from Constantinople's anti-Semitic pogroms of the 630s.

According to the eleventh-century Arab historian Al-Bakri, a high Khazar official advised the king that "those in possession of sacred scriptures fall into three groups." He suggested that the king should "summon them and ask them to state their case," and then "follow the one who is in possession of the truth."[7]

In another version (written by the tenth-century Khazar king Joseph), both the Romans and the caliphate sent envoys—this time uninvited—with "precious gifts and money and learned men to convert [the king] to their beliefs."[8]

"But," wrote Joseph, "the King was wise and sent for a Jew with much knowledge and acumen and put all three [the two envoys and the Jew] together to discuss their doctrines." After a lengthy debate, the Khazar monarch, a king called Bulan, adjourned the conference for three days. He then asked the Christian which of the other two faiths he preferred. The Christian envoy, probably a bishop, chose Judaism. The king then put the same question to the Muslim and received the same response.

It seems likely that the Khazar ruler—with political neutrality in mind—had already decided to opt for Judaism before the conference started, but had thought it expedient to give the others the opportunity to put their bids in, so to speak. Indeed, from a neutral second-preferences perspective, the Khazar king had seen to it that his choice of faith was, in a sense, actually seen to be in line with his superpower neighbors' wishes.

The conversion seems to have taken place sometime in the second quarter of the eighth century. But the Judaism the Khazar king followed appears to have been of a very basic variety. For possible internal reasons and probable external geopolitical ones, the newly converted king, Bulan, and his Jewish advisors seem to have kept exclusively or at least predominantly to the Old Testament and not to have paid much attention to Rabbinic law or the Talmud—the huge body of Jewish legal and cultural literature compiled in the fifth century. Within Judaism in the eighth century there was in some places—especially geographically peripheral areas—fierce doctrinal reluctance to accept Talmudic (originally predominantly Mesopotamian) interpretations of Jewish law and practice. In Mesopotamia itself, this actually developed into a major schism in which anti-Talmudic conservatives broke away to form a sect still known today as the Karaites.[9]

In Khazaria, the argument for embracing Judaism had been the commonality of the Old Testament's acceptability to Jews, Christians, and Muslims alike—and so geopolitically it would no doubt have been seen as "additionalist" to put any emphasis on the Talmud. After all, the Koran and the New Testament had not been embraced, precisely because they had not passed the commonality test. The dictates of political neutrality and a distinct lack of enthusiasm for the Talmud seemed to have given early Khazar Judaism a fairly conservative complexion.

It is likely that at that stage relatively few inhabitants of the empire converted, probably just the king and his immediate clan. However, the new religious situation must have led to at least some Jewish emigration by more pro-Talmudic elements and a steady flow of official and unofficial conversions to Judaism within the Khazar community as well as within other ethnic groups (also mainly Turkic) within the empire.

The anti-additionalist arguments of the 730s served their purpose but soon were no longer politically vital. Thus, by around 800, the Khazar king Obadiah, "a brave and venerated man," was able to "reform the Rule and fortify the Law according to tradition and usage." The reforming king then "built synagogues and schools, assembled a multitude of Israel's sages, gave them lavish gifts of gold and silver, and made them interpret the 24 [sacred] books, the Mishna and the Talmud and the order in which the Liturgies are to be said."[10] This seems to suggest that Talmudic knowledge did not exist in Khazaria at this time and that Talmudic experts had to be invited in from abroad, almost certainly to settle, as their theological interpretation of the Scriptures and the Talmud would have been a long-term and ongoing activity.

Obadiah's reform of Khazarian Judaism almost certainly stemmed, at least in part, from the king's own religious commitment and enthusiasm—and it is likely that at this stage conversion to the Jewish faith became more prevalent. Widespread conversions certainly must have started at some point, given the number of ethnically non-Jewish groups attested to in medieval times as adhering to Judaism or to Jewish customs in the Khazar region.

First of all, there were the Khazars themselves, the empire's ruling elite. Ethnically and linguistically Turkic, they probably numbered up to 750,000—at a guess perhaps 25 percent of the empire's total population of between 1.5 million and 3 million.[11]

Some of the Oghuz Turks—specifically those who worked for the Khazars in the ninth and tenth centuries—almost certainly became Judaized or even fully Jewish. It is known, for instance, that Seljuk, the founder of the dynasty that bears his name,[12] called one of his sons Israel, while his grandson was called Daud (David), both specifically Jewish names; and it is possible that their house of worship, referred to by an Arab chronicler,[13] was a synagogue.[14]

Some elements of another Turkic people, the Cumans, who swept west in the mid–eleventh century, also appear to have become either partially or fully Judaized. For instance, a Cuman prince by the name of Kobiak named his sons Isaac and Daniel.[15] Certainly some Turkic nomads on the south Russian (now Ukrainian) steppes were fully or partially Jewish. The twelfth-century Jewish explorer Pethahiah of Regensburg recorded that he had met nomads on the steppes—perhaps Cumans or Oghuz—who followed an unconventional form of Judaism, observed the Sabbath in total darkness (no artificial light being permitted), and prohibited even the cutting of bread on that day.

Then there was the Khazar influence on the Hungarians. The Magyar tribes originally lived in the Khazar sphere of influence on the steppe. In around A.D. 800 one of the Khazar tribes, the Kabars, fled from the Khazar heartland after a disagreement with the Khazar king. This tribe, as part of the Khazar nation, was almost certainly Jewish, and it became the leading group among the early Magyars.

Then, fifty or so years later, the Khazar monarch, as overlord of the Magyars, gave them the right to choose their own king. By 900, other tribes, the Pecheneg Turks, had forced the Magyars to migrate west to what is now Hungary.[16] But the old Magyar-Khazar link continued, and in c. 950 groups of Khazars (presumably Jews) were invited into Hungary by the Hungarians. In the fourteenth century many Hungarian Jews were still being officially categorized as Khazars.[17]

Cuman pressure in the early twelfth century on the Khazars themselves almost certainly led to a major new Jewish settlement being set up in what had once been Khazar land and was now the Viking principality of Kiev. This new town, established by c. 1117 and known as Bela Vezha (the same name as the Khazar empire's greatest fortress, just north of the Caspian Sea), was located near Chernigov, 90 miles north of Kiev. There must already have been a substantial and long-established Jewish community in the Kiev area, because tenth-century letters that refer to it still survive. Indeed, Kiev itself was probably founded by Jewish Khazars in or prior to the ninth century—well before it was taken over by the Vikings in 882.[18]

It was not only some Cuman and Oghuz tribes that seem to have become at least partially Judaized by their Khazar overlords or neighbors. Some north-Iranian-speaking Tat tribes of the Caucasus Mountains are still Jewish today, although academic opinion is divided as to whether their Jewish identity was derived from the Khazars, derived from the Iranian Jews, or influenced culturally or ethnically by both. A Russian chronicle of 1346 actually describes the eastern Caucasus as the "Land of the Jews."

Lastly, there are the ancient Jewish communities of Crimea (the Krimchaks), which are probably partially Khazar-derived or -influenced; although the original Jewish presence in Crimea had certainly started in pre-Khazar times. After the demise of Khazar power elsewhere, some sort of Jewish political survival probably continued in Crimea, for some Crimean Khazars tried to seize control of part of the Crimean peninsula as late as 1079, and the area was actually known as Gazaria (Khazaria) and the Jewish population as Gazari (Khazars) up till the fifteenth century. What's more, several Khazar Crimean fortress towns survived as Jewish centers into later medieval and early modern times.[19]

Of what long-term significance was the Khazar empire and the Judaization of substantial numbers of Turkic and other peoples? The effects were twofold.

First, the Khazar empire—and the fact that it was monotheistic—prevented the westward spread of Islam. If it had not been for the military might of the empire, Islam would likely have rolled west into pagan eastern Europe and possibly even into pagan Scandinavia in the eighth and ninth centuries A.D.[20] The Vikings, who later ended up as Christians, could well have become Islamicized instead if the Khazar block on Islamic expansion had not existed. Theoretically Poland, Hungary, Romania, eastern Austria, the Czech and Slovak lands, Germany, Denmark, Sweden, Norway, and Viking eastern England could all have become Muslim. If the Khazar empire had not prevented Islamic expansion, it is even possible that the Normans (originally Vikings from Denmark) might have already been Muslims for two hundred years by the time they conquered England in 1066. What's more, if the Arabs had occupied what is now the Ukraine and Russia, a Viking people known as the Rus would never have been able to push south and east from the Baltic to establish Russia.

But blocking the Islamic advance was not the only long-term historical role played by Khazaria. The Jewish empire's other legacy was the creation of a large pool of Jews of ethnically non-Jewish origin who subsequently became a major part—perhaps even the numerically dominant part—of northeast European Jewry and subsequently of world Jewry.

World Jewry was, and still is, divided into a number of distinctly different traditions, chief among which are the Sephardim (Spanish Jews) and the Ashkenazim (northern European Jews). By far the largest number of Ashkenazim originate from eastern Europe—especially Lithuania, Poland, and Russia—and almost certainly have a large Khazar or Khazar-influenced (i.e., ethnically Turkic, Slav, and Magyar) genetic component.

Potential physical evidence for this has recently been discovered by geneticists. DNA tests on Sephardic and Ashkenazi Jews have revealed the possibility that at least one key section of the latter community may have genetic evidence of a potentially large-scale or even mass conversion which must have taken place sometime after around A.D. 700—the time when the ancestors of the Sephardic and Ashkenazi communities started to become geographically differentiated. Historically it is known that such mass conversions have never occurred in western Europe and that in eastern Europe (including Russia and the Ukraine) no such conversions have occurred since at least A.D. 1200. This suggests that any such conversion must have taken place sometime between 700 and 1200 in eastern Europe—and the only known mass conversion within that time frame and in that geographical area was that of the Khazars in the eighth century. Significantly, the section of the Ashkenazi community whose DNA may suggest a partially convert origin is that section which up till now had traditionally been said to be wholly descended from the Assistant Priests of ancient Israel. This group, according to tradition, comprises the majority of the descendants of the ancient Israelite tribe of Levi—people who today still bear the name Levi or Levy. Significantly, it does not include a Levite subgroup—the Priests themselves—who often have the name Cohen. The Levi name, identity, and, even today, the Assistant-Priest status and role are only passed down in the male line, as is a specific piece of genetic material, the Y-chromosome—the DNA strand that actually determines maleness.

Genetic codes on the Y-chromosome are therefore inherited from a man's distant male-line ancestors. By analyzing Y chromosomes from a sample of both Levite and non-Levite populations in both Sephardic and Ashkenazi communities, geneticists have discovered that an astounding 30 percent of Ashkenazi non-Cohenic Levites have a particular combination of DNA material on part of their Y-chromosome that is not shared to any extent by either non-Levite Ashkenazi Jews or the Sephardic community as a whole.[22]

This genetic marker does not even show up among the Cohens (descendants of the ancient Israelite Chief Priests)—but only among the descendants of Assistant Priests, and then only within Ashkenazi (northern European) Jewry.

What seems to have happened is not only a potentially large-scale conversion of non-Jewish people, almost certainly Khazars, to Judaism, but also the adoption of Levite (Assistant Priest) status by a substantial number of the Khazar converts. This interpretation is implicitly supported by textual evidence that has survived from Khazar times. A tenth-century letter of recommendation from the Jewish community of Kiev to Jewish communities outside Khazaria was signed by Jews with traditional Turkic names whose almost certainly Turkic Khazar ancestors had adopted Levitical second names—in both cases the name Cohen (a Levite subgroup)—indicating that they saw themselves as descendants or close associates of the ancient tribe of Levi.

If some top Khazars were adopting Cohenic Levitical status (i.e., Chief Priest status), then it is more than likely that others—a larger number—were adopting ordinary Levitical status (i.e., Assistant Priest status). Adoption of Cohenic or ordinary Levitical status by converts was and is expressly forbidden by rabbinical law, so the Khazars had to develop a mythic national history that gave them the right to Levitical status. They claimed that they were the descendants of one of the lost tribes of Israel and were not converts at all but merely returnees to Judaism. Furthermore, the tribe they claimed ancestry from was that of Simeon, the brother of the founder of the tribe of Levi; in the Bible (Genesis 49) it is made clear that the descendants of Simeon and Levi were to have a common destiny. Probably it was the old pre-Jewish Khazar priests—the *qams*—who at the conversion had become Levites en masse while the rest of the ethnic Khazar population (and probably some other Khazar-influenced peoples) had become ordinary non-Levitical Jews.

In the tenth and eleventh centuries, as the Khazar state disintegrated, and into the thirteenth century, as the Cuman and Mongol hordes pushed large numbers of refugees westward, Khazar and Khazar-influenced groups professing Judaism—including the probably highly committed Levites—migrated into eastern Europe, where they mixed with other Jewish groups moving east from Germany and north from

Italy. As a result, many different peoples with different languages had to adopt a lingua franca, and that language became Yiddish—a composite language with a medieval German base but also including Slavic, Romance, Hebrew, Aramaic, possibly Turkic, and other lexical and syntactical components.

In time, the Ashkenazim became the dominant tradition in world Jewry, but the numerical strength that allowed them to achieve that status almost certainly derived, at least in part, from the Jewish empire of Khazaria, a state that vanished from the world stage a thousand years ago and has been forgotten even by most of the world's history books.

Thus did the climatic and consequent political events in sixth-century Mongolia lead, via Turkic expansion and the subsequent formation of the Khazar empire, to both the non-Islamic nature of Europe and the size, ethnic makeup, and predominant cultural orientation of world Jewry.

Courtesy of the climatic chaos of the mid–sixth century, Avars, Slavs, Arabs, Turks, and Khazars changed Europe's history forever.

PART SIX

WESTERN EUROPE

13

DISASTER IN
BRITAIN

The climatic problems of the sixth century—both directly and through the medium of the plague—were also inducing fundamental change, bringing ancient western Europe to an end and ushering in its protomodern successors. Many of the modern states of western Europe owe their genesis to the climatic and epidemiological turmoil of this period. It was, for example, arguably the single most pivotal era in British history, for it witnessed a decisive change in the balance of power between the island's two major ethnic groups.

Prior to the fifth century, Britain had been a predominantly Celtic (native British) land. Then, in the 440s, substantial numbers of Germanic peoples had crossed the North Sea and settled in parts of what is now eastern and southern England. Over subsequent decades, hundreds of tiny Anglo-Saxon kingdoms were established. Some then amalgamated to become slightly larger units—Sussex, Surrey, Kent, Essex, early Wessex, East Anglia, and early Mercia. By the early sixth century (perhaps by 510 or 520) Anglo-Saxon expansion had virtually ceased in the face of Celtic resistance. This was the period normally associated with the quasi-legendary figure of King Arthur, a successful pan-British war leader. The Germanic east and the Celtic west then began to develop independently and separately.

The historical evidence shows that on the whole the British disliked the Anglo-Saxons so vehemently that normally they did not wish to mix or even trade with them, and the archaeological evidence confirms that

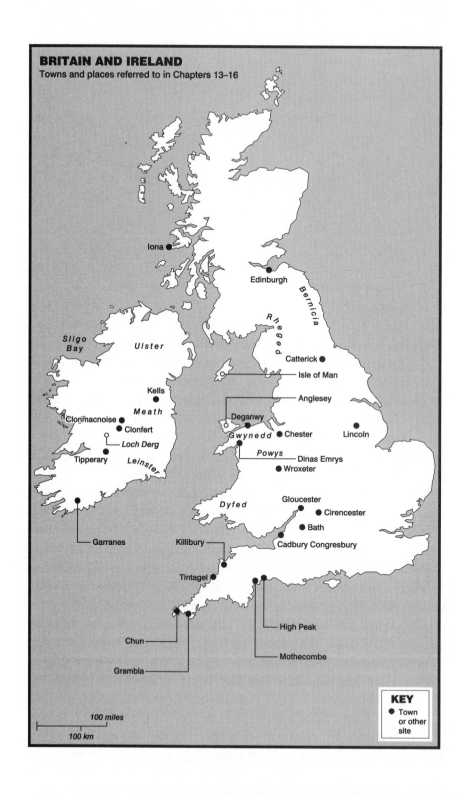

BRITAIN AND IRELAND
Towns and places referred to in Chapters 13–16

Iona ●

Edinburgh ●

Bernicia

Rheged

Sligo Bay

Ulster

Catterick ●

Isle of Man ○

Kells ●

Anglesey

Meath

Clonmacnoise ●
● Clonfert

Deganwy ○

Gwynedd

● Chester

Lincoln ●

○ *Loch Derg*

● Tipperary

Leinster

Powys

Dinas Emrys
● Wroxeter

Dyfed

Gloucester ●
● Cirencester

● Bath

Garranes

Killibury

Cadbury Congresbury

Tintagel ●

High Peak

Chun

Mothecombe

Grambla

100 miles

100 km

KEY
● Town or other site

there was indeed virtually no trade (and therefore probably little personal contact) between the Celtic west and the Germanic east.[1] In physical terms, vast forests separated the two peoples along most of what had become by the early sixth century a relatively stable frontier. And yet, by the early years of the following century, the Germanic Anglo-Saxons had taken over vast tracts of Celtic land, were engaged in further aggressive expansion, and had become the dominant geopolitical force. All this came about as a result, both direct and indirect, of the same worldwide climatic chaos that caused famines in China, snow in Mesopotamia, the first emergence of plague in East Africa, and the darkening of the sun, as reported in Constantinople.

Tree-ring evidence from Britain shows that tree growth slowed down significantly in 535–536 and did not fully recover until 555. The concentration of major climatic problems in the period 535–555 was seven times greater than in any other equivalent period during the rest of the 170-year span between 480 and 650.[2] Irish annals say that in Ireland there was a famine ("a failure of bread") in 538, almost certainly due to climatic problems. The Meteorological Office survey of British weather—*A Meteorological Chronology up to* A.D. *1450*—reveals that there were "floods in the Tweed with heavy casualties" in 536; that in 545 there was an "intensely cold winter"; that in 548, 250 people were killed in a "storm in London" in which "many homes were thrown down"; that in 550 "large hail stones like pullet's eggs fell in Scotland"; that in 552 there was "violent rain in Scotland for five months"; that in 554 "the winter was so severe with frost and snow that the birds and wild animals became so tame as to allow themselves to be taken by hand"; and that in 555 there were "severe thunderstorms all over Britain."

The significance of this information lies not in each individual entry but in the statistical concentration of them in the years 535–555, compared with the rest of the period. Yet despite the apparent severity of the climatic conditions and despite the famine (538 or possibly 536 in Ireland and almost certainly also in mainland Britain) associated with their onset, these events probably did not have any lasting impact, at least not directly. Interestingly, however, the period of the famine was much later (possibly as late as the mid–tenth century) reported—or more probably "selected"—as the death-date of King Arthur, A.D. 537. It was instead an indirect effect of the 530s climatic chaos which was to wreak major and permanent change on Britain.

In c. 549 the bubonic plague, having swept up from East Africa and across the Middle East and Europe, finally reached the shores of

BRITISH CLIMATE IN THE SIXTH CENTURY

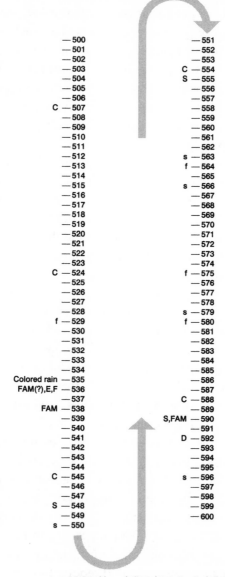

— 500	— 551
— 501	— 552
— 502	— 553
— 503	C — 554
— 504	S — 555
— 505	— 556
— 506	— 557
C — 507	— 558
— 508	— 559
— 509	— 560
— 510	— 561
— 511	— 562
— 512	s — 563
— 513	f — 564
— 514	— 565
— 515	s — 566
— 516	— 567
— 517	— 568
— 518	— 569
— 519	— 570
— 520	— 571
— 521	— 572
— 522	— 573
— 523	— 574
C — 524	f — 575
— 525	— 576
— 526	— 577
— 527	— 578
— 528	s — 579
f — 529	f — 580
— 530	— 581
— 531	— 582
— 532	— 583
— 533	— 584
— 534	— 585
Colored rain — 535	— 586
FAM(?),E,F — 536	— 587
— 537	C — 588
FAM — 538	— 589
— 539	S,FAM — 590
— 540	— 591
— 541	D — 592
— 542	— 593
— 543	— 594
— 544	— 595
C — 545	s — 596
— 546	— 597
— 547	— 598
S — 548	— 599
— 549	— 600
s — 550	

c	very cold	Letters denote types of climatic problems
f	flood	that were said, mainly by seventeenth–nineteenth-century
s	storm	scholars, to have occurred in any given year.
FAM	famine	Capital letters denote very major or exceptional
e	epidemic	climatic or climatically related events.
d	drought	

Main secondary source of data: C. E. Britton, *A Meteorological Chronology up to A.D. 1450*, London: HMSO, 1937.

the British Isles. In Ireland, the *Annals of Ulster* record that "a great epidemic" (a *"mortalitas magna"*) broke out. Of the aristocracy, at least six important figures—Finnia, Moccu, Telduib, Colam, Mac Tail, Sinchell, and Colum of Inis Celtra—are said to have perished. In Wales, the *Welsh Annals* also reveal that in 547 (corrected to 549 by some modern historians) the king of Gwynedd, a powerful monarch called Maelgwn, died of plague.[3]

The plague (which, as already described, had started in East Africa a decade earlier) almost certainly entered Britain on board ships that had come from either southwest France or, more likely, from the Mediterranean itself. As elsewhere, the carriers of the dread disease were stowaway black rats. There would have been plenty of opportunity for the epidemic to enter Britain because trade between the Mediterranean and the western part of the British Isles flourished in the first half of the sixth century, right up to the time of the plague.

Two key locations stand out as the most likely initial points of entry for the disease: Tintagel, on the north Cornish coast, and Cadbury Congresbury, on the river Yeo, two miles from the Bristol Channel. Both places were likely to have had direct contact with ships originating in the Mediterranean.

Tintagel—the mythical place of King Arthur's conception—appears to have been a royal citadel in the fifth century and the first half of the sixth. A substantial number of stone buildings from the period have been discovered on the site, as have considerable quantities of imported Mediterranean pottery. Excavations so far—in a relatively small percentage of the site—have unearthed three thousand fragments, and it is likely that tens of thousands more shards still remain to be discovered. An analysis of this unearthed material reveals that the royal elite at Tintagel were importing fine tableware from Phocaea in what is now western Turkey, other tableware items from the Carthage area (now Tunisia), jars from Sardis in western Turkey, and olive oil or wine amphoras from both Cilicia (southern Turkey) and the Peloponnese in southern Greece.

The Mediterranean influence at Tintagel may have gone even deeper than merely satisfying exotic tastes for fancy tableware and wines. Traders or even diplomats from the Roman world may well have lived at the royal court there. Excavations at a churchyard near Tintagel have unearthed two indications of a more pervasive Mediterranean influence—slate tablets bearing stylized crosses of a type more usually found in the

Mediterranean region, and remarkable evidence of graveside funerary feasts—again, things more normally associated with Mediterranean (specifically North African) practice.[4]

Thus mercantile and cultural contact was fairly strong. The Roman Empire, which was pushing west at this time, may even have viewed western Britain as simply a semidetached part of the Roman domain. Yet by the second half of the sixth century, Tintagel was substantially deserted. Almost certainly the culprit was the plague. The date fits, and the opportunities there for contact with the disease were probably the greatest in Britain.

A second mainland British entry point for the plague was probably the small town of Cadbury Congresbury on the river Yeo in Somerset. Excavations there have, as at Tintagel, produced evidence of trade with the Mediterranean. Fragments of wine amphoras from southern Greece, fine plates from western Turkey and North Africa, and olive oil amphoras from southern Turkey have been unearthed on the site. All date from the first half of the sixth century A.D.—and again, during the second half of the century, the site became deserted.

Additional British Isles entry points for plague rats may have included a coastal settlement north of Dublin called Lough Shinney, which ceased to exist in or immediately after the mid–sixth century; the fortress of Garranes near Cork, which also ceased to function then;[5] the north Welsh coastal site of Deganwy, a probable fifth- or sixth-century royal center associated with the known royal plague victim, King Maelgwn; and, also in Wales, the Porthmadog/Borth-y-gest area at the northeast corner of Cardigan Bay.

This last probable entry point is of particular importance because it is through the Porthmadog area that the great citadel of Dinas Emrys, ten miles farther north, would have been infected with plague. Dinas Emrys was abandoned in the mid–sixth century, like so many other British sites. The evidence for Mediterranean trade at Dinas Emrys is nowhere near as great as at the other sites, but excavations have yielded a fragment of west Turkish amphora and a shard of French-made plate (decorated with a Christian chi rho symbol).

After arriving in Britain through one or more of these entry points, the plague almost certainly proceeded to devastate vast areas of the southwest and Wales. Archaeology has revealed that at the very time the plague would have been raging, many settlements became totally depopulated, presumably as a direct result of the epidemic.

In Cornwall, a mile from the Atlantic coast, a settlement now known as Chun, with its twenty-foot-thick, twelve-foot-high stone defenses, became a ghost town in the mid–sixth century. It had likely been involved in the mining and export of tin and had therefore probably been in direct contact with overseas traders. A somewhat larger fortified Cornish settlement, Killibury, with a population of perhaps two hundred to three hundred, appears also to have become depopulated at the same time, as did a village at a site now called Grambla, near St. Ives.

In Devon, High Peak—a small fortified town, now a deserted series of earthworks on a windblown cliff top—ceased to exist after flourishing for more than seven hundred years. Another Devon coastal settlement, Mothecombe, also appears to have fallen into oblivion in the mid–sixth century. Dozens of other settlements almost certainly suffered the same fate but have not yet been detected archaeologically.

As well as those settlements that appear to have vanished into oblivion at the time of the plague, several other major archaeological sites have yielded fascinating evidence of rapid change or drastic population reduction at that time. The most important is the ancient Roman city of Viroconium (Wroxeter), which appears to have suffered a major drop in population followed by a complete reordering of the city's property boundaries.[6]

The evidence from the site suggests that in the mid–sixth century the city's major market fell into disuse, presumably because of a reduction in trade and number of customers.[7] Within a few decades this was followed by a complete redesign of the city's property boundaries within the much reduced urban area, and on the site of the marketplace a local magnate decided to build a large private house. This disrespect for previous property boundaries and former public property strongly indicates a substantial demographic discontinuity occurring at around the time of the plague.

On the eve of the plague, the city probably boasted several thousand inhabitants, spread over nearly two hundred acres and defended by almost two miles of timber palisade atop a substantial earthwork. It also likely had several churches, one of which has been recently discovered by archaeologists using ground-penetrating radar. But a few decades after the plague, the city was a very different place. It had shrunk to around twenty-five acres, its defenses were adjusted accordingly, and dozens of new houses were constructed on property plots that apparently did not respect their pre-plague predecessors. In part of the old Roman public baths (next to what had been the market) the inhabitants of a large new private house built a private chapel, the remains of which still survive today.[8]

It is likely that the plague recurred several times in the sixth century and that the cumulative result of the disease (together with the famine which preceded it) was a population reduction of up to 60 percent in southwest Britain (what is now southwest England, Wales, and the West Midlands).[9] No figures survive (and probably none were ever gathered) for the number of people who died of plague during that time. The only clues to the likely mortality rate are the much-better-recorded experiences of the fourteenth-century visitation of the plague (the Black Death), indications of the sixth-century plague mortality rates in the eastern Mediterranean, and the evidence for settlement discontinuity in sixth-century southwest Britain. It is also quite possible that in northern Europe, including southwest Britain, the disease was transmitted even more easily and more rapidly than in the warmer, drier south of the Continent. Plague bacteria survived for many hours in damp climates, compared to just a few minutes in the drier Mediterranean region. Both dry and damp regions would have suffered from flea bite–disseminated infection, but Britain would have been more vulnerable to infection caused by air-carried bacteria, which could be directly inhaled without the need for flea-bite transmission.

With up to 60 percent of the population dead in southwest Britain (perhaps up to 90 percent in some areas if typical plague devastation patterns pertained), normal life virtually collapsed, much agricultural land went out of use, and—as the archaeological record testifies—many towns and villages became depopulated and deserted.

With such devastation, the question must be asked: Why does there seem to have been no folk memory of this catastrophe?

The answer is that there may well have been.

14

THE WASTE LAND

Contrary to received wisdom, the sixth-century plague catastrophe may indeed have been preserved in the oral tradition and in literature that, centuries later, acted as source material for particular aspects of the medieval Arthurian romances—especially those associated with the quest for the Holy Grail.

The concept of the "Waste Land" occurs in at least half a dozen Arthurian romances dating from the twelfth to the fifteenth centuries.[1] It also occurs in a totally non-Arthurian, mid-eleventh-century Welsh epic called the *Mabinogi* and possibly in the twelfth-century *History of the Kings of Britain*, by Geoffrey of Monmouth.[2] In several of the romances the phenomenon is specifically referred to as the "Waste Land," while in several others—and in the *Mabinogi*—the concept is manifestly in evidence but is not given a formal name.

Three key pieces of circumstantial evidence suggest that the Waste Land concept may derive in part from the real sixth-century catastrophe. For one thing, there is the similarity of date. All but two of the stories involving the concept of the Waste Land are in works associated with the semilegendary Dark Age *dux bellorum* (warlord) Arthur, who is said to have died in either 537 or 542; the mid-tenth-century *Annales Cambriae (The Welsh Annals)* gives the former date, the twelfth-century *History of the Kings of Britain* the latter. Certainly the *History of the Kings of Britain* (and quite possibly other now long-lost texts) would have been known to the

113

writers of the Arthurian romances, who would therefore have been well acquainted with Arthur's sixth-century vintage.

Additionally, there are similarities in the nature of the literary and real "Waste Land" catastrophes. *The Welsh Annals* actually refer to the 530s famine in the very same sentence in which the death of Arthur is recorded; the entry for 537 calls it a *"mortalitas"* (mass death) that took place in Britain and Ireland. This *mortalitas* is almost certainly the same event as the "failure of bread" (the famine) referred to in the *Annals of Ulster* for the years 536 and/or 538.[3]

The *History of the Kings of Britain*, on the other hand, refers to devastation due to a war taking place sometime after the death of Arthur. Perhaps significantly, the date given for Arthur's demise is the very date Continental historians have given here for the beginning of the plague catastrophe in Constantinople and Europe. It is interesting that the dates "selected" for Arthur's death are those in which key recorded natural disasters occurred.

The medieval Arthurian romances are seen as being associated with famine and/or disease and/or war—a potentially significant reflection of the real circumstances of the mid- to late sixth century, in which famine was followed by plague, which in turn was followed by invasion and war. The relative chronology is, not surprisingly, somewhat confused in the Arthurian romances, but all the elements are there.

Even the type of disease—namely plague—may be hinted at in the nature of the mysterious wound that the king of the soon-to-be-wasted land suffers from. This royal wound—which magically causes the land to be wasted and is therefore symbolic of the Waste Land as a whole—was a bleeding injury to the thigh region in general and the groin/genital area in particular. In the real events of the sixth century, it was the plague that was the main cause of the Waste Land, and the key physical manifestation of plague were the buboes (great boils), which erupted bloodily into open sores, specifically in the groin and armpits.

The Arthurian romance *The Quest for the Holy Grail* (early thirteenth century) actually refers to "a great pestilence" in its description of the Waste Land phenomenon.[4] And *The Post-Vulgate* (also of the thirteenth century) talks of half the people in the villages lying dead and "labourers dead in the fields"—exactly the sort of situation one would expect to see from plague. Indeed, there are strikingly similar historical accounts from Constantinople and Anatolia for the 540s.

The first brief mention of anything approximating a "wasting" of the land in Britain is in the *Welsh Annals* entry for 537, as previously noted. It states: "The battle of Camlann in which Arthur and Medraut fell and there was *'mortalitas'* [mass deaths] in Britain and Ireland."

But, as I touched on earlier in this chapter, the earliest proper description of the Waste Land phenomenon (though without any Arthurian connection) is in the *Mabinogi*, an epic Welsh folktale, eventually written down in the eleventh century. The story relates how a magical mist descended and that when it eventually lifted, everything had gone—"no animal, no smoke, no fire, no man, no dwelling." The houses of the princely court were "empty, deserted, uninhabited without man or beast in them."[5] Later, there is a symbolic threat of famine when all the ears of wheat are magically stolen (by an army of mice) from the stalks on which they had been growing: "In the grey dawn only the naked stalks" remained. In the end, it transpires that this proto–Waste Land was caused by an evil wizard, possibly symbolizing death, called "The Grey One."

There are geographical similarities between the literary Waste Lands and the real ones of the sixth century. Indeed, most of the Waste Lands in the Arthurian romances and other medieval literary sources were said to be located in Wales[6] or, more specifically, south Wales[7] or Logres/Loegria.[8]

More generally, Britain or Listenois (probably another name for Britain or a part of Britain) is cited as the location of the Waste Land. The Arthurian romances in general—the literary backdrop for the Waste Land—tend to be associated with the Somerset/south Wales region. Thus, the southwest quadrant of Britain is often seen as the area that was wasted—and this corresponds with what was probably the case (due mainly to the plague) in the real world of the sixth century.

The next description of the Waste Land phenomenon was written down by Geoffrey of Monmouth in his *History of the Kings of Britain* in the mid–twelfth century and describes how some years after Arthur's death—conceivably in the 560s or 570s—the city of Cirencester was captured and burned by advancing barbarians. The British were chased over the river Severn into Wales. Then the leader of the barbarians "ravaged the fields, set fire to all the neighbouring cities and gave free vent to his fury until he had burnt almost all the land in the island, from one sea to another.

"All the settlements were smashed to the ground with a great force of battering rams. All the inhabitants were destroyed by flashing swords and crackling flames. Those left alive fled, shattered by these dreadful disasters," wrote Geoffrey in a work that, while inaccurate in terms of names and dates, may be illuminating in terms of more general themes.[9]

Next, in the late twelfth century, the French writer Chrétien de Troyes in his *Story of the Grail* (sometimes also just called *Perceval*) describes the first truly Arthurian Waste Land associated with the castle/town the hero, Perceval, visits just before discovering the home of the Holy Grail—the so-called Grail Castle.

As a result of war and lack of food, the men-at-arms of the castle were "so weakened by famine and long vigils that they were wonderously changed." And just as Perceval "found the land wasted and impoverished outside the walls [of the town], he found things no better within, for everywhere he went he saw the streets laid waste and the houses in ruins, for there was no man or woman to be seen. Thus he found the town desolate, without bread or pastry, without wine, cider or beer."[10]

A further account written in the thirteenth century, *The Perlesvaus* (sometimes called *The High History of the Grail*), describes "a waste land, a land stretching far and wide where there dwelt neither beasts nor birds, for the earth was so dry and so poor that there was no pasture to be found." The walls of the huge city were "crumbling round about and the gates leaning with age." It was "quite empty of inhabitants, its great palaces derelict and waste, its markets and exchanges empty, its vast graveyards full of tombs, its churches ruined."[11]

Then, in a thirteenth-century addition to one of the manuscripts of *The Story of the Grail* (an addition known as *The Elucidation*), there is a further Waste Land story with a spectacularly Celtic flavor to it. Unlike the Geoffrey of Monmouth story or Chrétien de Troyes' version, the advent of this particular Waste Land is set years before the time of Arthur—and it is Arthur's Round Table knights who are said to have vowed to bring it back to health by rediscovering the Grail Castle.

The story starts with a wicked king and his men, who rape the mysterious, otherworldly maidens who guard a sacred well and who serve water in golden cups, virtual proto-Grails, to all travelers. The rape and the theft of the golden cups drive the maidens away and disrupt the flow of goodness from the wells. The wells dry up and the land becomes waste: "The kingdom [of Logres] turned to loss, the land was dead and desert in such wise as that it was scarce worth a couple of hazel-nuts. For they lost the voices of the wells and the damsels that were therein."[12]

Another thirteenth-century Arthurian romantic description appears in *The Quest for the Holy Grail* in which, for the first time, the Waste Land is regarded as a term of geographical nomenclature—a proper noun—and is seen as the direct result of the maiming of a king (ostensibly by a sword), though on this occasion it is set in a time before Arthur. It is also the occasion in which a great epidemic is seen to flow from the maiming: "This was the first blow struck by that sword in the Kingdom of Logres. And there resulted from it such a great pestilence and such a great persecution in both kingdoms that the earth no longer produced, when cultivated. From that time on, no wheat or other grain grew there, no tree gave fruit and very few fish were found in the sea. For this reason, the two kingdoms were called the Waste Land [for] they had been laid waste by this unfortunate blow."[13]

Another blow (ostensibly by a lance), the so-called dolorous stroke, features in the thirteenth-century *Merlin Continuation*. This assault, seen in the narrative as having occurred at the time of Arthur, was regarded as the cause of the Waste Land. Balaain (Balain), the knight with the two swords, is described as having seized the sacred lance (the weapon used to wound Christ on the Cross) in both hands. He "struck King Pellehan who was behind him so hard that he pierced both his thighs." The king fell to the ground, severely wounded. Then the palace trembled and shook, a great voice was heard throughout the castle, and people fainted everywhere. "The true history says that they lay unconscious two nights and two days and of this great fear more than one hundred died in the palace."

Balaain then left the castle. "As he rode thus through the land, he found trees down and grain destroyed and all things laid waste, as if lightning had struck in each place, and unquestionably it had struck in many places, though not everywhere.

"He found half the people in the villages dead, both bourgeois and knights, and he found labourers dead in the fields. He found the Kingdom of Listenois [Britain] so totally destroyed that it was later called by everyone the Kingdom of the Waste Land and the Kingdom of the Strange Land, because everywhere the land had become so strange and wasted."[14]

The Arthurian romances and other medieval Waste Land texts are all, of course, essentially nonhistorical.[15] Nonetheless, in terms of the period in which the action is set, in terms of the locations where the action takes place, and in terms of the mixture of famine, groin-area injury, pestilence, depopulation, and war, the idea of the Waste Land may have been partially derived, through oral and lost written accounts, from the real famine-hit, plague-ridden, war-torn, depopulated Waste Land of mid- to late-sixth-century southwest Britain.

15

THE BIRTH OF
ENGLAND

Cynddylan's hall is dark tonight,
There burns no fire, no bed is made.
I weep awhile, and then am quiet.

Cynddylan's hall is dark tonight,
No fire is lit, no candle burns,
God will keep me sane.

Cynddylan's hall. It pierces me
To see it roofless, fireless.
Dead is my lord, and I am yet alive.

Cynddylan's hall is desolate tonight
Where once I sat in honour.
Gone are the men who held it, gone the women.

Cynddylan's hall. Dark is its roof
Since the English destroyed
Cynddylan, and Elvan of Powys.[1]

A Welsh poet whose name has been lost in the mists of time wrote these words, probably in the third quarter of the seventh century. They still speak across the centuries with tragic power about the end of the Anglo-Saxon conquest of what is now England. Cynddylan was a mid-seventh-century ruler of the central Welsh kingdom of Powys,

and his hall (his royal palace) was almost certainly located in the city of
Wroxeter—the same city that a century earlier had been hit by the plague.

The plague epidemic in the mid–sixth century and the fall of Wroxeter in the mid–seventh century are two events that at first sight appear
unconnected. But nothing could be further from the truth, for it was the
plague that fundamentally destabilized the geopolitics of Britain.

Whereas much of the British-ruled west was devastated, the Anglo-
Saxon east was not. Almost certainly the plague did not reach the
Anglo-Saxon part of the country until well into the seventh century.[2] Essentially, sixth-century Britain was an ethnically partitioned land. The
contemporary British monk and historian Gildas wrote that pilgrims
weren't even able to visit sacred martyrial shrines in the east because of
"the unhappy partition of Britain." For virtually the entire sixth century
(until the 590s) not a single west British monk is recorded as having even
attempted to preach to the pagan Anglo-Saxons in the east.

On the whole, the British absolutely hated the Anglo-Saxons and refused to have much contact with them. Even abroad, several continental
writers were shocked at the stubborn refusal of the British to dine with
Anglo-Saxons or even to sleep under the same roof when they encountered each other abroad.

Gildas did not even like uttering the word *Saxon*. Speaking of "impi-
ous easterners," "villains" with "dreadful claws," he described them as
"ferocious Saxons (name not to be spoken), hated by man and God."[3] Indeed, he, and no doubt most other Britons in the west, would have dearly
liked to see them exterminated.

There was very little trade between the two halves of partitioned
Britain. Archaeologically, virtually no Anglo-Saxon items made before
c. 570 have been found in western Britain, and no western British products that can be definitely attributed to the sixth century have been found
in the Anglo-Saxon east. None of the early- to mid-sixth-century medieval
pottery types used in western Britain ever seems to have reached the east
of the country. Anglo-Saxon trade with the near Continent was virtually
nonexistent. The archaeological evidence suggests that even Kent, so near
to France, only started regular trade with the European mainland in the
580s or 590s. Indeed, there are very few Continental coins found in Kent
that were minted before approximately 570.

By contrast, western Britain was busy trading with not only the Continent but also the Mediterranean. One can assume direct shipping links

with southwest France (Bordeaux, for example) and Spain, and either direct or indirect links with North Africa, Greece, and Asia Minor. The artifacts excavated at Tintagel (see Chapter 13) and evidence of burial feasts suggest that not only Mediterranean goods but Mediterranean people were arriving as well. Western Britain was wide open to plague infection—and was devastated. Anglo-Saxon eastern Britain—shut off from the west by ethnic hatreds, British fear, and large forests—escaped, at least till the seventh century.

The main geopolitically important effect of the plague was demographic. Population levels dropped in the west but not in the east (see Chapter 13). In the west, the plague had hit in 547, and it is highly likely, given the normal behavior of the disease, that it struck again in the 550s. Before long, Anglo-Saxon settlers were pushing west to fill what must have been in many areas a demographic and political vacuum. The Anglo-Saxon advance, which had paused for some forty years, thus restarted.

By the 560s the renewed movement west was under way. Clashes were reported in the *Anglo-Saxon Chronicle* as having occurred in the 550s.[4] In 571 the south Midlands appears to have fallen to the Saxons, and six years later Gloucester, Cirencester, and Bath fell. At around the same time, the Saxons advanced into Dorset.

Meanwhile, in the southwest Midlands, other Anglo-Saxons—the Hwicce—were penetrating Worcestershire and north Gloucestershire by c. 580. By around 600 another group, the Magonsaete, were beginning to penetrate Herefordshire and south Shropshire.

The filling of the demographic vacuum often substantially preceded the filling of the consequent political one. Demographically weakened Celtic areas would be slowly colonized by Anglo-Saxon groups, thus weakening traditional native British political authority. At some stage in each area, political reality would catch up with demographic reality and Anglo-Saxon political power would replace increasingly irrelevant, weakened, and isolated British political power.

In south Shropshire this last stage in the process happened in c. 656, when King Cynddylan was killed and Wroxeter finally fell. The poet of Wroxeter—the same Welsh bard whose name is now lost to us—wrote movingly after his city had fallen:

> Gone are my brethren from the lands of the Severn
> Around the banks of the Dwyryw
> Sad am I, my God, that I am still alive.[5]

It isn't known whether northwest Britain was also affected by the plague, but even if it wasn't (as seems possible), the geopolitical ripples from the British southwest's demographic and political catastrophe would have had an indirect effect on the situation in the north. The precise political and other mechanisms by which this happened are not fully understood, but at virtually the same time that the Anglo-Saxon advance was relaunched in the south, the same thing began to happen in the north.

By 570 an Anglo-Saxon group called the Bernicians had used military muscle to declare themselves independent of the weakened local British political authority. At roughly the same time, another Anglo-Saxon group, the Pecsaete, began to expand into the Peak District. By 590 other groups had taken over the Lincoln area in the east and what is now the Leeds and Huddersfield area in the north. By 595 the geopolitical balance had deteriorated to such an extent that one of the greatest of the British kingdoms, that of Rheged in the north Pennines, began to collapse.

Even the military intervention of the far northern British kingdom of Edinburgh failed to stop the takeover. In 595 the Edinburgh rescue expedition was routed in one of British history's most historically important battles, that of Catterick in Yorkshire.

A poetic lament lends immortality to its heroes:

> *Men went to Catraeth [Catterick]*
> *Shouting for battle*
> *A squadron of horse.*
> *Blue their armour and their shields,*
> *Lances uplifted and sharp,*
> *Mail and sword glinting*
> *Though they were slain, they slew.*
> *None to his home returned.*
> *Short their lives,*
> *Long the grief,*
> *Among their kin.*
> *Seven times their number,*
> *The English they slew.*
> *Many the women they widowed*
> *Many the mothers who wept.*
> *After the wine and after the mead*
> *They left us, armoured in mail.*
> *I know the sorrow of their death.*
> *They were slain, they never grew grey*

> *From the army of Mynydawc, grief unbounded,*
> *Of 300 men, but one returned.*[6]

The intervention had failed, much of Rheged had fallen, and as the Wroxeter bard had recalled the sadness of his king's wasted palaces, so a northern poet was soon to describe the fate of Rheged's once warm royal hearth and hall.

> *This hearth, wild flowers cover it.*
> *When Owain and Elphin lived*
> *Plunder boiled in its cauldron.*
> *This hearth, tall brambles cover it.*
> *Easy were its ways.*
> *Rheged was used to giving.*
> *This hearth, dock leaves cover it.*
> *More usual [once] upon its floor*
> *Mead, and the claims of men who drank.*
> *This pillar and that pillar there.*
> *More usual [once] around it*
> *Shouts of victory, and the giving of gifts.*[7]

Within ten years of the partial collapse of Rheged, ancient Chester fell to the Bernicians. For the first time, Wales was cut off from the other remaining Celtic British territories—the Cornwall/Devon peninsula and the northwest. In a sense it was then that Wales, as a separate cultural as well as purely geographical entity, was born. By 680 the takeover of what is now England was virtually complete, with only Cornwall remaining outside Anglo-Saxon control.

Although "England" was still split into more than a dozen different kingdoms, first one and then another dominated. The ruler of the dominant state was not just king of his particular polity, but was also Bretwalda (overlord) of all England.[8] In a way, then, England was born out of the demographic and political changes that took place in the hundred years following the mid-sixth-century climatic crisis and plague. Plague could be said to have been England's midwife, not just in a geopolitical sense, but also in a linguistic and cultural one.

The demographic vacuum, or partial vacuum, explains to an extent why Celtic was entirely wiped off the linguistic map in most of what was to become England. Indeed, only ten Celtic words have transferred into

English from the language once spoken by England's inhabitants. In terms of law, government, and even folk tradition, England owes its inheritance to its Germanic past, not its Celtic one.

In a sense, Anglo-Saxon expansion never really stopped. By 840 Cornwall had lost most of its independence, and it was fully taken over by 930. By 1200 most of eastern Ireland was under English (Anglo-Norman-led) control. By 1300 Wales was occupied. First moves toward intercontinental expansion took place in the late fifteenth century and the sixteenth century. In 1607 the English colonization of North America began in earnest. By 1624 and 1630 colonization of the Caribbean and Central America, respectively, had begun. The Kingdom of Scotland was integrated into the British state in 1707. The year 1801 saw Ireland follow suit. The eighteenth century witnessed the takeover of India and Australia, while the nineteenth century saw the empire grow to include New Zealand, much of Africa, and many other territories worldwide. English is now the most widely spoken language in the world (after Chinese) and the most widely distributed. English culture has been successfully transplanted to North America and Australasia and has merged with local cultures in India, Africa, and elsewhere to produce world history's most influential cultural-linguistic complex. Today the world's most powerful country, the United States, is very substantially an English creation in origin.

The dominoes that fell in Britain over the centuries following the climatic and epidemiological events of the sixth century ultimately changed the world, perhaps even more spectacularly than the legacies of most other nations from that period.

And in similar, though far from identical, ways, the climatic and epidemiological chaos of this era also helped give birth to three other key western European nations.

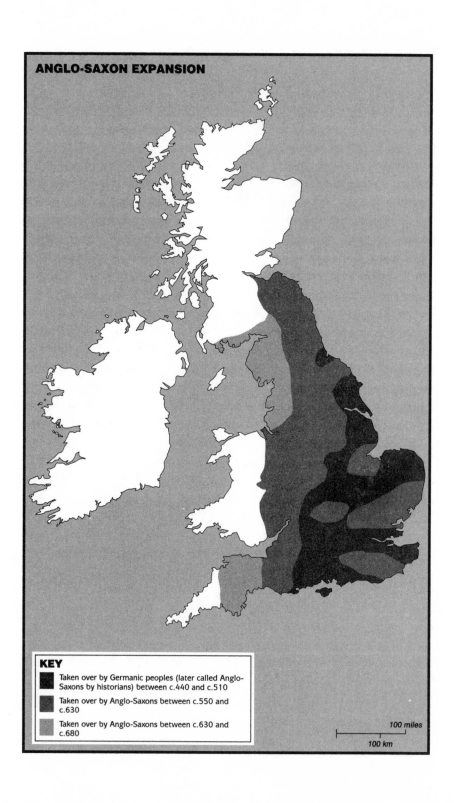

ANGLO-SAXON EXPANSION

KEY

Taken over by Germanic peoples (later called Anglo-Saxons by historians) between c.440 and c.510

Taken over by Anglo-Saxons between c.550 and c.630

Taken over by Anglo-Saxons between c.630 and c.680

100 miles

100 km

16

IRISH CONCEPTION

Weapons press forward, men press forward
In the great [Derry] swamp of Daire Lothair
A cause of strife discomforted
Around the King of [Ulster's] Cruithin [Dynasty],
  Aed Brecc [Fiery Freckles!]
The battle of all the Cruithin is fought
They burn [the subkingdom of] Eilne
The battle of Gabar Liphi is fought
And the battle of Cúil Dreimne
Hostages are taken after the war
Away, west, like a human harvest
[Captured by the Lords] Forgus, Domnall, Ainmire
And Nannid son of Daui.
Splendid moves
[King] Baetán's steed upon the host
Well satisfied is Baetán of the yellow hair.

With these words the *Annals of Ulster* describe a series of battles that helped to unite vast tracts of Ireland under one high king.[1]

Fought in the 560s, they marked the beginning of a long and bloody military struggle that would eventually lay the foundations for the unification of the island of Ireland four centuries later.

The second half of the sixth century saw the conception, if not the

125

birth, of protomodern Ireland in other ways, too—especially in terms of religion and language. And, as in England, it was almost certainly the natural catastrophes of the mid–sixth century that destabilized the geopolitical and cultural status quo, opening up the way for massive and rapid change.

The period 538 to 553 was one of almost total disaster in Ireland. The worldwide climatic chaos of the mid-530s led, in Ireland, to crop failure and famine. As noted in Chapters 13 and 14, the *Annals of Ulster* say that there was a "failure of bread" in 538. This crop failure was part of a particularly severe overall disruption of plant growth in Ireland that is testified to in the tree-ring record for 536 to 540—a record that has been compiled by cross-sectioning and analyzing the trunks of waterlogged ancient oaks discovered in Irish peat bogs.[2]

Then in the early or mid-540s a terrible epidemic broke out. Irish sources provide two conflicting dates for this disaster. One of them, the medieval *Cronicum Scotorum*, gives 541, a date suggesting that the epidemic (perhaps smallpox or a similar disease) was triggered by the 538 famine.[3] More likely is the date provided by the *Annals of Ulster*, 545. In that year both France and Spain were already infected with plague, and it is probable that it spread to Ireland from either of these areas or directly from the Mediterranean. As mentioned in Chapter 13, some Irish population centers (Lough Shinney, near Dublin, and the royal fortress of Garranes, near Cork) are known, from archaeology, to have ceased to function in or immediately after the mid–sixth century. Even the greatest in the land were taken by the epidemic; the annals record that one of the country's leading churchmen, Mo Bí Clárainech, died of it.

But worse was to come, for in 550 Ireland was engulfed by a second epidemic—this time almost certainly plague. Referred to in the annals as the *Mortalitas Magna* (Great Death), the disease must have wiped out a substantial proportion of the population, including a large element of the relatively small literate and governing elite.

The *Annals of Ulster* actually record the deaths of five prominent victims—senior churchmen from Bangor in the northeast, Tipperary in the south, the Dublin area in the east, and Leinster and Lough Derg in the center and west of Ireland. The dead clerics probably represented the loss of 20 to 30 percent of the top tier of churchmen in this one outbreak alone.

Then in 553, practically before the survivors had recovered from the horrors of the 550 outbreak, a third epidemic, again without doubt plague, broke out.

From a geopolitical standpoint, the plague and even the pre-plague period had been relatively peaceful. In the forty-five years prior to 555 there were only eleven battles recorded in the Irish annals.[4] But immediately after the depopulating experience of the famine and plague years, all hell seems to have broken loose. In the forty-five years after 555, twenty-seven battles are recorded—almost two and a half times more than in the equivalent preceding period. Indeed, in the ten years from 556 to 565 there were no fewer than eight recorded battles—more than three times the average known warfare rate for the previous four and a half decades.

As in other parts of Europe, the plague affected certain parts of Ireland more than others. If normal plague patterns pertained, areas that were more densely populated and often richer were devastated to a relatively greater extent than sparsely populated ones. The pandemic therefore had the effect of reducing population-level differences between fertile and less fertile areas. This afforded a rare opportunity for post-plague expansion to less prosperous warlords in less fertile and therefore less densely populated districts—especially those farthest from contact with the Continent.

That is precisely what seems to have occurred. The warfare that engulfed Ireland after the pandemic was characterized by the rise to power and prominence of a hitherto little-known family from the relatively infertile northwest of Ireland—the Uí Néill. Prior to the arrival of the plague, the Uí Néills had been local warlords, little known outside the Sligo Bay area on the Ulster-Connacht border. Yet within a decade of the end of the pandemic, they had seized much of west and central Ulster and large tracts of Meath. The poem quoted at the beginning of this chapter records their victories in Ulster and central Ireland in the 550s. "Well satisfied" was "Baetán of the yellow hair," say the *Annals of Ulster*, referring to the delights of conquest enjoyed by the king of the Uí Néills.

The wars of the second half of the sixth century were very much Uí Néill conflicts or the results of them—often battles in which Leinstermen or Meathmen or Ulstermen tried to repel or throw off the ever-expanding Uí Néill yoke. The period from the seventh century to the ninth was an era in which the Uí Néill family, originally from the remote northwest, increasingly brought most of Ireland under their direct or indirect control.

It was this loose hegemonic unification that paved the way for the gradual emergence in the ninth to eleventh centuries of a single united Irish kingdom. Uí Néill Ireland was thus the ultimate political ancestor of the modern Irish nation-state. As in England, the plague had been midwife to a nation.

But it was not simply in political terms that famine and plague forged the character and nature of Ireland. In religious terms the experience of the famine and the plague appear also to have had an effect, as the plague years and immediate post-plague period saw the founding of the first really important churches and monasteries in Ireland. Four are specifically mentioned in the various Irish annals: the monasteries of Derry (in 546), Clonmacnoise (sometime in the period 543–548), Bangor (in 557), and Clonfert (in 562). Although Ireland's aristocracy had been officially Christian for two or three generations and there must have been many small churches already in existence, the churches founded in this era were the first to be recorded in the annals.

It is likely that the experience of the great famine and the three epidemics had created a strengthened demand for divine intervention. The traditional quasi-druidic gods and spirits of popular paganism had not produced a shield against starvation, disease, and death, and there must have been a sincere longing for more effective access to divine protection and an increased chance of life in the hereafter.

Major new churches and monasteries, run as they were by members of the ruling elite, were also important in political terms. If, through the Church, rulers—often Uí Néills—could have both God and people on their side, then vital political as well as religious objectives could be realized. Increasingly, the ecclesiastical expansion ran parallel to the political one. Uí Néill churchmen staged takeovers (probably of doubtful legality) of rival churches and monasteries, just as Uí Néill warriors took over rival territories and kingdoms. But the net long-term religious effect of the plague itself, and the related church-founding phenomenon, was to Christianize the mass of the population to a degree that had not been achieved before. Residual druidic influence must have withered on the vine as Christianity offered salvation to the afflicted and a helping hand to the emerging Uí Néill ruling elite.

The mid-sixth-century catastrophe also forced changes in lifestyle generally. As warfare became endemic (following the geopolitical destabilization), the general level of security seems to have dropped. From the mid–sixth century onward, even the lowest of farmers began to construct defenses around their relatively humble homesteads. Typically they would build small stone ramparts or earthwork enclosures around their farms, mainly in order to protect themselves and their livestock in troubled times. As warfare increased so, no doubt, did banditry and cattle rustling conducted by robber gangs and small armies living off the land. Between the mid–sixth and ninth centuries an estimated seventy thousand of these defensive farm enclosures (now known to archaeologists as ring forts) were built, and forty-five thousand still survive as deserted ruins.[5]

The chaos and disorder that followed the plague-induced geopolitical destabilization did more than create a security-conscious mentality. It also helped shape the nature of Irish linguistic and literary culture.

Modern Irish is essentially an evolved version of a form of Celtic that came into existence in the late sixth century. Prior to the great famine and the plague epidemics of the middle of that century, the Irish spoke a form of Common Celtic (the ancestor of all the surviving Celtic languages in the British Isles). Then, in the mid– to late sixth century, there was a very rapid linguistic landslide: Many word endings were dropped in a process known to linguists as apocope, and middle syllables were lost in many words in a parallel process known as syncope. What is more, the way words were pronounced changed. A new accent evolved (or an existing one spread more widely) in which very powerful stress was put on the beginnings of words while noninitial long vowels were shortened. Linguists have deduced this by studying the changes in surviving inscriptions and texts from the fourth to the seventh centuries and by applying an understanding of known mechanisms of linguistic change to those texts.

This virtual linguistic revolution took place because of alterations to the demographic balance caused by the mid-sixth-century plague disaster. The old establishment, based as it was in the more densely populated areas of southern and eastern Ireland, was decimated, and new accents from the periphery flowed into the linguistic vacuum as peripheral warlords took advantage of this demographic equalization. Furthermore, as the small traditional literate class was most likely severely reduced in size, there may have been a partial scribal discontinuity, after which new scribes would have been more open to nontraditional linguistic influences. Even the nature of Irish poetry changed, with the traditional long-line meters of ancient Ireland replaced by meters based on Latin Christian hymns.

Amid disaster and untold suffering, protomodern Ireland had been conceived, along with its language, popular religion, and even aspects of its literature. But the climatic events of the mid–sixth century and their epidemiological consequences were also forcing change on the mainland of western Europe.

17

FRENCH GENESIS

"When the Plague finally began to rage, so many people were killed off throughout the whole region and the dead bodies were so numerous that it was not even possible to count them. There was such a shortage of coffins and tombstones that ten or more bodies were buried in the same grave. In [one] church alone on a single Sunday, 300 dead bodies were counted. Death came very quickly. An open sore like a snake's bite appeared in the groin or the armpit, and the man who had it soon died of its poison, breathing his last on the second or third day."[1]

Thus wrote the great sixth-century Gallo-Roman bishop and historian Gregory of Tours in *The History of the Franks*, describing the depredations of the bubonic plague in the city of Clermont in central France. In Gregory's century, the disease devastated parts of what is now France on at least four occasions: 543–544, 571–572, 581–584, and 588–590. And just as it helped shape Britain's future, the pandemic appears to have had a substantial effect on the nature of subsequent French history.

During the first and second centuries B.C., Gaul (the old name for what is now France) was conquered by the Romans. As the centuries wore on, Roman culture and language became firmly established, but in the mid–third century A.D. Germanic peoples—including a group called the Franks—raided deep into Gaul. After several decades they were repulsed, but a century later further incursions took place, and this time the Frankish invaders could not be dislodged. They were allowed to remain as Roman allies on Gallo-Roman territory in what is now Belgium. Then in the fifth century, as the western Roman Empire began to disintegrate under pressure from a plethora of Germanic invaders, the Franks seized parts of northern Gaul and by 507 controlled all of what is now France, except Brittany, Burgundy, and the far south (including Provence). By 537 Burgundy and Provence had also fallen, and the Franks were beginning not only to build an empire but also to see themselves as the heirs of Rome in the west.

They adopted Roman law and language, Roman-style governmental practice and court protocol, the Roman Catholic religion, and even Roman titles. But in one vital and surprising respect, they did not follow Roman precedent: They did not base themselves in the traditional high-status seats of former Roman political power in the southern half of France. The great Roman palaces of Arles and Lyons remained unused—at least by Frankish monarchs.

The reason for this is that by the time the Franks had the opportunity to adopt a southern power base, in the mid–sixth century, the key southern cities were experiencing a particularly savage decline at the hands of the plague. The pandemic did not affect all of Gaul equally; the more urban south appears to have been hit far worse than the less urban north. As a result (and as in Britain), there was a political and economic realignment, with the once gloriously imperial, once wealthy south losing its appeal from every conceivable point of view.

If the Franks had taken control of the south half a century earlier, they might well have based themselves there, just as the invading Visigoths in Spain had adopted Roman Toledo, the Ostrogoths in Italy had adopted Ravenna, and the Vandals, in what is now Tunisia, had adopted Carthage. But Frankish power began to extend to southern Gaul just half a dozen years before the plague began to wreck the lives and economies of the southern cities in the 540s.

In 543 Arles (and no doubt other southern cities) was decimated. In the 550s or 560s it is possible that plague hit the south again, as it broke out again in other parts of the Mediterranean, but no record has survived. In 571 it returned to devastate Clermont and the Auvergne region, Lyons, Bourges, Dijon, and Chalon-sur-Saône. Then in 581–584 the disease swept through Narbonne, Albi, Nantes, and other unnamed districts, while in 588–590 it decimated Marseilles, Avignon, and the Rhône Valley as far north as the Lyons area.

The plague, of course, affected not only Gaul but most other Mediterranean territories as well. Trade declined throughout the entire area, and by the end of the century the taxes and tolls that could be extracted from the southern ports had shrunk to a level that was no longer attractive to the Frankish political authorities. With trade reduced, population down, and wealth diminished, power evaporated from the former southern Gallo-Roman imperial seats of power. The differential way in which the plague had struck had simply made the south less politically and economically important than it had been, while conversely increasing the power of the north.

The decision by the Frankish kings to stay put in northern Gaul was, in retrospect, a momentous one. It ensured that the Paris basin became the political epicenter of the emerging French state. It probably also ensured that the Frankish kingdom evolved into modern France. A state based in Arles or even Lyons would eventually have had less interest in maintaining control over the north, fringed as it was in later medieval times by potentially aggressive powers in England, Scandinavia, and Germany. It was, by contrast, probably easier for the north to keep the south (flanked partly by the Mediterranean, rather than wall-to-wall rivals) than it would have been for the south to keep the north. In addition, the emergence of the north as the political epicenter of proto-France played a pivotal role in encouraging the development of a North Sea/Channel mercantile economy that helped lead to the eventual rise of Holland, England, and France, as Atlantic rather than Mediterranean powers. This provided them with outlooks that were ultimately global rather than purely Mediterranean- and European-oriented.

The plague also had consequences that were less geopolitical. As cities were faced with mass death, the phenomenon of the plague helped provoke a new public response. Instead of people praying or becoming pilgrims as individuals, entire urban populations embarked on mass pilgrimages. Pilgrimage became a corporate activity, a public exercise in the power of devotion and prayer.

These events—in which thousands of citizens would march in desperation for miles—were known as rogations. The concept had first been invented in the late fifth century in Vienne in southern Gaul in an attempt to solicit divine help in quelling an earthquake. The technique was then refined and became widespread in the mid– and late sixth century as entire urban communities tried to repel successive plague epidemics.

(Gregory of Tours refers to the institution of a very large annual rogation near Clermont when the plague first reached France in 543.) In the end, the rogation tradition began to spread beyond the borders of the Frankish empire and gradually became popular all over western Europe.

In the fraught atmosphere of plague-ridden sixth-century France, two other religious phenomena also took hold. From at least the time of the 581–584 outbreak, there appears to have been an increase in official anti-Semitism. In 582 the Frankish king ordered the forcible baptism of a large number of Jews. And in 587 and 590 Gregory of Tours reported in his *History of the Franks* the emergence of false prophets and saints and even a false Christ. He wrote that as the plague was attacking Marseilles, a man from central France, dressed in animal skins, made his way south. On reaching Arles, he claimed to be Jesus Christ.

"Great crowds of people flocked to see him and brought out their sick," begins Gregory's account. "He laid hands upon them, to restore them to health. Those who gathered round him gave him clothes, and gifts of gold and silver. All this he handed over to the poor. He would lie on the ground saying prayer after prayer. Then he would rise to his feet and tell those who stood round to begin worshipping him again.

"He foretold the future, prophesying that some would fall ill and that others would suffer affliction, while to a few he promised good fortune. A great number of people were deceived by him, not only the uneducated, but even priests in orders. More than 3,000 people followed him wherever he went. Then he began to rob and despoil those whom he met on the road, giving to the poor and needy all that he took.

"He drew up a sort of battle line and made ready to attack Aurelius, who was at that time Bishop of the Diocese. He sent messengers ahead to announce his coming, men who danced naked and capered about.

"The Bishop was quite put out. He chose some of the toughest of his servants and told them to go and find what it all meant. One of them, the man in charge, bowed low as if to kiss the man's knees and then held him tight. He ordered him to be seized and stripped. Then he himself drew his sword and cut him down where he stood. So fell and died this Christ, more worthy to be called an anti-Christ."

The bubonic plague pandemic that impacted so heavily on France in the sixth century had, of course, originally been triggered by climatic disruption of the wild-rodent ecology of East Africa in the 530s.[2] But the worldwide climatic problems of that period had also affected French history more directly, with the bizarre behavior of the weather actually stopping a war and quite likely changing the course of French history.

At that time the Frankish world was divided into three kingdoms whose rulers—two brothers and a nephew—were at each other's throats. Childebert, the king of Paris, and Theudebert, the king of Metz, were about to attack Lothar, king of Soissons. It was through Lothar that the entire Frankish (Merovingian) dynasty continued to flourish after the mid–sixth century, so his death in battle would probably have changed French history forever. There might well have been no Carolingians, no Charlemagne, and no medieval or modern state of France.

But that attack, though planned, never took place. From the account of Gregory of Tours:

"Childebert and Theudebert assembled an army and prepared to march against Lothar. When he heard of this, he realised that he was not strong enough to resist their combined forces.

"Lothar took to the woods, built a great circle of barricades among the trees, and put his trust in the mercy of God. Queen Clothilde [the mother of two of the kings] learned what had happened. She went to the tomb of Saint Martin [in Tours] where she knelt in supplication and spent the whole night praying that civil war might not break out.

"Childebert and Theudebert advanced with their troops, surrounded Lothar's position and made plans to kill him in the morning. When day dawned, a great storm blew up over the spot where they were encamped. Their tents were blown down. Their equipment was scattered and everything was overturned. There was thunder and lightning and they were bombarded with hailstones.

"They threw themselves on their faces on the ground, where the hail already lay thick, and they were severely lashed by the hailstones which continued to fall. They had no protection except their shields, and they were afraid that they would be struck by the lightning. Their horses were scattered far and wide. The two kings were cut about by the hailstones as they lay on the ground.

"They did penance to God and begged him to forgive them for having attacked their own kith and kin. None can doubt that this miracle was wrought by Saint Martin through the intercession of the Queen."

It might seem at first like a somewhat fanciful story, but there are similar accounts of giant hailstones from around the same time, all associated with the 530s climatic downturn, in Britain and in China.[3]

Certainly if Childebert and Theudebert had succeeded in killing

Lothar, a massive war of succession would have broken out within a generation, because there would have been no obvious successors. The Frankish empire might well have disintegrated or been taken over by the Burgundian element within it. In either event, subsequent French history would no doubt have been quite different. Thus perhaps through hailstones, but more definitely through the plague, did the climatic crisis of the 530s change the history of France.

18

THE MAKING
OF SPAIN

For Spain, as for so many other nations, the sixth century has a special significance, for in a sense it was then that modern Spain was born.

Spain had been the Roman Empire's first major overseas province, and it remained an integral part of the empire for more than six hundred years, from the third century B.C. to the fifth century A.D. But during the fifth century, Rome lost control of the Iberian Peninsula.

The saga started in A.D. 375 when a German tribal confederation, that of the Visigoths (living in what is now southern Romania), was threatened by an Asiatic people, the Huns. The Visigoths asked for and were granted permission to enter the Roman Empire. They were allowed to settle in the Balkans but soon ended up at war with their Roman hosts. In 410 they captured and sacked Rome itself. Despite that, two years later they became allies of the empire and were given the job of subduing four other groups of German barbarians who had invaded the Empire in 406, marched across France, and occupied much of Spain.

The Visigoths succeeded in their Spanish mission and as a reward were granted land in southwest Gaul. However, the Germanic barbarians in Spain soon regrouped, and in 455 Rome asked the Visigoths to intervene again. The barbarians were defeated once more, but in 468 Rome switched sides and formed an alliance with one of the barbarian groups they had asked the Visigoths to subdue.

The Visigoths responded to this Roman treachery by seizing vast tracts of officially Roman territory, thus forming a virtual empire of half of Gaul (including their original territory) and three-quarters of Spain. Because of a parallel Germanic takeover in Italy, the Roman Empire in western Europe collapsed in 476, and like Spain, Italy became an independent Gothic kingdom by 493.

Roughly from 457, therefore, the Visigoths were the major power in Spain. In 508 they lost most of their territories north of the Pyrenees, so that their kingdom was from then on mainly confined to the Iberian Peninsula.

According to their own legends, the Germanic people called the Goths came originally (in or before the first century B.C.) from southern Scandinavia. However, Roman sources record that by the first century A.D. they were settled on the southeast coast of the Baltic Sea around the mouth of the river Vistula. But in the second half of the following century they migrated right across eastern Europe and settled along the north and northwest coast of the Black Sea, an area they then used as a base from which to attack the Roman province of Dacia (modern Romania). In the 270s the Goths forced the Roman Empire to abandon Dacia, and took the territory for themselves. These Gothic raiders became known as the Visigoths (valiant Goths), while those Goths farther east came to be known as Ostrogoths (eastern Goths).

Christianity was first introduced to a small number of Visigoths in the mid–third century A.D. by Christian prisoners who had been captured during raids on Roman Anatolia (modern Turkey). Just over a century later, in 376, the Visigoths were allowed to settle within the Roman Empire, in what is now Serbia. There they were converted to Christianity (as a condition of their admittance to the empire) by a priest of Visigothic origin called Ulfilas, who translated the Bible into Gothic. Ulfilas, however, espoused a non-Catholic form of Christianity known as moderate Arianism—a faith that had imperial backing in 376 but lost that support and became heretical after a Church council held in 381.

Although Christian, Arian theology was fundamentally different from Catholicism. Catholicism taught that Christ and God were both manifestations of the same Godhead—that although they are different and distinct "persons," they are of the same nature. Arianism, on the other hand, believed that although God was eternal, Christ was not. He was simply the first thing created by God. Moderate Arians said Christ was a supernatural being, but not God in the same sense as God the Father. Radical

Arians went further and held that Christ had no divinity at all, and that although an inspiration to humanity, he was merely one of God's creations. Both these views were seen by Catholics as undermining the central Christian concept that Christ could save sinful humans from eternal damnation. If Christ were not God, that power would be in doubt. It was this Arian dimension that was to affect much of subsequent Visigothic Spanish history.

Appearing first in 542, the plague appears to have had at least two major effects on Visigothic-ruled Spain. As in other areas, it caused substantial social, economic, and political destruction. It also seems to have upset the balance of power between the Visigothic ruling class and their Romano-Spanish subjects.

Plague reduced tax revenue by killing off both taxpayers and tax collectors. As well as killing large numbers of ordinary people, it also wiped out a large number of individuals of great personal, political, and military power. In history, the creation of an abnormally large number of vacancies at the top most frequently creates a large bout of competitive—and often violent—activity to fill them.

And as for the relationship between ruler and ruled, this too appears to have been upset by the depredations of the plague. The population of Visigothic-ruled Spain on the eve of the plague was around four million, only three hundred thousand of whom were Visigoths. So demographic reductions would have been absorbed relatively painlessly by the majority Romano-Spanish population, but not so easily by the already much smaller ruling Visigoths.

A combination of all these factors likely played a role in tipping Spain into chaos in the years immediately following the plague outbreak. During the sixth and seventh centuries, only four Visigothic kings were murdered, yet three of those four assassinations took place in the twelve-year period that followed the outbreak of plague. King Theudis was murdered in his palace in Toledo in 548. Theudigisel was done to death while drunk at a banquet in Seville in 549. His successor, Agila, was murdered by his own troops in 555. Being a Visigothic king was most certainly a risky business in the mid–sixth century.

The first plague epidemic and its immediate aftermath (roughly 545–552) was also characterized by political disintegration. The Romano-Spanish urban population of Cordoba—probably led by the local senate—rose in revolt against the Visigothic-ruled Spanish state in or slightly before 550. King Agila tried to suppress the revolt and failed miserably, losing his son, his royal treasure, and most of his army as a result. Other urban revolts in Orense, Asturias, and Cantabria (all in the north) probably also broke out at this time, although the historical sources refer to them only when these uprisings (along with the Cordoba revolt) were being brought to an end two decades later. A sixth-century revolt of a somewhat different flavor broke out in 551 when a Visigothic nobleman called Athanagild, taking advantage of Visigothic royal weakness, seized Seville and challenged King Agila for the throne.

The Roman imperial authorities, who controlled much of the Mediterranean at this time, had seized control of Ceuta on the southern side of the Strait of Gibraltar in 534 and doubtless had been waiting patiently for an opportunity to reconquer Spain—a land the empire had not ruled for some eighty years. The mid-sixth-century chaos in Spain—and more specifically the revolt in which Athanagild played a role—gave them the opportunity they had been waiting for. In late 551 the rebel Visigoth appealed to the Roman emperor Justinian for help. The emperor, eighteen hundred miles away in Constantinople, responded immediately, and a Roman army landed in Spain (probably in or near Malaga) in June 552. At the battle of Seville later that summer, the combined imperial and rebel forces defeated Agila, who was forced to retreat.

At this stage, the imperial forces acted merely as Athanagild's allies, but having established a bridgehead in Spain, they were not content to play second fiddle to a barbarian rebel for long. Thus in 555 the Romans are believed to have launched a second invasion of Spain, this time seizing the great coastal city of Cartagena directly from the much-weakened King Agila. It must have been a surprise attack, and it probably dismayed Athanagild just as much as it upset Agila, inasmuch as it turned the Romans from Athanagild's allies into rivals for control of Spain. For Agila, it spelled the end; the loss of Cartagena appears to have disgraced him totally.

And so it was that in March 555 Spanish history was turned on its head. The rebel Athanagild disowned his alliance with the Romans, and at the royal headquarters in Merida, Agila was murdered by his own men, who then proceeded to proclaim their enemy, the rebel Athanagild, as king.

The united Visigothic forces were now able to at least stem the Roman advance, but for the next seventy years, they were unable to expel them from Spain.

*   *   *

Roman Spain formed part of a resurgent—almost reborn—Roman Empire. The modern public perception of the Roman imperial system is that it died, at least in the west, in the fifth century A.D. Most people's image of the end of the empire is colored both by its retreat from its British provinces in A.D. 410 and the Goths' sack of Rome in the same year, vividly described by the immortal Gibbon.

However, in the second quarter of the sixth century, the Roman emperor, Justinian, launched an extraordinary project, the reconquest of the western lands. In the main, his policy was to act opportunistically—to seize territory when and if he saw weakness and when he perceived opportunity. And that is just how the far south of Spain became part of the empire once again, with the opening provided by Athanagild's revolt.

Justinian succeeded in seizing back for the empire not only southern Spain but also North Africa, Italy, all the islands of the western Mediterranean (Sardinia, Corsica, Sicily, and the Balearics), and the territories now known as Bosnia and Croatia. In thirty years he increased the empire's size by some 50 percent, so that it once again stretched from the borders of Persia to the Atlantic Ocean. Although the expanded imperial system lost its Spanish territory in 625, Justinian's sixth-century Roman reconquest of the western lands was not finally extinguished until the Normans seized southern Italy more than four centuries later, in 1050.

The Roman reconquest of parts of southern Spain, therefore, brought a revived empire to the very doorstep (or, indeed, halfway into the front hall) of Visigothic Spain. The governor-general of the new Roman province gloried in the title of the "master of the soldiers in Spain" and reported directly to the emperor in Constantinople. However, important textual evidence has survived suggesting that the pope also exercised a degree of unofficial influence over him.

The Roman province (known as Spania) also controlled a significant portion of Visigothic Spain's trade, for it occupied around seven hundred miles of coastline, including several key ports.[1] The importance of Spania to subsequent Spanish history has usually been underestimated. The surviving evidence strongly indicates that it had crucial direct and indirect effects on Visigothic Spain. Spania tended to act as a sort of political and cultural magnet, distorting the direction of events in the rest of the Iberian Peninsula.

A whole series of these distortions had the cumulative effect of altering the balance of power in the Visigothic world. Although there is no conclusive evidence of any direct connection, the first probable consequence on the wider political scene of the Roman intervention was the decision by the Visigoths' enemies in the western Iberian Peninsula, the kingdom of the Sueves, to convert from Arianism to Catholicism.[2] The conversion took place in the 550s at virtually the same time as, or very shortly after, the Roman intervention and subsequent invasion of Visigothic Spain.

The Visigoths were, of course, Arian, while the Roman Empire was staunchly Catholic. So the Suevian conversion would have been seen by the Visigoths as a hostile pro-Roman move at a time when the Visigothic kingdom was discomfited by a Catholic empire. Then, of course, it had been the Roman intervention that had ultimately led to the demise of King Agila, who was probably the most anti-Catholic of all Visigothic monarchs. It was he who appears to have been responsible for initiating the ban on Catholic Church councils—a ban that lasted some three and a half decades. Agila was admittedly replaced by another Arian, but one who, prior to the second phase of the Roman intervention, had been prepared to ally himself with a Catholic empire against his Arian king.

And then there was the native Romano-Spanish anti-Visigothic revolt in Cordoba that erupted in or probably shortly before 550. It is very likely that that insurrection would have been snuffed out in the 550s or 560s if the Roman seizure of southern Spain had not occurred. As it was, the Cordoban rebel ministate formed a sizable independent Catholic enclave sandwiched between Roman imperial and Visigothic territory. It certainly would have had some community of interest with the Catholic Romans and the Roman presence probably helped prolong its independence.

The Roman-Visigothic border was an open frontier. Private individuals, merchants, clergy, and others passed freely through it. So, without doubt, the presence of a substantial imperial Roman community in the occupied province led to much-increased trade with the eastern Mediterranean world, not only by Spania but also (via the province's two major ports, Malaga and Cartagena) Visigothic Spain itself. This has been detected archaeologically, with Gothic fashions in clothing beginning to disappear in the late sixth century. The Visigoths seem also to have been much taken with eastern Mediterranean ideas of urbanism. In 578 and 580 the Visigothic king, Leovigild, became the only Germanic ruler in Europe to start founding new cities, and although he almost certainly peopled them with Visigoths, he decided to give them Greek and Latin names. The first city he established was in honor of his youngest son, Reccared, and he called it Reccopolis (the city of Reccared).[3] Leovigild was almost certainly aping the name of the capital of the Roman Empire, Constantinopolis (Constantinople), which had been named after its founder, Emperor Constantine.

In 581 the king founded a second Gothic city, and again he chose a Roman-style name, Victoriacum (Victory).[4] At around the same time, Leovigild started adopting imperial eastern-Roman court ritual in his royal palace in Toledo.

But by far the biggest way in which the Roman province distorted the progress of Visigothic history was its involvement in a second revolt against the Visigothic monarchy, which broke out in 580. Not only was the insurrection of great political importance for subsequent Spanish history, it was also arguably one of the most tragic in personal terms.

The saga started in the year 578 when the Visigothic king, Leovigild, decided to marry his oldest son, Hermenegild, to the daughter of the Frankish ruler, Sigibert. The Franks were Catholics, but Leovigild presumably hoped that Sigibert's daughter—a princess called Ingundis—would convert to Arianism. After all, he must have reasoned, Visigothic princesses who married Frankish royals had always converted to the Frankish religion, Catholicism.

However, on arrival in the Visigothic capital, Toledo, Ingundis—who was barely twelve years old and might have been expected to be fairly malleable—refused point-blank to convert. Leovigild's second wife, Goisuintha (Hermenegild's stepmother), was, because of dynastic intermarriage, also Princess Ingundis' grandmother. But she failed to display any grandmotherly love and patience and proceeded to use somewhat unconventional methods of persuasion to convince the young princess of the rightness of Arian theology. Goisuintha started off by pulling the girl's hair, then graduated to hurling her to the ground and kicking her till she bled. When the stubborn twelve-year-old would still not comply, Goisuintha had her taken outside, stripped, and thrown in a fish pond. But still the princess stood her ground.

Whether partly because of these appalling personal antagonisms or for totally different reasons, the king decided to put Hermenegild in charge of the province of Baetica, a strategically key region bordering on the Roman-held south. Accordingly, Hermenegild and his young wife then left Toledo to take up residence in the main city of Baetica, Seville. There, the tables were turned. The princess joined forces with a leading Catholic monk called Leander (the brother of the local bishop, or possibly even the bishop-elect) to persuade her husband to convert from Arianism to Catholicism. Remarkably, they succeeded. For the heir to the throne to take such action in obvious defiance of his father's wishes was a direct challenge to the Visigothic state and monarchy.

Traditionally, Visigoths had defined their national identity through their religion (Arianism) and their language (Gothic), while the subject population, the native Romano-Spaniards, had defined their identity in similar terms (Catholic faith and Latin language).[5] Visigothic Spain was, in effect, a binational state. Indeed, it even had two legal systems—one for the ruling Gothic-Spanish nation (the Visigoths) and one for the native Romano-Spanish nation. Intermarriage between the two was illegal. It was a sort of apartheid, although the Romano-Spaniards were certainly not oppressed and lived in relative freedom, even controlling (at municipal level) most of the towns.

Whether he intended it to be or not, Prince Hermenegild's conversion was therefore a challenge to the political system as a whole. The king desperately tried to avert disaster by attempting to open negotiations with his errant son, but the prince would not even discuss the issue. Instead, Hermenegild sent Leander off to the Roman emperor in Constantinople to ask for help. The prince then took to calling himself king (of what is not clear; presumably just of Baetica) and started minting his own coins. Hermenegild controlled two of Visigothic Spain's five provincial capitals, Seville and Merida, and formed an alliance with the Roman Empire and the Kingdom of the Sueves. It is likely also that thousands of Visigoths in Baetica also converted to Catholicism along with their leader.

Initially Hermenegild was doubtful about converting, and it is probable that if Baetica had not been adjacent to imperial Roman territory and Roman military strengths, he would not have taken such an enormous risk.[6]

As it was, he took out what he thought was a reliable insurance policy by signing a treaty with the empire that guaranteed Roman military help if he needed it. With Roman backing, Hermenegild's Catholic minikingdom began to force the Arian king Leovigild to make major politico-religious changes.

Hermenegild's propaganda against his father was overwhelmingly religious in content. He claimed that Leovigild was persecuting his son on purely religious grounds—a propaganda spin designed to appeal to Catholics, whether Romano-Spaniards, recent Visigothic converts, or the authorities in the papally influenced Roman province of Spania.

King Leovigild was therefore obliged to try to portray himself as highly liberal in his attitude to Catholicism if he wanted to spike his son's propaganda guns and therefore reduce his son's ability to rally his rebel troops. It was under such political pressure that Leovigild took two dramatic courses of action in 582, just as he was preparing to attack his son.

First, he announced that he would henceforth be prepared to worship at the shrines of Catholic martyrs and even, on occasion, in Catholic churches—something the Arian Visigothic kings had never done before.

Second—and much more fundamentally—he made a statement saying that Christ and God were equally important and equally divine. Although he did not extend this equality to the third part of the Trinity (the Holy Spirit), his statement brought his theological viewpoint as an Arian king very close to that of his Catholic son and of his imperial Roman backers.

In putting Christ on an equal footing with God, the royal announcement of 582 jettisoned in a few words the central belief of Arianism as it had been for more than two centuries. It was a breathtaking concession, virtually negating the theological raison d'être of the entire Arian faith. What had begun as a tactical PR maneuver to outpropagandize the rebel prince had the effect of preparing the ground for even more fundamental change just five years later.

With his new Catholic-friendly, highly diluted religious beliefs in place and on record, the king moved swiftly against his son. The city of Merida fell, and Leovigild minted special commemorative coins bearing the legend "Victoria." Then, early in 583, just a few miles from Seville, he seized the key rebel fortress of Osset and the ancient town of Italica.

Leovigild then faced the prospect of doing battle with the imperial Roman army, which had been called in by Hermenegild under the terms of his treaty with the empire. But the king succeeded in bribing the imperial general with thirty thousand gold coins, and the imperial army stayed in its camp as Leovigild stormed Seville. His son, Hermenegild, however, managed to escape and took refuge in independent Catholic Cordoba. His father seized control of that city and cornered his son, who had sought sanctuary in a church.

The king sent his younger son, Reccared, into the building to persuade the rebel prince to give himself up and appeal for royal mercy. Hermenegild prostrated himself before his father, and in an apparent act of mercy the king helped him up and kissed him. And yet the prince was rapidly sent into exile to Valencia and then to some sort of prison in Tarragona, where he was kept in chains. Then, at Easter 585, the king tried to trick Hermenegild into accepting Holy Communion from an Arian bishop. The prince—still a Catholic—refused, and his father, the king, ordered his murder. The Hermenegild saga was over.

The tragedy remained a forbidden subject in Spain for many generations, but the process of politico-religious change that had been set in motion could not be stopped.

In 586 several top Catholic clergymen who had gone into exile during the war with Hermenegild returned to a warm welcome—and some contemporary Catholic sources even claimed that the Visigothic king, Leovigild, converted to Catholicism in secret shortly before he died in April 586. Leovigild's younger son, Reccared, took the throne, and ten months later converted to Catholicism—secretly, for fear of how the Arian nobility would react.

First the new king called a conference of Arian bishops to try to persuade them to move in a Catholic direction, but with little success. Then he called a joint meeting of Arian and Catholic bishops, and finally he convened a meeting solely for Catholic bishops at which he announced his conversion. There followed at least two Arian assassination attempts and an armed Arian revolt, but all three failed, and Arian church property was given to the Catholic Church. The ban on Catholic Church councils was lifted, and Arianism became an illegal heresy in Spain, just as it had been for many years in much of the rest of Europe.

In Toledo in 589, Reccared presided over the first Catholic Church council to be held in Spain for forty years. Addressing the assembled bishops, he criticized his father's Arianism and proposed the adoption of a specifically oriental eastern-Roman element into church services, namely, the Creed of Constantinople. This, he said, should be recited in unison by congregations before the Lord's Prayer "so the people would believe that which they had to repeat regularly, and would therefore be unable to plead ignorance of the true faith."[7]

Perhaps more sinisterly, he also accepted the Catholic clergy's demands for a clampdown on the Jews. In an effort to further ingratiate himself with the Catholic clergy, he introduced new legal restrictions on Spain's Jewish population. Jews were banned from holding a whole array of public offices, and all sexual contact between Jews and Christians was banned. In some areas the Church further decreed, or tried to decree, that

Jews were forbidden to chant the Psalms at funerals and that Jewish slaves would be whipped a hundred times if they did not rest on the Christian Sabbath.

Reccared's conversion in 587 marked, in a real sense, the birth (or more accurately, the conception) of modern Spain. Before 587, Spain had been a strictly binational state, with two utterly distinct legal systems, languages, religious traditions, and political systems. Now suddenly there was only one religion—Catholicism. Gothic, as a language, was fading and a local Latin dialect, proto-Spanish, was coming into general use. Roman dress and fashion prevailed. Intermarriage between Visigothic Spaniards and Romano-Spaniards had been allowed for a decade or so, and Spanish anti-Semitism had snarled its way into existence and would reach horrific proportions within a generation, remaining a key aspect of Spanish culture for centuries.

The more accessible monarchy of the Germanic past, with its lack of hereditary law, had already been dead for fifteen years, replaced by a more centralized, exalted, semihereditary system that enhanced its power by making the Catholic Church of the majority Romano-Spanish population a virtual tool of government. The internal needs of the monarchy and the catalytic role of the external force of the Roman Empire brought about a state that was fast developing as a more centralized, devoutly Catholic, nationalistic, and stridently anti-Semitic entity, the key traditions and characteristics of which were revived in opposition to the Islamic conquest and occupation, survived in exile during the Islamic interlude—and reemerged as the ideological foundations of imperial and modern Spain.

Spain—and indeed Europe as a whole—had been transformed by the climatic and epidemiological developments of the sixth century.[8] In a very real sense, 535 and its aftermath had helped bring ancient Europe and the ancient Middle East to a close and had given birth to their proto-modern successors.

PART SEVEN

DISASTER IN THE ORIENT

19

CHINESE
CATASTROPHE

China is today the world's most populous nation, accounting for around 20 percent of the world's total population. In terms of area, it is the third biggest on the planet. Its unity and its huge number of inhabitants are likely to combine to make this giant among nations one of the prime political and economic players of future world history. The concept and even the name of China as a united political entity go back to the Qin (pronounced "chin") Dynasty of the third century B.C., but in terms of real political continuity, the unification of China dates from the late sixth century A.D.

Although China had been politically united between 221 B.C. and A.D. 220, for most of the succeeding 369 years the country was politically fragmented at any given time into a number of independent states (up to sixteen in the north and just one or two in the south). Thus, with the exception of 60 years of total fragmentation in the tenth century and 180 years of a straight north-south split in the twelfth and thirteenth centuries, China has since the sixth century enjoyed almost a millennium and a half of political unity.

It was the history of the sixth century that produced that unity—and it was the climatic disaster of the 530s that, probably more than any other factor, shaped that century's history.

"Yellow dust rained down like snow."

Thus wrote the author of one of the great chronicles of sixth-century

China, the *Nan shi*, or *The History of the Southern Dynasties*, describing the beginning of a terrible and fateful sequence of events that began sometime between mid-November and early December 535.

A similar entry, adding only that the dust (*ch'en* in Chinese) could be "scooped up in handfuls," was included for the month of December 536. And a third entry (for 1 February 537) reported that on that day "it rained *hui*" that was "yellow in colour." The word *hui* was also used in another record of the 536 event, one contained in the *Sui-shu*, or *The History of the Sui Dynasty*. Whereas *ch'en* means "dust" or "dirt," *hui* means "dust" or "ashes."

The potential difference in meaning lies at the heart of a great climatic conundrum. The mysterious *ch'en* or *hui* falling from the sky in late 535 and the winter of 536–537 must have been either volcanic ash or a totally extraordinary and unseasonable series of very severe dust storms caused by massive climatic disruption. But whatever the nature of the celestial dust, its arrival was the first evidence in China of a period of severe climatic dislocation.

Other evidence of climatic chaos was not slow in coming. In July 537 China was hit by frost, while in August it snowed. *The History of the Southern Dynasties* recorded that "in July in Qingzhou and [another province] there was a fall of frost" and that "in August in Qingzhou there was snow," which "ruined the crops." Qingzhou, a low-lying province, is roughly at the same latitude as southern Spain and central California; summer frost and snow were, in normal times, virtually unknown.

With the crops destroyed in Qingzhou and several other provinces, there was a widespread famine. The crop failure must have lasted for two years, for in September 538, "since there had already been deaths from famine," there was an amnesty of rents and taxes.

All these entries come from the *Ben ji* (the basic annals) of *The History of the Southern Dynasties*. However, the northern Chinese annals (the *Bei shi*) also record a sharp climatic deterioration and a series of famines for the mid-530s.

"Because of drought, there was an imperial edict which ordered that in the capital [Ch'ang-an], in all provinces, commanderies and districts, one should bury the corpses," says the *Bei shi* for late April to early May 535.[1] "[There was] great drought. [The government] had to provide water at the city gates [of Ch'ang-an] and the hall gates [of the palace] as well as the gates of the government offices," says the entry for late June and early July of the same year. Then in September 536, in the north Chinese

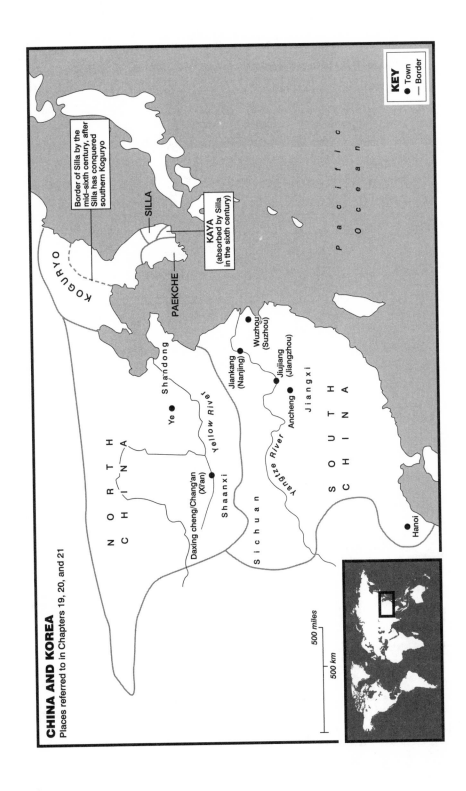

CHINA AND KOREA
Places referred to in Chapters 19, 20, and 21

KEY
- Town
- Border

KOGURYO

Border of Silla by the mid-sixth century, after Silla has conquered southern Koguryo

SILLA

KAYA (absorbed by Silla in the sixth century)

PAEKCHE

Pacific Ocean

Shandong

Ye

Yellow River

Wuzhou (Suzhou)

Jiankang (Nanjing)

Jiujiang (Jiangzhou)

Ancheng

Jiangxi

NORTH CHINA

Shaanxi

Daxing cheng/Chang'an (Xi'an)

Sichuan

Yangtze River

SOUTH CHINA

Hanoi

500 miles
500 km

MAJOR CLIMATIC EVENTS IN SIXTH-CENTURY CHINA

Plus rent and tax amnesties and imperial ploughing rituals

NORTH CHINA	Year	SOUTH CHINA		NORTH CHINA	Year	SOUTH CHINA
D	500				551	a
D	501				552	
D	502	D			553	
	503				554	
	504				555	
	505				556	
D	506				557	
	507				558	
D	508				559	
	509				560	
	510				561	
D	511				562	
D,F	512	D			563	
D	513	P			564	
	514				565	
	515				566	
	516			F	567	
D	517	P			568	
D	518				569	
	519				570	H
	520				571	
	521				572	
	522				573	
	523	P			574	
	524			F	575	
	525				576	
	526				577	
	527				578	H
	528				579	
	529				580	
	530				581	
	531				582	
	532				583	
	533	P		D	584	
	534				585	
D,D	535	P,Y		F,D	586	
D,D,D	536	P,Y			587	
D	537	P,D,F,S,Y		D	588	
F	538	P,A,D,F			589	
	539				590	
	540	P			591	
	541	A,P			592	
	542	a			593	
	543	a		D	594	
D	544	a		F	595	
	545	a			596	
	546	A			597	
	547	P,a		F	598	
	548	D,a			599	
D	549	D,a			600	
D	550	D,Y,a				

D drought   P ritual ploughing   Y yellow dust   a amnesty years

F flood   S snow in summer   A rent and tax amnesty announcements   H hail in summer

Source of data: The *Nan shi* and the *Bei shi*.

"provinces of Bian, Si, Zhuo and Jian, hail fell" and there was "a great famine." By December the situation had deteriorated to such an extent that the government had to send special inspectors "to investigate [the conditions of] the famished refugees who were roaming around north of the Yellow River."

And in Shaanxi province, "the land within the Passes," *The Annals of the Western Wei* in the *Bei shi* state that there was "a great famine," and that "the people practiced cannibalism and 70 to 80 percent of the population died."

"In the following year [in March], because there had been hail and drought in nine provinces, there was a great famine and as the people fled [in search of food] I begged [the emperor] that the [state] granaries should be open to give relief," wrote a senior government official, as the climatic dislocation continued. In the summer of 538 in what is now the province of Shandong there was a massive flood. The waters rose so high that "the toads and frogs were croaking from the trees."[2]

The climatic chaos and its resultant agricultural failures appear to have had two immediate political consequences. First, the emperor of southern China tried to invoke the powers of heaven to improve the situation.[3] He decided that he personally would carry out the state's major annual agricultural religious ritual, the ceremonial plowing of the imperial wheat field.

In this ritual, in March the emperor personally plowed the first furrow in the field. The three highest governmental officials then did the next nine furrows (three each), followed by other top officials, who did five each. Selected commoners did the rest. The ritual plowing was preceded by a grain offering to a Chinese-style agriculture god, the Divine Husbandman, who they believed had long ago given the knowledge of agriculture to the Chinese people.

The imperial plowing ritual had fallen into disuse for most of the fifth century and was performed only infrequently in the first third of the sixth century. Then in 535 climatic disaster and crop failure seem to have forced the southern authorities to make it an annual ritual, and it was held each year from then until 541, excepting 539. They had to be seen by the population to be doing something to remedy a situation in which tens of thousands of people—perhaps even hundreds of thousands—were dying.

The second political consequence of the famine was far more serious.

The crop failures and the result of social dislocation and poverty undermined the economy of the southern Chinese state. The tax system virtually collapsed, presumably because there was no surplus wealth to collect. The 538 tax amnesty—introduced in twelve provinces because of famine deaths—was repeated in 541, but this time throughout southern China and for a period of five years. After that it was extended three more times, until 551.

The initial reason for the collapse of the tax system was certainly the poverty caused by the famine, but other related causes lay behind the constant renewal of the amnesty. As poverty persisted and the lack of tax revenue destroyed the government's ability to rule effectively, popular revolts began to break out.[4] Three are known—one ethnic, one probably partly religious, and one political—but there were probably others of which no record survives.

The ethnic revolt almost certainly owed its genesis to the weakened state of central government at this juncture. Its epicenter was the Hanoi area of Vietnam, which was then part of the southern Chinese state. Under the leadership of a commoner called Li Fen (probably a Sinicized Vietnamese), the rebels defeated the local Chinese governor in 541 and then two years later humbled an army led by a member of the emperor's family, the Prince of Linyi. Soon the rebel leader, buoyed with confidence, started calling himself emperor. With central government massively weakened in financial terms, it took another two years to suppress the revolt. But eventually—in 546—Li Fen was captured and thrown into a cave, where presumably he perished.

The second revolt was briefer but, in a way, perhaps more serious than the Vietnamese uprising. It broke out in 542, engulfed an area only three hundred miles southwest of the capital, near the city of Ancheng, and owed its origins to the famine in two ways. Like the Vietnamese insurrection, the Ancheng rebels almost certainly took advantage of the tax-starved central government's weakness. Perhaps more significant, the rebels probably saw the famine and the ensuing poverty in millenarian religious terms.

In conventional Buddhist belief, the next Buddha—the Maitreya—will return to save the world when the last Buddha's message of ethical enlightenment has been forgotten and the world is again totally steeped in evil. This "second coming" is not thought of as being imminent. It is something that will be necessary only thousands of years hence. But in nonconventional "heretical" Buddhism—the so-called Left Way—the

Maitreya was expected rather sooner. It is likely that the Ancheng rebels included just such messianic radicals who regarded the increased levels of poverty and suffering as evidence that the world had entered a period of darkness and decay and that the coming of their Messiah was imminent. They may well have seen their revolt as preparing the way for their savior.

The entry in the *Nan shi* for early 542 is quite terse—it suggests the probable heretical affiliations of the rebels in its note that "the commoner Liu Jinggong from Ancheng commandery, embraced the Left Way and rebelled." His followers, who numbered tens of thousands, took over some five thousand square miles of what is now northern Jiangxi province. In the end, the emperor's son, Prince Yi (of whom more later), sent an army that successfully defeated the rebels and captured their leader, Liu Jinggong, who was taken to the capital and beheaded in the city's central marketplace.

By 546 the country was in such an appalling financial state that the currency began to lose its value. In 547 it was said that more rebellion was brewing. As in other parts of the world, the climatic events of the mid-530s ushered in a period of climatic instability, and in 544, 548, and 549 China was hit by three more droughts.

In the northern Chinese *Bei shi*, a major drought is cited for 548, while *The History of the Southern Dynasties* records extremely serious droughts and subsequent famines in 549 and 550, in which the population was reduced to cannibalism in some areas. The accounts say that in the famine of 549 "people ate each other" in the great city of Jiujiang (now Jiangzhou) on the south bank of the Yangtze, and in 550 "from spring until summer there was a great drought, people ate one another and in the capital [modern Nanjing] it was especially serious."

As these new droughts raged—and with the government weak and starved of taxes—a third revolt broke out with substantial peasant backing. In 547 a northern Chinese general, Hou Jing, defected to the south, and as a result, the huge tract of northern territory he controlled became at least nominally part of the southern state.

The northern government understandably took immediate action to recover its lost land, and within a year Hou Jing had been defeated, his territory fell again under northern control, and the defeated general fled south. The southern government then made peace with the north, and Hou feared he would be handed over to his former northern colleagues as part of the peace treaty. Faced with such a fate, and knowing the weaknesses of the southern Chinese state, the general rebelled in August 548.

His revolt, though caused by the political pressures of the day, would not have stood any chance of success if it had not been for the massively increased levels of poverty and government weakness that were results of the drought and famines.

He openly courted the poverty-stricken rural peasantry and the urban poor, and it is very likely that at least some of his peasant supporters harbored Left Way messianic hopes, as the peasants in Ancheng had six years earlier.

He marched on the southern capital, Jiankang (now Nanjing), and camped outside its massive walls. After a siege of just four months, the city surrendered. The general—who was of Turkic, not Chinese, origin—despised the Chinese aristocracy. Many of the capital's poorer citizens had escaped from the city and were welcomed by the rebels. Indeed, when the rebels entered Jiankang, they found senior aristocrats starving to death in their palaces and deserted by their retainers, yet still clad in their traditional finery. The emperor himself, now in his eighties, was captured by the rebels, and is said to have been left to starve to death in his imperial palace.

Hou Jing was finally defeated in 552, but the southern state was exhausted and shattered. The general's revolt had become in many ways a popular revolution against poverty, famine, and traditional aristocratic rule. One of China's greatest epic poems—*The Lament for the South*, written by a southern civil servant—described in metaphoric terms how the circumstances of the mid–sixth century made disaster inevitable:

> *We were sailing over leaking-in water,*
> *In a glued-together boat,*
> *Driving runaway horses with rotten reins,*
> *Trying with a worn-out sieve to make the salt lake less brackish.*[5]

The 520-line epic also described how Hou Jing incited popular revolt and attacked the imperial capital:

> *He then stirred up the unruly,*
> *And invaded the royal domain,*
> *Halberds hacked the twin towers [of the palace],*
> *Arrows struck the thousand gates.*

The defeat of the imperial forces at the siege was a disastrous and bitter experience for the aristocracy, including the author of *The Lament*:

> Drums toppled, standards broken,
> Riderless horses lost from the troop,
> Confused tracks from fleeing chariots,
> Brave warriors kept inside the walls,
> Wise advisers held their tongues,
> As if the [fierce] elephants had fled to the forest,
> Or the [ever-resourceful] snake was to flee to its hole.

But catastrophe did not cease at the fall of Jiankang. In a sense, the revolt simply exacerbated it. The Hou Jing rebellion, successful because of the increasing weakness of the state, totally destabilized south China. The rebel victory had created a sort of political vacuum. Because Hou Jing was an outsider, a populist rebel who had no connection to the ruling dynasty and was not even ethnically Chinese, his brief regime was not regarded as having any legitimacy at all. His puppet emperor—a virtual prisoner whom he murdered in the end—must have been seen as no more than a captive marionette.[6]

From the day the capital fell to the rebels, a bloody, often multisided civil war broke out within the remnants of the old ruling dynasty. Over the next eight years, south China was to have no less than ten emperors—puppets, children, and assorted megalomaniacs. Usually there were two, sometimes three, claiming to be emperor at any one time, and most ended up as murderers, murder victims, or both. The warlord with the most blood on his hands was one of the previous emperor's children, Xiao Yi, who killed his nephew and his own brother and drove a second brother to his death. The murderer was then slaughtered by another nephew.

South China broke into three major power centers—Jiankang in the east, Sichuan in the west, and, in the middle, the central Yangtze. While dynastic brother fought dynastic brother in the south, the north Chinese powers of Northern Qi and Western Wei busied themselves grabbing as much southern territory as they could digest.

The Western Wei seized most of Sichuan and the central Yangtze and dragged most of the population of the capital of the latter region off into slavery. This multisided struggle for power was brutal in the extreme, and desperate men resorted to desperate measures. Whole families were wiped out. The rebel Hou Jing had taken the precaution of slaughtering the sons of his erstwhile puppet emperor, whom he murdered in 551, shortly before he himself was killed and, reportedly, cooked and eaten—his skull being retained by his enemies as a drinking vessel!

When the great warlord Xiao Yi perished at the hands of his nephew in 554, most of Yi's sons were murdered, too. Yi, quite apart from murdering numerous members of his own family, is also said to have indulged in black magic. In early 553 he apparently had a wooden effigy made of his brother and proceeded to drive nails into it. At any rate, nails or no nails, by August his brother Chi had been defeated, captured, and beheaded.

The Lament for the South—a truly appropriate title for a poem about the period—suggests that Yi trusted no one and that in his own character lay the seeds of his destruction:

> *Sunk in suspicion he followed only his own desires,*
> *Concealing his faults, he prided himself on his accomplishments,*
> *The business of the empire came to naught.*

Recording the end of Prince Yi, *The Lament* describes the pathetic state of his imperial territory in 554:

> *Now, territory reduced to a wart,*
> *With a fortress like a crossbow pellet,*
> *His enemies bitter,*
> *His alliances cold,*
> *This vengeful bird could fill up no sea,*
> *This simple old man could move no mountains.*

In the end, with the rebel Hou Jing and most of the imperial family dead, two southern generals seized power and enthroned one of the last remaining members of the southern royal house, a son of Xiao Yi. Northern Chinese pressure, however, forced one of the generals to put an alternative southern royal—a northern nominee—on the throne. The second general, named Chen, promptly attacked and executed his erstwhile colleague and restored the original puppet emperor, but not for long. In 557 the surviving general forced the emperor to abdicate, took the throne for himself, and founded China's last independent southern dynasty.

The author of *The Lament* was clearly puzzled as to how God could have allowed the iniquities that had afflicted southern China:

> *As the greatest gift of Heaven and Earth is Life,*
> *So the greatest treasure of the sage is the throne,*
> *By employing worthless upstarts,*
> *They took the whole South and threw it away,*
> *One grieves that the empire united in one household,*
> *Should have met with [Hou Jing's] rebellion,*
> *And to have given the quail's head to Qin*
> *How could God have been so drunk.*

Climatic disaster had produced famine and poverty, which in turn had produced in the south Chinese state a collapse of the tax system and weakened government. Increased poverty (and sometimes the resultant messianic religious fervor) and financial and administrative weakness in the government had then combined to produce social unrest and rebellion. And rebellion—plus all the other factors—had then finally destabilized the old southern imperial regime and had led to its fragmentation and its demise.

In its place, a new southern imperial system developed, but it was a totally different edifice from the old imperial system that had flourished before the chaotic period from 535 to 557. The old system had been a relatively centralized one, whereas the new order was highly decentralized. During the years of chaos, local warlords had increased their power vis-à-vis the weakened central authority, but now that the troubles were over, the decentralization could not be reversed. What's more, political continuity had been destroyed and could not be resurrected. A very large number of the traditional ruling class had been liquidated by rebels and by each other during the years of chaos. On top of all this, the new decentralized southern state was much smaller. The northern Chinese states of the Western Wei and the Northern Qi had seized huge tracts of southern territory while the south was busy cutting itself to pieces.

It was now only a matter of time before the northerners—who had not suffered such dire political consequences as a result of the mid-sixth-century famines—decided finally to finish the job.[7] The powerful northern state of Zhou took spectacular advantage of the new southern regime's weakness in 575–577 when it turned on the south after tricking them into joining an anti–Northern Qi alliance. The southerners were routed and lost huge amounts of military equipment and men. Only political distractions in northern China saved the south from being swallowed up there and then.

But the southern state had been further enfeebled and could only be regarded by the north as prey awaiting slaughter, a crop waiting for the harvester's sickle.

20

THE REBIRTH
OF UNITY

"You are a wasteful and licentious ruler and have neglected your proper imperial duties and have oppressed the people, executed the righteous, exterminated the blameless, and disregarded the forces of Heaven."[1]

The emperor of northern China wrote these words to his weaker southern counterpart in the third month of A.D. 588. The southern ruler was presented by a northern envoy with an imperially sealed list of his twenty alleged political crimes—wastefulness, neglect of duty, moral laxity, and so on—and was accused of responsibility for virtually all the ills of the world, from the appearance of malevolent phantoms to the repeated occurrence of natural disasters. The sealed letter may have looked like a private warning to a weaker neighbor, but the northern emperor then published three hundred thousand copies and illicitly distributed them throughout southern China.

The northern harvester had indeed sharpened his sickle. A new dynasty, the Sui, had come to power in northern China in 581, and its first emperor, Wendi, was determined to finally finish off the job of devouring what was left of the south Chinese state. By 584 a new military communications system, involving roads and canals, was being built. Key military appointments had been made by 586. A special purchasing commission had bought a hundred thousand fresh horses from stud farms throughout north China.

In 587 the north had invaded and occupied a small yet strategically vital independent state and had thus gained control of the whole of the north bank of the Yangtze River frontier with the south. By 588 two great fleets had been built—one maritime, the other constructed purely for river warfare on the Yangtze. Then finally, seven months after the propaganda war had been launched with the distribution of the three hundred thousand tracts, all southern diplomats in the north were arrested and final preparations for invasion began. Within a matter of days, the greatest military campaign the world had ever seen was under way.[2]

The invasion force consisted of 518,000 infantry, horse soldiers, sailors, and marines. Pouring across the Yangtze in a massive eight-pronged assault, the invading force also boasted hundreds of maritime and riverine battleships. In what was a reflection of the weakened political state of the south, the southern empire was almost totally unprepared. The southern emperor was, in fact, too drunk even to read his own general's urgent military dispatch informing him that northern troops had crossed the frontier. Later, when the invaders captured the southern capital, the dispatch was found unopened under the southern emperor's bed!

As northern forces closed in on the south's capital, southern generals were quick to submit. One key commander virtually defected and helped the invaders gain entry to the city. The southern emperor, Chen Shubao, in a pathetic attempt at escape or suicide, threw himself down a well and had to be rescued by the invaders, who heard screams at the bottom and winched him up, wet, bedraggled, and with two concubines still clinging to him.

Meanwhile, most of the south Chinese aristocracy surrendered and the resistance in the capital quickly came to an end after a few isolated yet bloody battles. However, elsewhere in the southern empire, fierce fighting broke out. On the Yangtze itself, four giant 110-foot-high, five-deck battleships—each manned by eight hundred sailors, crossbowmen, and marines—used their fifty-foot-long battering rams to demolish ten southern warships. Other southern defeats followed, and soon virtually the whole of the Yangtze Valley was in northern hands.

Then, in a desperate but doomed attempt to turn the tide, surviving southern forces gathered around the city of Wuzhou, located between the fallen capital and the sea. But a virtual blitzkrieg by northern land and sea forces took the city. The southern general who was in charge fled disguised as a Taoist monk, and his forces fell back to a last refuge, an island in the middle of a nearby lake.[3] As a last stand, it was a heroic failure.

Soon the entire southern empire was under northern control, and the

THE CONSEQUENCES OF A.D. 535 FOR CHINA

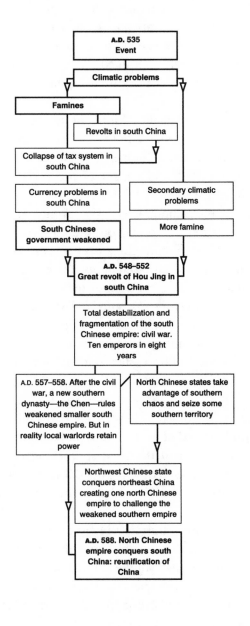

southern emperor, his family, and his entire aristocracy were being marched into permanent exile in the north. According to one ancient source, the column of high-ranking southern prisoners, plus their retainers and their northern military guards, stretched for 170 miles without a break.[4] Some on foot, others on horseback, many in carts, and the highest-ranking in exquisitely appointed sedan chairs, the exiles wound their way through China to the northern capital, Daxing Cheng (near modern Xi'an).

As they marched into exile their former home—the capital city of the southern empire for the previous 282 years—was razed to the ground. Like Carthage at the hands of Rome, its walls, temples, palaces, and houses were all obliterated, and the site of the vast metropolis was returned to agricultural use.

And when at last the column of weary exiles entered the capital city of their captors, they were made to play out the very last act of the drawn-out tragedy that had begun amid climatic chaos and famine more than half a century earlier. In a bizarre ceremony, the captured ex-emperor of the south, his imperial regalia, his ex-ministers, and his ex-generals were paraded into the Sui emperor's vast ancestral shrine to be presented as prizes of war to the northern emperor's ancestors. It must have been the strangest of meetings, for many of these aristocratic prisoners were descended from northerners who had fled south almost three hundred years earlier, when the Chinese state had first fragmented. For some, it was not only a surrender but a sort of ancestral, even spiritual, homecoming.

The next day, the ex-emperor, twenty-eight of his most senior princely relations, and two hundred of his former top officials were assembled in the vast open plaza south of the great southern gate of the imperial palace. There, they were offered official imperial sympathy for their sufferings as a defeated dynasty—and then blamed for bringing south China to ruination.

"Chen Shubao and his ministers all held their breath and prostrated themselves on the ground; filled with shame, they were unable to reply," says the contemporary chronicle of the Sui dynasty.[5]

The southern empire had taken half a century to unravel, but its demise made possible the unification of China, a state that has survived, with only a few interludes, till the present day.

21

KOREAN DAWN

As much of China began its half-century-long journey into chaos, and as societies throughout the world began to be destabilized by the climatic events of the 530s, those same events played a pivotal role in the long-term history of another part of the Far East—the Korean Peninsula.

In A.D. 535—the very year the climatic disaster started in China and almost certainly in Korea as well—the only surviving pagan state in the peninsula, the Kingdom of Silla, decided to adopt Buddhism. It was a momentous decision that was to play a key role in creating the circumstances that led to the emergence of a united Korea. Once again, the sixth-century climatic events seem to have helped realign geopolitics and redesign history, bringing to a close the era of ancient Korea and ushering in its protomodern successor. But how did the climatic events of the 530s lead to the adoption of Buddhism, and how did the adoption of that particular religious faith lead ultimately to the unification of a country that over the centuries was to grow into an important regional political power and then, more recently, into a major second-tier world industrial power?

According to the record of Korean history of the sixth century, the so-called *Samguk sagi*, 535 seems to have marked the start of a period of climatic chaos in the peninsula.[1] The climate in the period 535–542 was among the two worst bouts of weather experienced in Korea during the whole of the sixth century.

Although some of the *Samguk sagi* material covering the sixth century

165

KOREAN CLIMATE IN THE SIXTH CENTURY

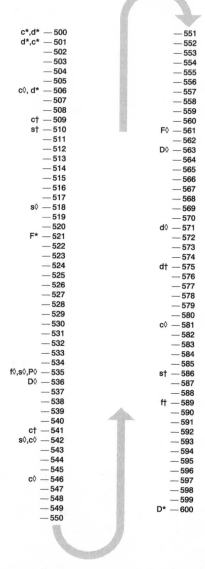

c*,d* — 500	— 551
d*,c* — 501	— 552
— 502	— 553
— 503	— 554
— 504	— 555
— 505	— 556
c◊, d* — 506	— 557
— 507	— 558
— 508	— 559
c† — 509	— 560
s† — 510	F◊ — 561
— 511	— 562
— 512	D◊ — 563
— 513	— 564
— 514	— 565
— 515	— 566
— 516	— 567
— 517	— 568
s◊ — 518	— 569
— 519	— 570
— 520	d◊ — 571
F* — 521	— 572
— 522	— 573
— 523	— 574
— 524	d† — 575
— 525	— 576
— 526	— 577
— 527	— 578
— 528	— 579
— 529	— 580
— 530	c◊ — 581
— 531	— 582
— 532	— 583
— 533	— 584
— 534	— 585
f◊,s◊,P◊ — 535	st — 586
D◊ — 536	— 587
— 537	— 588
— 538	f† — 589
— 539	— 590
— 540	— 591
c† — 541	— 592
s◊,c◊ — 542	— 593
— 543	— 594
— 544	— 595
— 545	— 596
c◊ — 546	— 597
— 547	— 598
— 548	— 599
— 549	D* — 600
— 550	

s	storm	Letters denote types of climatic problems that occurred in any given year.
d	drought	
c	unusually cold	
f	flood	Capital letters denote very major climatic events and climatically induced problems
p	pestilence	

Relative kingdom within Korea where climatic problems occurred.
* Paekche
† Silla
◊ Koguryo

Source of data: The *Samguk sagi*

is often regarded skeptically by historians, the climatic details (especially the 530s and 540s entries), correlate so well with data from the rest of the world that the Korean material has to be considered to have some credibility. Taken together, the climatic data for north China, Korea, and Japan for 535 and 536 is quite striking.

In north China, only 120 miles west of Korea, the *Bei shi* (the north Chinese annals) say that by March 535 drought conditions were so intense that "there was an imperial edict which ordered that in the capital, in all provinces, commanderies and districts, one should bury the corpses." By May 535 not only had the crops failed (almost certainly the cause of the deaths referred to in March), but even supplies of drinking water were running short.

In Korea itself, the *Samguk sagi* records that in 535 there was flooding and that in 536 "there was thunder and also a great epidemic" followed by "a great drought." To add to the problems, an earthquake hit Korea in late 535. All these Korean records for 535 and 536 pertain to the northern and central part of the peninsula, not the southern part; there is no information available at all from the south for these years, but records from Korea's eastern neighbor, Japan, suggest climatic chaos there, too. The 536 entry in the Japanese chronicle *Nihon shoki*, suggests that people were suffering from appalling hunger and were "starving of cold."[2]

It is virtually inconceivable that, alone in the region, the Kingdom of Silla escaped the climatic disaster of 535–536. It is therefore vital to look at the adoption of Buddhism in Silla against the background of natural catastrophe.

Prior to the 530s, the dominant system of religious beliefs in Silla appears to have been one in which nature spirits and ancestors were seen as being able to influence all natural phenomena. There was no one religion, just a series of local cults centered around local spirits and deities. Nevertheless, there were common rituals, feast days, and beliefs, and religious matters were broadly in the hands of shamanic priests or priestesses.

There was a belief in immortality, at least of the soul, and the elite were buried along with golden jewelry they had worn in life and winged crowns and caps that may have symbolized their shamanic power to ascend to heaven. Certainly in the neighboring region of Kaya, the dead had at one time been supplied with pairs of large bird wings to facilitate their flight to eternity. Magic, divination, and ancestor worship were practiced, and the entire population celebrated key holy days, probably including the seed-sowing and harvest festivals when drums may have been played to invoke the help of, or to thank, the spirits or deities of the harvest or those of the sky.

Buddhist ideas first began to take permanent root in Silla early in the sixth century, when a Chinese diplomat and Buddhist missionary arrived at its royal court. The king was sympathetic, but most of the aristocracy was stubbornly opposed to the new faith. Indeed, a previous attempt to introduce Buddhism in the mid–fifth century had also run into massive opposition and had failed.

But then came the climatic disasters of 535–536, which must have been so severe that they had, by 536, led to a massive outbreak of disease (the "great epidemic" referred to above), presumably following on the heels of famine. Buddhism must have been seen by the Silla monarchy, and no doubt by much of the population, as essentially a more powerful form of magic than their own assorted spirit deities. It was identified with the power and the glory of the Chinese empire and regarded with some awe. Only the conservative aristocrats, with their vested interest in the social and religious status quo, were opposed, and it is likely that as the climatic chaos started to bite and crops started to fail, the balance of power between pro- and anti-Buddhist camps at court tipped in favor of what was seen as the strongest brand of disaster-curing magic on offer.

The official adoption of Buddhism by the Silla government in 535 can now be seen as the key watershed in Korean history, for it launched Silla on an expansionist path that ultimately led to the creation of a united Korea.[3] But how did this happen? After all, the two other Korean kingdoms—Paekche and Koguryo—had been Buddhist for more than 150 years and their conversion had not led to such developments.

It was essentially a matter of timing. The fact that Silla was the last to be converted gave it considerable advantages in the peninsula's geopolitical struggles. In a sense, it gained what its competitors had gained from Buddhism—an aggressive sense of national identity and destiny. But because the two other Korean kingdoms, Paekche and Koguryo, had converted a century and a half earlier, it was Silla alone that was also able to benefit from the positive political organizational aspects of its very recent pre-Buddhist past.

Buddhism in Paekche, Koguryo, and elsewhere had tended to encourage the development of absolute monarchies at the expense of aristocratic/royal oligarchies. Although there were some advantages to absolute kingship systems, they were, on the whole, more vulnerable to political destabilization. On the other hand, pre-Buddhist, pre-absolutist, more oligarchical systems in which royalty and top aristocrats essentially shared some aspects of power were, in many cases, probably more stable and had deeper social roots through the traditional aristocratic network.

In a sense, in the decades following the 535 conversion, Silla enjoyed the benefits of being Buddhist without its political drawbacks, and it also enjoyed the pre-Buddhist political system, which did not immediately die with the introduction of the new faith and which, at least for a time, guaranteed social organization and the loyalty of virtually everybody who mattered.

It was based on a principle known as *kolp'um*—literally, "bone rank"—which held that everyone had a specific inherited niche in society. The whole population was divided into eight ranks. Some members of the royal family belonged to the top group, the *songgol* (hallowed-bone rank); minor royals and a few top aristocrats belonged to the *chin'gol* (true-bone rank); and most aristocrats belonged to "head ranks," six, five, and four. The rest of the population belonged to head ranks three and two and, at the very bottom, head rank one. The daily life of this extraordinarily organized and ordered society was determined utterly by the rank system. True-bone houses could be a maximum of twenty-four Korean feet in length or width. One rank down (head rank six) and you were restricted to twenty-one feet. Head rank five had to content themselves with eighteen-foot-wide homes, while everyone else was forbidden to exceed fifteen feet.

Bone rank and head rank even governed what color clothes an individual was permitted to wear and what color trappings his horse could have. All state positions were also ranked so that, for instance, those in head rank six could not have jobs above office rank six, and those in head rank five could not aspire to anything more than office rank ten. And in a system mirrored in the British army in the nineteenth century, only true-bone aristocrats were allowed to hold the top military positions.

To express its new Buddhist-inspired determination—and despite the climatic disaster still raging in East Asia (presumably including Silla)—the king announced in 536 the beginning of a new era, the *konwon* (literally "the initiated beginning"). Buddhism was usually beloved of monarchs because it defended and promoted the concept of the state as being of almost supreme importance. Indeed, a massive nine-story Buddhist shrine, the Temple of the Illustrious Dragon, was later built in Silla's capital, and the population, from the lowest-ranking to the highest, maintained that its nine stories symbolized their nation's destiny to conquer nine other countries—including Japan and China. Silla Buddhism also began to claim that some of its bravest fallen warriors—boy-soldiers of the so-called *hwarang* (flower of youth)—had been reincarnations of Lord Buddha (technically, incarnations of the reborn Buddha, the Maitreya).

Inspired by Buddhist-derived nationalism and strengthened by its still strong pre-Buddhist social traditions, Silla succeeded in trebling its territory between 550 and 576. Interestingly, another development initially set in motion by the 530s climatic destabilization—China's move toward unity—helped create, in turn, a Korean desire to unify their peninsula in the face of Chinese aggression.

This unity was achieved in 675 under Silla direction and survived the demise of the kingdom of Silla itself. Its successor state, Koryo (Korea), rose in the early tenth century like a phoenix from its ruins and preserved the Sillan legacy of a united Korea—a legacy that has endured from that day till this, except for the north-south division of the past forty years.

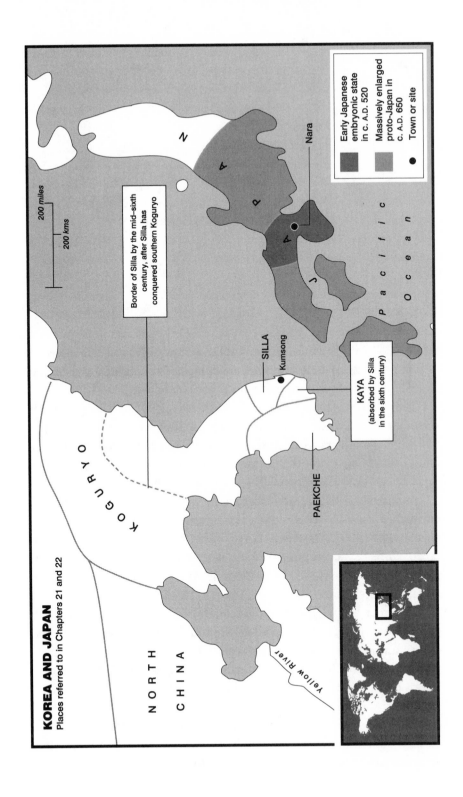

KOREA AND JAPAN
Places referred to in Chapters 21 and 22

200 miles
200 kms

NORTH
CHINA

Yellow River

KOGURYO

SILLA
Kumsong

PAEKCHE

KAYA
(absorbed by Silla
in the sixth century)

Border of Silla by the mid-sixth
century, after Silla has
conquered southern Koguryo

J A P A N

Nara

Pacific
Ocean

Early Japanese
embryonic state
in c. A.D. 520

Massively enlarged
proto-Japan in
c. A.D. 650

• Town or site

22

"TEN THOUSAND STRINGS OF CASH CANNOT CURE HUNGER"

"Food is the basis of the empire. Yellow gold and ten thousand strings of cash cannot cure hunger. What avails a thousand boxes of pearls to him who is starving of cold?"[1]

Thus says the major chronicle of early Japan, the *Nihon shoki*, in words attributed to an edict issued by the Japanese king Senka in the year 536.[2] It is the only entry of its type in the entire 120,000-word chronicle, and it is no coincidence that its date coincides precisely with the climatic disaster that was unfolding worldwide at exactly that time.

As with so many countries around the world, Japan's crucial period of emergence was the sixth century A.D., a century in which the climatic chaos of the 530s had acted as one of the key initial motors for change. In Japan, climatic catastrophe was translated into massive political and religious change through four key interrelated factors: climate, migration, disease, and religion.

The crucial sequence of events actually began in Korea, where in 536 (and probably already in 535) drought and famine had struck. The pattern of drought followed by intense famine is documented in greater detail in the north Chinese annals pertaining to areas just 120 miles from Korea, but it is probably safe to assume that Korea would have suffered equally.

Typically, famines force their desperately hungry victims to move around, often traveling substantial distances, in search of food—and then to congregate at those few places where food or water is still available.

172

The combination of population movement and temporary population concentration triggers epidemics. The increased mobility spreads disease much faster than normal, as do the higher population densities, achieved where starving people congregate. Thus, endemic disease quickly becomes epidemic disease.

Significantly, the Korean chronicle, the *Samguk sagi*, says that an epidemic did strike in exactly the right year—536. It is the only epidemic recorded by the *Samguk sagi* for the entire sixth century, so it must have been very serious indeed. Evidence from Japanese sources suggests that the disease was probably smallpox (or possibly measles, a malady capable of causing almost as many deaths as smallpox in nonimmune populations).

For centuries there had been intermittent waves of migration from Korea to Japan, and during the first four decades of the sixth century there was a steady flow of Korean immigrants—farmers, scribes, metalworkers, and others. The numbers involved were so substantial that they began to affect Japanese politics. One of Japan's top aristocratic families, the Soga, aligned themselves with the foreigners and with foreign—that is, Buddhist and Chinese—culture in general.

The *Nihon shoki*, referring specifically to immigrants in an entry for the year 540, says they were gathered together to be counted and that there were 7,053 households. The counting operation—the first of its kind mentioned in the chronicle—suggests that the 530s had seen a particularly large flow of migrants to Japan, probably partially as a result of the famines and epidemics.

In Japan, the "yellow gold cannot cure hunger" edict, reported by the *Nihon shoki*, suggests that the king and his court were extremely concerned about the situation. That entry is quickly followed by one outlining how supplies of grain are to be transferred from various districts to other areas. Grain was to be dispatched, for instance, to one district where a granary was to be built, "thus making provision against extraordinary occasions and long preserving the lives of the people."

The East Asian region seems to have continued to endure climatic problems and famine for several years. Mainland sources cite problems in China between 535 and 538 (see Chapter 19), and it is likely that Japan experienced similar problems.

Against the background of these problems (and perhaps specifically as a worthy and placatory religious act in troubled times), the king of southwest Korea (Paekche) decided in 538 to send a religious mission to the Japanese royal court. The mission presented the Japanese king,

Senka, with a gold and copper image of the Buddha, several ritual Buddhist banners and umbrellas, and a number of sacred books. The head of the mission is said to have told the king that Buddhism "is, among all doctrines, the most excellent," and that "every prayer is fulfilled and naught is wanting."[3]

Paekche had been Buddhist for 150 years and is not known to have ever bothered to send a religious mission to the Japanese royal court before. And despite the fact that most of Korea and much of China had also been Buddhist or partially Buddhist for 150 and more than 350 years, respectively, Japan—even the continentally inclined aristocrats of the Soga family—had shown no interest in converting to Buddhism. But the situation in the 530s was unprecedented. The entire region was suffering from famine, and—as in Silla three years before—many must have felt that the strongest possible magic and/or the help of the strongest possible god was required to return nature to normalcy.

Yet there were others who were frightened that during a crisis it might be particularly unwise to offend the traditional native gods of Japan by worshiping a foreign deity. The ironworking, armor-making Mononobe aristocratic clan and the Nakatomi military aristocratic family warned the king of this in no uncertain terms, according to the *Nihon shoki*: "Those who have ruled [this kingdom] have always made it their care to worship in spring, summer, autumn and winter, the 180 gods of heaven and earth, and the gods of the land and of grain. If, just at this time, we were to worship in their stead foreign deities, it may be feared that we should incur the wrath of our national gods."

The king therefore decided on a compromise. The leading enthusiast for adopting Buddhism, the head of the Soga clan, would be allowed to worship the foreign deity—as an experiment.

The Soga clan leader, Oho-omi, "knelt down and received [the statue of Buddha] with joy," says the *Nihon shoki*. "He enthroned it in his house," and then converted a second building into a temple. But then disaster struck. A catastrophic epidemic (probably smallpox) broke out in Japan. Vast numbers of people died. Because Japan had almost certainly not experienced smallpox for many generations, if at all, there was virtually no immunity.

"Pestilence was rife in the land, from which the people died prematurely. As time went on, it became worse and worse and there was no remedy," notes the *Nihon shoki*. In those areas of Japan that were affected—certainly all those with relatively high population densities—it is likely that 60 percent of the population died. At first the disease would have produced flulike symptoms (fever, backache, headache), often followed by coughing and diarrhea. A rash—similar to that experienced in scarlet fever—would then have appeared. Victims would have felt as if they were on fire or constantly being scalded with boiling water. The *Nihon shoki* later describes sufferers as saying "our bodies are as if they were burned." Then the nature of the rash would have changed. Starting densely on the head and progressing downward, but particularly dense also on the hands and feet, hundreds of sores (also referred to later in the *Nihon shoki*) would have began to appear on the victim's skin. Each sore would have started as a small bump, metamorphosing into a clear blister and finally into a larger pustule.

Five percent of the sufferers would have died in the first few days from internal bleeding, while a further 5 percent would have perished as the sores took hold and their fever soared to 104 degrees Fahrenheit. The great majority of sufferers would probably have survived the smallpox virus but been killed by pneumonia (30 percent) and septicemia (also 30 percent) after the virus had stripped away the protective mucosal cells in the nose, throat, and eyes, thus allowing secondary bacterial infection.

In the devastated areas of Japan, nine out of every ten people probably contracted the virus, and only three out of those nine are likely to have survived it. In these circumstances it was therefore not surprising that the king's decision to allow the Buddha to be worshiped was seen as the cause of the epidemic.

Opponents of Buddhism reasoned that the native gods of Japan were understandably angry. Those gods were the deities of what is today the Japanese Shinto religion. Known as the *kami*, they fell into five main categories: those that lived in trees, tall thin rocks, mountains, and other naturally occurring objects; those associated with particular crafts or skills; those that protected a specific family or wider community; those that were once living human beings, including some ancestors; and special elite deities such as the sun goddess and the two gods who were said to have created the islands of Japan.

The *kami* were regarded as having no shape of their own and had to be summoned by a shaman (priest) to enter an object whose form they could then adopt. It was generally believed that the spirits preferred long thin vessels to inhabit—magic wands, banners, long stones, trees, specially made dolls, and even living human beings. These humans—mediums—tended to be women and allowed their bodies and their voices to be literally taken over by the gods. The king himself may even have been seen as a rare male medium whose body was permanently "borrowed" by his divine ancestor, the sun goddess. Thus, the king was seen as a receptacle, a vehicle of the divine.

As the smallpox epidemic devastated Japan, the Mononobe and Nakatomi clan heads are said in the *Nihon shoki* to have implored their king to get rid of the Soga leader's Buddha statue: "It was because thy servants' advice on a former day was not accepted, that the people are dying thus of disease. If thou dost now retrace thy steps before matters have gone too far, joy will surely be the result! It will be well promptly to fling [the statue] away and diligently to seek happiness in the future."

The king had little option but to agree. In a sense, the Buddha had indeed been responsible for the epidemic, for the disease had arrived from Korea as an unwelcome part of the package of "things foreign" that the Soga had been enthusing about.

"Let it be done as you advise," the *Nihon shoki* says the king told his critics. "Accordingly," the chronicle continues, "officials took the image of the Buddha and abandoned it to the current of the canal of Naniha. They also set fire to the [Soga leader's Buddhist] temple, and burned it so that nothing was left."

The row over Buddhism and the smallpox catastrophe must have opened up a vast political rift within the body politic of Japan, for in the midst of the epidemic and the religious recriminations (or immediately after them) the king was assassinated. It was the first known royal assassination in Japanese history. It is likely that the slaying of King Senka was carried out by the Soga clan, presumably angry at the way in which the monarch had capitulated to Mononobe and Nakatomi demands in the Buddhism row.[4] Certainly the next king, Kimmei, was backed by the Soga clan, and Soga notables became his key advisors, ministers, and affines. The Buddhism row and opposition to the Soga and their foreign friends and ideas forced the clan to push ruthlessly for a stronger monarchy over which they alone could have control. The rest of the aristocracy experienced a comparative decline in power.

The king was a vehicle through which the Soga, with their ideas of Chinese and Korean origin, reconditioned and transformed Japan. It was important, therefore, from their perspective to build up the status of the king vis-à-vis the rest of the non-Soga elite. When Kimmei died in 571, he (in contrast to everyone else) appears to have been buried in a huge moated tomb over a thousand feet long—the Mise Maru Yama, near the ancient city of Nara. In traditional Japanese elite style, it was built as a vast keyhole-shaped step pyramid, its sides bedecked with ritual vessels and parasols protected by life-size ceramic guardsmen, its summit topped by an elaborate replica palace. It was the last giant tomb of its type ever constructed.

The Soga appear to have soon tried once again to introduce Buddhism. In 584, apparently in an attempt to use Buddhist prayer to defeat another smallpox outbreak (of which there had been several since the disease's initial incursion in the 530s), they set up a temple and had it consecrated by a Korean Buddhist priest. But the anti-Buddhist (and anti-Soga) political elements seized on the opportunity to revive the objections that had been raised four and a half decades earlier.[5] The new generation's Mononobe and Nakatomi clan leaders are said in the *Nihon shoki* to have chastised the new emperor, Bidatsu, for allowing the Soga to build a temple: "Why hast thou not consented to follow thy servant's counsel? Is not the prevalence of disease from the reign of [the old king] down to thine, so that the nation is in danger of extinction, owing absolutely to the establishment of the exercise of the Buddhist religion by [the] Soga [leader]." The king replied: "Manifestly so: let Buddhism be discontinued."[6]

The Soga had misjudged the situation. Power was visibly slipping from their grasp as their archrivals, the Mononobe clan, demolished the temple and burned it together with the Soga's cult statue of Lord Buddha. The *Nihon shoki* even describes how child Buddhist nuns of the Soga clan were imprisoned and flogged.

The very outbreak of smallpox that had encouraged the Soga to call for the Buddha's help in 584 and which had rekindled the religious hostilities now spread to the royal palace, and the king himself died of it.

"The land was filled with those who were attacked with sores and died thereof. The persons thus afflicted said: 'Our bodies are as if they were burned, as if they were beaten, as if they were broken.' " The words do accurately describe the experience of having smallpox, especially during the second week of the disease, but the phrases were also no doubt meant to reflect the notion of divine vengeance upon those who attacked Buddhism, its practitioners, and its houses of worship. After all, the *Nihon shoki* was written by the eventual victors in this long process—the Buddhists.

The Soga clan soon saw the need for ruthless action to regain political control after this debacle. So when the next emperor, Yomei, contracted smallpox in 587, and when his wish to seek Buddha's help in saving him

THE CONSEQUENCES OF A.D. 535 FOR JAPAN AND KOREA

```
                          ┌─────────────────┐
                          │    A.D. 535     │
                          │     Event       │
                          └────────┬────────┘
                          ┌────────┴────────┐
                          │  Climatic chaos │
                          └────────┬────────┘
          ┌──────────────────┐     │      ┌──────────────────┐
          │ Drought and smallpox │◄──┴────►│  Famine in Japan │
          │ epidemic in Korea │           └─────────┬────────┘
          └─────────┬────────┘                      │
                    │       ┌──────────────────┐   ▽
                    │       │ Korean emigration to │  ┌──────────────────────┐
                    │       │     Japan        │   │ Introduction of Buddhism │
                    ▽       └──────────────────┘   │     into Japan          │
    ┌──────────────────┐   ┌──────────────────┐   └────────────┬───────────┘
    │ Conversion of the Korean │ Smallpox epidemic in │  ┌──────────────────┐
    │ Kingdom of Silla to │   │     Japan        │   │ Anti-Buddhist backlash │
    │    Buddhism      │    └──────────────────┘   └──────────────────┘
    └─────────┬────────┘   ┌──────────────────┐
    ┌──────────────────┐   │   A.D. 536/590   │
    │ Silla expansionism │  │ Struggle of pro-Buddhist │
    └─────────┬────────┘   │ elements for political │
              ▽            │    supremacy     │
    ┌──────────────────┐   └──────────────────┘
    │ Unification of Korea │  ┌──────────────────┐
    └──────────────────┘   │ Buddhists victorious │
                           └──────────────────┘
                           ┌──────────────────┐
                           │ Sinicization of Japan and │
                           │ ultimately the emergence │
                           │ of the Japanese nation │
                           └──────────────────┘
```

from death was thwarted by the opposition, a pro-Soga royal prince murdered a key member of the opposition, the Nakatomi clan leader.[7] The murder may have helped bring life to Japanese Buddhism, but it certainly did not save the king, whose "sores became worse and worse" before he finally expired.

Soon the Soga discovered that the main remaining anti-Buddhist opposition element, the Mononobe clan, was planning a coup, so in a ruthless preemptive strike, the Soga and elements of the royal family massacred the Mononobe. Some were killed in battle, while others appear to have been rounded up and executed. At one execution site, a dried-up riverbed, hundreds lay dead. "Their corpses had become so rotten that their identities could not be ascertained, but by the color of their clothing their bodies were identified for burial by their friends," says the *Nihon shoki*.

By 590 numerous Buddhist temples were being built, and it seemed that with the anti-Buddhist opposition liquidated, the Soga position was secure. But the new king, Sujun, seems to have wanted a greater degree of independence from his Soga minders and was reportedly gathering armaments in his palace. So once again the Soga launched a preemptive strike, this time murdering the king himself. He was the clan's second royal victim, the first having been Senka, half a century earlier.

With King Sujun disposed of, a pro-Soga monarch and enthusiastic Buddhist—a powerful lady called Suiko—was placed on the throne.[8] She had much experience of power politics, being the daughter of King Kimmei by a Soga wife and having been married to the former King Bidatsu. Her nephew—a prince called Mumayado (later, posthumously, known as Shotoku)—was also pro-Buddhist and pro-Soga.

The great ideological and political conflict for the soul of Japan, which had begun in the 530s, was now almost over. The traditionalists and isolationists had lost and the pro-Buddhist, pro-foreign reformers had won. Over the next twenty years, religious, political, economic, administrative, fiscal, artistic, and calendrical ideas were imported wholesale from the Asian continent, mainly from China. In 603 a more meritocratic system replaced the traditional hereditary hierarchy at court. In 604 Chinese Confucian principles of harmony, duty, and decorum were introduced. In 607 the first Japanese embassy was sent to China. Soon students were going to China to study. Deliberately copying the Chinese emperor, Queen Suiko even styled herself the "heir of heaven."

In a sense, Buddhism had been merely the Trojan horse within which all these other changes were waiting to enter Japan. The process that had been kicked into motion by the climatic and epidemiological events of the 530s had been completed by the early seventh century, and Japan was an utterly different place from what it had been in the early sixth. Ancient Japan had died, and protomodern Japan had been conceived. Today's Japanese nation-state has its distant yet essential origins in the tragic yet catalytic sixth century.

PART EIGHT

CHANGING THE AMERICAS

23

COLLAPSE OF THE
PYRAMID EMPIRE

J ust as Europe, the Middle East, and the Orient had experienced massive geopolitical change in the century following the climatic disasters of the 530s, so too did the Americas. Both in Mesoamerica and
the Andes, there was a total geopolitical realignment, driven ultimately by
the engine of climatic change. In North America and in non-Andean
South America, the sixth century was also one of transformation—an era
of new beginnings.

When the Spanish, under the conquistador Hernán Cortéz, conquered
Mexico between 1519 and 1521, they stumbled upon the deserted ruins
of a vast city with wide avenues, great plazas, and huge pyramids—the
largest of which was almost as big in terms of volume as Egypt's Great
Pyramid of Cheops. The Spanish conquerors asked the defeated Aztecs to
tell them who had constructed such magnificent buildings. The Aztecs
replied that the deserted city had been the Place of the Gods (Teotihuacan
in Nahuatl, the local language), and that it had been built long ago by a
race of giants. To prove the truth of this latter assertion, they produced
what they claimed were massive thighbones of these gigantic supermen.
However, unbeknownst to both the Spanish and the Aztecs, the giant
thighbones were in fact those of an extinct species of prehistoric elephant.

But it was an understandable error, given the sheer scale of the pyramids and the ruined city they lay at the heart of. The largest building was
the vast Pyramid of the Sun—a towering 215-foot-high mass of over 1.2
million tons of rubble and sun-dried mud bricks. The city itself covered

eight and a half square miles, and modern archaeologists now estimate that it must have been home to between 125,000 and 200,000 inhabitants.

The Spanish account of what the Aztecs told them about the Place of the Gods is the earliest historical information that exists about Teotihuacan. And yet archaeological investigations of the site have now revealed that the city had been deserted almost a thousand years earlier—at virtually the same time that saw population collapse in so many places in the Old World.

In the early sixth century Teotihuacan was at its peak—a flourishing metropolis, the heart of an economic, ideological, and probably partially military empire that had as its sphere of influence the southern half of Mexico and much of what is now Guatemala and Belize. It was a heterogeneous empire of different peoples, tribes, and states. Some were conquered tributaries, while others were long-term allies or client states who probably would never have dared defy the hegemony of Teotihuacan.

The empire was bound together by religious ideology and by trade. With its huge number of inhabitants, the city was by far the largest population center in the Americas. Indeed, at the time, Teotihuacan was the sixth largest metropolis on earth. It must have sucked in vast quantities of imports from all over Mesoamerica. And it must also have pumped out substantial quantities of exports and reexports.

The livelihoods and economic survival of several million Mexicans and Maya depended on the maintenance of Teotihuacan and its power. The city was the heart of ancient Mesoamerica's equivalent of today's steel industry—the mass manufacture of millions of artifacts made of volcanic glass (obsidian). Artisans in dozens of workshops worked in what was probably a partially state-controlled industry to produce a wide range of obsidian items—everything from spearheads and blowpipe darts to knife blades and exquisitely made human figurines. Hundreds of other workshops specialized in making baskets, mats, pottery, and textiles, as well as jewelry made out of imported seashells and sculptures made out of basalt.

The construction industry must also have been substantial. To provide the raw materials for dwellings for up to two hundred thousand people, let alone the specialist skills to repair and intermittently replace them, and to build and maintain dozens of often vast public buildings, would have required a large workforce to extract and make lime, make bricks, cut stone, obtain and work wood, and paint the frescoes that adorned the interior walls of so many houses in the city.

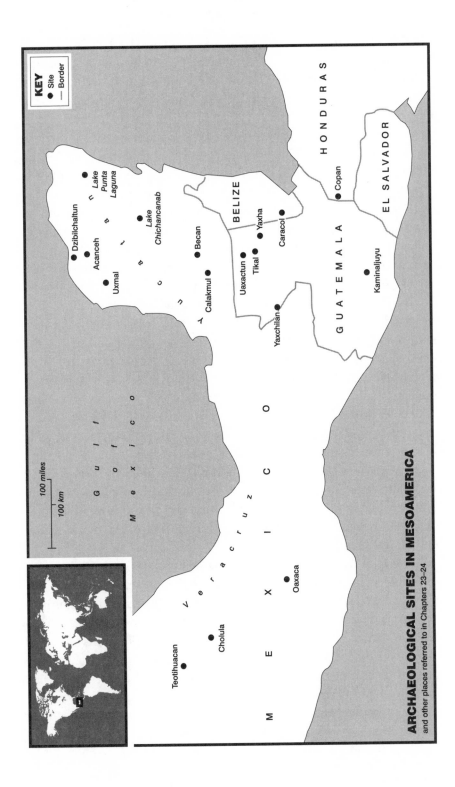

KEY
● Site
— Border

100 miles
100 km

Gulf of Mexico

Dzibilchaltun ●
● Lake Punta Laguna
Acanceh ●
● Lake Chichancanab
Uxmal ●
● Becan
● Calakmul
Uaxactun ●
Tikal ●
Yaxha ●
● Caracol
Yaxchilan ●

BELIZE

HONDURAS

● Copan

EL SALVADOR

GUATEMALA

● Kaminaljuyu

Teotihuacan ●
Cholula ●
● Oaxaca

Veracruz

MEXICO

ARCHAEOLOGICAL SITES IN MESOAMERICA
and other places referred to in Chapters 23–24

Other industries that would also have flourished—albeit on a smaller scale—must have included mica and feather working and papermaking. Although no actual paper has survived in Teotihuacan, the technology for manufacturing it did exist in Mexico at the time, and stone paper beaters have been unearthed on the site. Made from the pounded inner bark of particular types of trees, paper would have been used not just for writing on, but also for making ritual clothes and jewelry and as an easily inflammable base on which to daub incense, rubber, and blood to be burned as offerings.

There was also a large merchant community in the metropolis; archaeological evidence suggests that entire suburbs of foreign merchants and artisans existed. The import business was on a truly massive scale—a remarkable feat bearing in mind the substantial distances involved and the complete absence of wheeled vehicles or even pack animals.

Seashells (for making jewelry) had to be imported from the Gulf of Mexico and the Pacific coast, 150 and 180 miles away, respectively. Rubber (for balls) had to be obtained from Veracruz, on the Gulf coast—and Guatemala, 500 miles to the east. Much of the cotton textile needed to manufacture clothes also probably came from the Maya regions far to the east, and from the Oaxaca and Veracruz areas, respectively 270 and 150 miles from Teotihuacan. Feathers—including those of the green-blue quetzal—had to be traded from the jungle areas in or near what is now Yucatán and Guatemala. And minerals used for making paint pigments were obtained from the north; some cinnabar, hematite, and malachite came from mines, probably controlled by Teotihuacan, hundreds of miles away from the capital. But the most exotic of all imports, turquoise, had to be obtained from what is now the northern part of New Mexico, 1,200 miles away.

Although a good 30 percent of the population was probably involved in craft or manufacturing activities, most of the remainder, the great majority, would have been agricultural workers. Whether agricultural land was owned by individual families, larger kinship groups, or by the state itself is not known. However, archaeological survey work has yielded settlement data that suggests that the population was concentrated in the metropolis as a matter of deliberate political policy.[1] In the countryside for miles and miles around Teotihuacan and its immediate vicinity, there were very few settlements. It appears that almost the entire population of the surrounding two hundred square miles had at some point been forced to live in the city, thus preventing the development of any potential rival population centers. This politically induced phenomenon of rural depopulation must have led not only to overintensive use of farmland within walking distance of the metropolis, but also to underuse of potential farmland beyond the city's immediate environs.

Agricultural prosperity was not only at the heart of the city's—and the empire's—survival; it also lay at the core of Teotihuacano religion. The most important deity was almost certainly the rain god Tlaloc, who not only was seen as the power behind rain, thunder, and lightning but was also closely associated with the staple food (maize) and aspects of creation itself. He was believed to take the form of a fanged animal, perhaps a roaring jaguar or raging crocodile, who lived in a deep cave inside a sacred mountain. Yet he was also seen as being immanent within the clouds themselves.

It's not known for sure which temple at Teotihuacan belonged to Tlaloc, but the prime candidate is probably the vast Pyramid of the Sun—the largest structure in the city. In 1971, almost twenty feet beneath the 215-foot-high pyramid, archaeologists discovered a man-made passageway over three hundred feet long leading to a mysterious cloverleaf formation of four subterranean caves. There they found ducts for channeling water through the caverns and evidence of ritual activities, some of which even predated the building of the pyramid itself. The known primacy of Tlaloc at Teotihuacan, the caves underneath the pyramid, and the presence of channels to carry water combine to suggest that Tlaloc was probably the deity to which this huge structure was dedicated.

Water lay at the heart of Teotihuacan's politico-religious and economic systems. Indeed, the Nahuatl words for "water mountain" (referring to the extinct volcano that dominates Teotihuacan and which still gurgles with the sound of water trapped inside it) and "community/city" are one and the same, *altepetl*. The three most important deities, Tlaloc (the rain god), the feathered serpent Quetzalcoatl (also linked with rain and water), and the Mother of Stone (the personification of the water mountain) were all associated with life-giving water.[2] The link between rain and agricultural fecundity was symbolized by Tlaloc's association with corn, the city's staple food, while Quetzalcoatl's traditional association with the ideology of divinely sanctioned rulership underpinned the political aspect of Teotihuacano religion.

The city (and the empire) was a religious state to the extent that the rulers no doubt saw their power as divinely derived, and probably identified themselves and the metropolis with the birth of humanity and the beginning of time itself, which is how the later Aztecs saw Teotihuacan. In an uncanny New World equivalent of Christian divine sacrifice theology—evidence, if ever there was, of the global commonality of the human psyche—Teotihuacan was seen, at least by later cultures, as a sort of Mesoamerican Jerusalem where the gods had sacrificed themselves so that humanity might live.

Ancient Mesoamericans believed in a cyclical series of universes. At the end of the life span of each universe it was destroyed, and a new universe then had to be created. The site on which Teotihuacan was built was seen—again, at least by later cultures—as the place where the present universe (the fifth) was born. However, in order for this new universe to be created and life to start again, a divine sacrifice was required.

Thus it was that, according to a legend known from Aztec sources, the gods assembled where Teotihuacan now stands and discussed which of their number would sacrifice himself, become the fifth sun, and so bring light to a reborn world. In a poignant sequence of pain-filled anthropomorphism, the humblest of the gods, Nanahuatzin (literally, "the pus-filled one"), leaped into the flames of creation and became the reborn sun. But the rest of the new universe did not show any signs of materializing, and so the remaining gods had to sacrifice themselves as well.

From their self-sacrifice, the cosmos and the world began to take shape. In the end, almost everything had been formed, from stars to animals, mountains to humans themselves. The establishment of government on earth was also probably seen as having a divine origin. And it was at the very place, Teotihuacan, where the gods had created the universe that there emerged the most powerful government of the Mesoamerican world—the lords of Teotihuacan, "the wise men, knowers of the occult things."[3]

The way in which the religious/ideological basis of society was inextricably interwoven with the economic basis (agriculture) and the political basis (divinely sanctioned government) was the fundamental strength that unified and sustained the metropolis and its power for so many centuries. Yet it was the same close integration of religion, economy, and political ideology that made collapse total when the metropolis and its empire came under unprecedented stress following the worldwide climatic problems of the 530s.

Teotihuacan was simultaneously the Athens, the Rome, and the Jerusalem of the ancient Mesoamerican world. In religious, economic, and political terms, in terms of perceived ancient wisdom, and even in

terms of population concentration, the empire's eggs were all in one bas-
ket. Thus, when disaster struck, it struck with a totality and finality that
was probably more clear-cut than anywhere else on earth, even at that
time of global change and catastrophe.

Because there is as yet no tree-ring or other comparable data from central
Mexico, archaeologists have no direct way of detecting an individual ancient episode of drought there. There is broad evidence for a general dry-
ing of the climate in Mexico in the third to sixth centuries A.D., but to find
out when any particularly severe crisis-inducing episodes or periods of
drought occurred in Mesoamerica, a picture has to be deduced from ar-
chaeoclimatic data obtained from adjacent regions, from the world as a
whole, and from correlation with potential consequences, in the form of
archaeologically detectable events, such as the demise of Teotihuacan.

   A detailed analysis of all the available data from the Americas does reveal that a fairly dramatic climatic event occurred across both continents
and must therefore almost certainly have affected central Mexico. There is
compelling evidence from seven different areas—California, southern
Mexico, Colombia, Peru, Brazil, Chile, and Argentina—to suggest that
there was severe climatic disruption throughout the Western Hemisphere
in the mid–sixth century A.D.

   In the late 1960s an American tree-ring specialist, Valmore La Marche
of the University of Arizona, collected a substantial number of high-
altitude bristlecone pine tree-ring samples from Campito Mountain in
California suggesting climatic deterioration—probably colder and drier
weather—beginning in 535–536, with a much more serious deterioration
in 539. Growth did not then return to normal until the late 550s. Other
evidence collected in the 1980s by another American academic, Louis
Scuderi of Boston University, from California's Sierra Nevada Mountains
told a similar story, although the data suggested that the episode of climatic deterioration lasted even longer, till around 570.

   In Yucatán (southeast Mexico), just five hundred miles east of Teotihuacan, painstaking analysis of lake deposits has revealed evidence of a
severe twenty- to fifty-year-long drought that seems to have started in the
mid–sixth century. At one lake, Punta Laguna, evidence of this great
drought has been provided by water snails and tiny crustaceans called ostracods. The amount of different types of oxygen isotope found in their
shells varies according to the climatic conditions prevalent at the time
they died. Because oxygen with an isotopic value of 16 evaporated more

easily than the heavier oxygen 18, an extended period of dry weather left behind an abnormally high percentage of the latter. The drought can be dated by carrying out radiocarbon dating tests on wood fragments and ostracods, and research carried out by scientists from the University of Florida has revealed that it occurred in the sixth century, was the first such event for almost a thousand years, and was not repeated for another three centuries.[4] Similar results were found at a second Yucatán location, Lake Chichancanab, where a massive sixth-century drought was detected by measuring the varying percentages of a particular mineral in the lake sediments.[5]

In South America, tree-ring data obtained from ancient Fitzroya conifer timbers have revealed that a dramatic cooling of temperature took place in A.D. 540. The main evidence is from Chile—but supporting evidence has recently also been obtained from Argentina. The Chilean material—from Lenca, in the south of the country—shows that 540 had the coldest summer of the past 1,600 years.[6]

In the northern half of South America, there is no tree-ring data going back as far as the sixth century, but there is other evidence of two different kinds, mainly from Peru and Colombia.

Back in 1983 a team of U.S. scientists from Ohio State University's Institute of Polar Studies climbed Peru's 18,711-foot-high Quelccaya glacier and succeeded in extracting two ice cores roughly 525 feet long.[7] Because there were no helicopters in Peru capable of flying to that height, refrigeration equipment could not be flown in and the ice cores had to be moved out overland. The cores had to be broken up into six thousand samples about two inches long, each of which was then packed in its own individual container and allowed to melt. The Ohio team then had to carry all six thousand samples down from the glacier during a two-day mountain trek, sometimes on 45-degree slopes. The analysis of the samples revealed several episodes in which there had been a decrease in ice accumulation, lower levels of oxygen 18, and an increase in the amount of regionally originating dust—almost certainly evidence of dust storms caused by drought. By far the most intensive and long-lasting episode, and the one that started most abruptly, was a period of drought that appears to have struck in the mid–sixth century and to have lasted around thirty years.

Further confirmation of climatic disaster comes from data on ancient river levels collected from the lower San Jorge Basin in Colombia in the

1970s and 1980s. An analysis by Colombian archaeologists Clemencia Plazas and Anna Falchetti revealed that the mid– to late sixth century was the driest period in the entire 3,300-year-long sequence.[8] Similar evidence was discovered in the lower Amazon basin in Brazil and in lakes in the Colombian Andes.[9]

The Colombian and Brazilian evidence—together with the data from Peru, Chile, Argentina, Yucatán, and the United States—shows that there was a severe pan-American mid-sixth-century climatic disaster. The combined evidence strongly suggests that Mexico must also have suffered.

In consequential terms, this is confirmed by the date and nature of the collapse of the great Mexican metropolis of Teotihuacan and its empire. Until recently the depopulation and virtual demise of this vast ancient city was believed to have taken place in the eighth century A.D., but a recent reassessment of the evidence has now led archaeologists to redate the collapse to 150 years earlier—to the sixth century A.D.[10] The redating shows that Teotihuacan started to collapse probably around the middle of the sixth century and had disintegrated demographically, economically, and politically by the end of the century.

Teotihuacan has no written history—or at least, none has ever been discovered. Although this extraordinary urban civilization has its own home-grown rudimentary script, it appears to have been relatively unsophisticated, and only parts of it have so far been deciphered.[11] So to untangle the sequence of events that led to the collapse of Teotihuacan and its empire, the only data available are those provided by archaeology. But the information yielded by a series of excavations at the site does tell a fascinating story.

In fact, archaeological data from Teotihuacan provide heartrending evidence of different aspects of the end of the metropolis—burned temples, deaths from malnutrition, deserted houses, smashed idols, and murdered members of the city's elite. Untangling the evidence, it is possible to construct a reasonable model of what actually occurred in the terminal decades of this Mesoamerican Jerusalem.

The climatic disaster that drastically slowed the growth of so many trees in North and South America, dried up rivers in Colombia, and caused dust storms in Peru certainly involved a massive drought. The probable effects of that drought can be seen all too graphically in the archaeological record. In a detailed study, an American anthropologist, Rebecca Storey, of the University of Houston, has analyzed data from more than 150 skeletons unearthed in a small cemetery in an ordinary working-class apartment compound on the southern fringe of the city.[12]

Her findings reveal that in the years prior to the collapse, people had already begun to die at an earlier age, almost certainly as a result of the great drought and the accompanying massive agricultural failure. Indeed, the death rates for those under twenty-five virtually doubled—68.3 percent of the working-class population were dying before the age of twenty-five, compared to 38.5 percent in more normal times.

The research shows that infectious disease was common in Teotihuacan at all times. However, when the agricultural system failed, nutritional deficiency seems to have substantially reduced the population's ability to counteract infection. Infection then would have manifested itself in several major ways, often including severe diarrhea and a tremendous reduction in the digestive system's ability to absorb nutrients. As a result, it was nutrient starvation rather than total unavailability of food that resulted in death.

High death rates in the city (creating demand for new laborers) coupled with economic collapse (due to agricultural failure) in the countryside would have led to substantial migration into the metropolis. But Storey's research suggests that most of these migrants, with lower immunity to urban disease, died within a few years of their arrival. In the final period (probably the final decades) of Teotihuacan, deaths in the prime migrant age group (fifteen to twenty-four) trebled, from 8.3 percent to 27 percent of total deaths. Another factor in the particularly high level of deaths in this age group must have been the increase in the overall circulation of disease caused by the higher frequency of infection suffered by the migrants.

Because the root cause of the problem was food shortage, it is likely that the Teotihuacano elite would have used their political muscle (and probably at some stage, their military power) to secure sufficient food for themselves. Social divisions would therefore have grown not only in terms of health and wealth, but also in terms of age, intergenerational cultural continuity, parental control, geographic origin (the migrant element), and loyalty to the system.

With so much of the working population dying before the age of twenty-five, the mechanisms of social continuity and control would have broken down. There would have been insufficient numbers of older citizens to pass on cultural traditions to the younger generation. There would also have been large numbers of young orphans who, if they survived, would have passed through their teens with a much-reduced level of adult supervision. And with the rural-to-urban migration referred to earlier, the percentage of people with a lower level of loyalty to the city and its traditions would have increased substantially.

There is also archaeological evidence for change at the top of society. In the terminal period of Teotihuacan, there was a big increase in the amount of military iconography. Wall paintings that had previously been almost exclusively religious in nature were now joined by frescoes that seem to depict members of military sections of the city's elite. This apparently increased importance of the army developed *before* the final collapse of the civilization and probably reflects serious divisions in a ruling class faced with agricultural and commercial collapse as well as increasing social division and unrest. If examples from the history of later centuries in other parts of the world are any guide, then it is more than likely that division within the ruling elite would have led to some sort of military coup, after which strong-arm measures would increasingly have been used to maintain the social and religious status quo.

The religious dimension in the gathering catastrophe was almost certainly of prime importance. As already outlined, the major deities— Tlaloc, the feathered serpent Quetzalcoatl, and the Mother of Stone— were all associated, to one extent or another, with rain. So when the rains failed and continued to fail dramatically, probably for several decades with little respite, there was almost inevitably a crisis in religious confidence. It is very likely that the water mountain representing the Mother of Stone herself would have dried up and stopped gurgling.

Rain underpinned not only the city's agricultural and religious systems but also, indirectly, the system of political control itself. Government was seen as having divine origins. The rulers of Teotihuacan certainly governed with divine sanction and possibly even as representatives of the gods—perhaps even as deities, or incarnations of deities, themselves. Certainly Quetzalcoatl was a god associated with the institution of rulership, and the cream of the city's elite are thought to have actually lived within the complex of palaces and other structures built around the great Temple of Quetzalcoatl.

Teotihuacan, as the religious heart of the Mesoamerican cosmos, was almost certainly a sort of theocratic state in which religion, nurtured by the life-giving divine gift of rain, played an overwhelmingly important role. And so it is easy to see how persistent drought led—through agricultural failure, famine, and disease—to religious and therefore political disillusionment.

As disaster unfolded in the metropolis, the empire began to unravel—the weakened center was disintegrating, and the mainstay (and raison d'être) of empire, trade, was also disintegrating. Evidence from another major central Mexican site, Cholula, suggests that it (and presumably many other centers) were equally badly hit by the drought. Famine-induced population reductions and increased poverty throughout much of Mexico would have drastically reduced trade levels. What commerce was left would no doubt have been further restricted by increased social disorder, population movement, and banditry.

The obsidian industry—and probably several others—were under some form of Teotihuacano state control, and the reduction in trade must have robbed the government of revenues and power. Archaeological evidence from all over Mesoamerica shows Teotihuacano trade and influence shrinking in the latter half of the sixth century.

The end of the Mesoamerican Jerusalem and its empire was now fast approaching. Only one final and violent act remained to be played out—for all the archaeological evidence indicates that the lights finally went out in Teotihuacan in a veritable orgy of flames and bloody murder.

The selective way in which the destruction was carried out and the obviously emotional zeal with which individual members of the elite were slaughtered strongly suggests that the forces that ended Teotihuacano civilization were internal, not external.

During what appears to have been an extraordinarily violent popular insurrection nearly every major building in the city associated with the ruling elite was ransacked, torn apart, and put to the torch.[13] In the city center, archaeological excavations have yielded evidence that between 147 and 178 palaces and temples were burned to the ground in an orgy of systematic, hate-filled destruction, quite possibly of an intensity without parallel in human history. In the rest of the metropolis between 50 and 60 percent of the temples were torched. Religious buildings (and the palaces in the city center) were the main targets. Relatively few apartment compounds were attacked, and those that were probably belonged to extended families that were somehow associated with the government or with the failed religious system.

Thousands of angry citizens must have surged into the city center and broken into the main palace complex, where they would have come face-to-face with those members of Teotihuacan's elite who had not already fled—and who now stood no chance at all. Still wearing their jade, obsidian, and onyx mosaic crowns bedecked with iridescent blue and green feathers, many were cut down with the utmost barbarity. Archaeological detective work has revealed how one nobleman or priest was seized in the west room of the Ciudadela Palace's northwest apartment and dragged some distance into the complex's central patio, where most of his body was left. His skull had been shattered and his body hacked to pieces, bits being scattered on the ground all the way from the west room to the patio. The archaeological investigation revealed that he was a very high-status individual. Pieces of a jade mosaic (probably from a headdress) and jade, onyx, and shell beads (probably from a necklace) were found around his shattered corpse.[14]

Another similarly dismembered victim was found nearby, and a third was in the south palace. The small number of skeletons discovered so far suggests either that much of the elite had succeeded in escaping in the days immediately before the insurrection, or that they had been seized by rebels and murdered elsewhere.

After hunting down and killing the last remaining members of the ruling elite, the mob set about the systematic destruction of the politico-religious heart of the city. The presumably wooden (and perhaps textile) constructions at the bottom and sides of temple platform staircases, and the partly wooden temples themselves, were set afire. Archaeological excavations have revealed evidence of intensely destructive burning in these particular locations in most temple complexes.

In the temple in the Ciudadela Palace complex, a structure closely associated with traditional government, archaeologists discovered that five statues had been deliberately removed from the sacred area and smashed. Dozens of fragments were then equally deliberately thrown in every conceivable direction. The shattered remnants of one of the figures—a two-foot-high statue of a goddess—were found scattered over nearly a thousand-square-foot area!

In the same governmental complex, at the spectacular seven-tiered pyramid temple of Quetzalcoatl, sacred sculpted stone heads were hurled down into adjacent passageways and even into the patios of one of the neighboring palaces. In the palaces themselves, six smashed images of the discredited and now presumably hated rain god, Tlaloc, were found among the ash and the debris.

The rebels had systematically torn apart and shattered the objects of their anger. The depths of vengeful hatred that must have driven this wave of destruction can hardly be imagined, but must have reflected the sufferings endured prior to the revolt by the mass of Teotihuacan's population.

As the flames consumed one part of the city center, angry mobs surged into other central areas. At the pyramid temple of the Mother of Stone (now known as the Pyramid of the Moon) the huge stone blocks that flanked a great staircase adjacent to the pyramid were hurled down and ended up a hundred yards away. The homes of priests or nobles associated with the temple were ransacked. Twelve massive carved pillars, adorned with military insignia, were pulled over.

And at a temple in another part of the city—in the Puma Mural group of buildings—archaeologists again found evidence that stone blocks had been deliberately removed and tossed down into a plaza. The force of each impact was so great that the blocks literally bounced across the surface of the square, leaving a trail of telltale impact marks. There too a sacred statue—a valuable green onyx figure of a god—had been violently smashed. The temple was then torched; 1,500 years later, archaeologists even found where the burning beams had fallen.

As Teotihuacan destroyed itself—or in the run-up to the final crisis— a huge 200-ton statue, probably depicting the god Tlaloc, was being carved—perhaps on the orders of the doomed Teotihuacano government and priesthood—far away from the metropolis, on the slopes of a sacred mountain[15] associated with the god. The statue, one of the largest in the world and certainly the largest ever made in Mesoamerica, seems to have symbolized the religious conflict that must have raged as the Teotihuacan endgame unfolded. Traditional Tlaloc loyalists—the government and members of the ruling class—may well have ordered the creation of this unprecedentedly huge idol in a last, desperate bid to persuade the god to produce rain.[16]

But the rains didn't come, insurrection broke out, the Mesoamerican Jerusalem destroyed itself, and Tlaloc's two-hundred-ton bulk was abandoned for one and a half millennia on the slopes of his own holy mountain—a fitting symbol for the end of the greatest civilization ever to have flourished in the ancient New World.

THE CONSEQUENCES OF A.D. 535 FOR MESOAMERICA

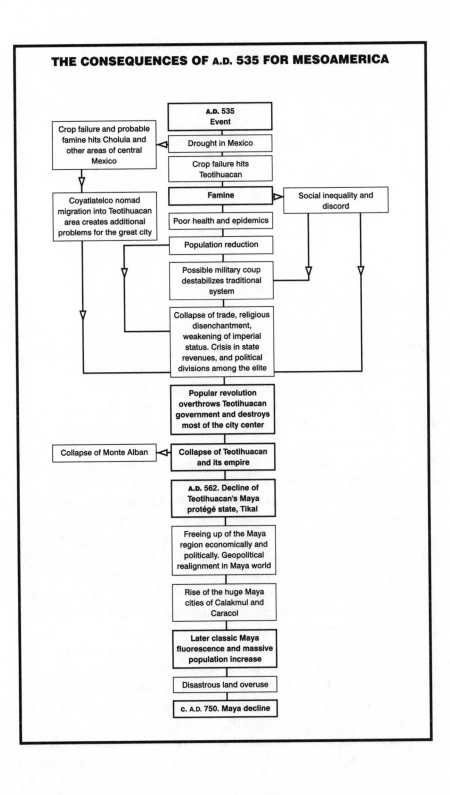

A.D. 535 Event

Crop failure and probable famine hits Cholula and other areas of central Mexico

Drought in Mexico

Crop failure hits Teotihuacan

Famine

Social inequality and discord

Coyatlatelco nomad migration into Teotihuacan area creates additional problems for the great city

Poor health and epidemics

Population reduction

Possible military coup destabilizes traditional system

Collapse of trade, religious disenchantment, weakening of imperial status. Crisis in state revenues, and political divisions among the elite

Popular revolution overthrows Teotihuacan government and destroys most of the city center

Collapse of Monte Alban

Collapse of Teotihuacan and its empire

A.D. 562. Decline of Teotihuacan's Maya protégé state, Tikal

Freeing up of the Maya region economically and politically. Geopolitical realignment in Maya world

Rise of the huge Maya cities of Calakmul and Caracol

Later classic Maya fluorescence and massive population increase

Disastrous land overuse

c. A.D. 750. Maya decline

24

THE DARTS OF
VENUS

ometime in late 561 or early 562, the enemies of one of Mesoamerica's greatest cities, Tikal, began to plan to destroy its power.

To bring down Tikal, a city of some thirty thousand people,
would require nothing less than the fiercest form of conflict known to the
Maya, namely, cosmic war. It was the job of the priests, with their deep as-
tronomical knowledge, to enlist the support of an appropriate divine cosmic body. So in late 561 or early 562, the priests of Tikal's great rival, the
city of Calakmul, recruited no less an ally than Venus himself.

For the Maya, Venus was no Old World goddess of love, but a very
male god of war and disaster. They were confident that he would rain
down cosmic darts and destruction on their Tikali enemies. But to ensure
the deity's support, Venus had to be in precisely the right place at the right
time so that he might strike down the enemy and guarantee victory.

The Calakmul soldiers would simply be the instruments of the god—
not independent human beings dependent on chance, but warriors im-
plementing a divinely ordained destiny. For fate to smile on Calakmul's
cosmic plan, just one human choice had to be made absolutely correctly:
the selection of the day for the attack. It had to be one that would enable
Venus to strike with all his power, and so the Calakmul priests chose 29
April 562—the only day in the planet's eighteen-month cycle on which it
actually appeared to stand stock-still, ready to pounce.

And so it was that Calakmul and its allies attacked and humbled the
great city of Tikal. Backed by his divine Venusian war patron, the ruler of

198

Calakmul—the appropriately named King Sky Witness—took control and appears to have installed as the city's ruler a puppet king, a young boy called Animal Skull, who could not have been much more than nine years of age at the time.[1]

For the Tikal elite, the aftermath of conquest was a time of ignominy and bloodstained suffering. The attack had almost certainly not been a purely external event. A fifth column of disgruntled members of the ruling family probably collaborated with the conquest of their city, and it is likely that Animal Skull was the son of one of the members of this alienated group. Indeed, it was probably this fifth column that was responsible for deliberately and very selectively smashing up the intricately carved royal commemorative monuments in the city's great plaza. The four previous monarchs who had ruled successively from 511 until the 562 conquest appear to have been absolutely loathed by the incoming Animal Skull regime, for it was their monuments that were selected for destruction. Their two predecessors' monuments (covering the period 458 to 511) were ostentatiously left untouched.

A disproportionate share of this dynastic hate seems to have been reserved for the first of the post-511 rulers—a woman known to Mayanists as the Lady of Tikal. Female succession was very rare in the Maya world, and it has to be assumed that her accession was the result of a major political crisis—perhaps a sort of coup d'etat in which powerful nonroyal figures sought to gain power by placing her on the throne.

It seems likely that the change of regime in 562 was the violent denouement of a dynastic sequence of events that had started in 511 with the presumably irregular accession of the Lady of Tikal. The splendidly ignominious aspect of this pivotal year would have been symbolized by the enthronement of the boy king. A powerless puppet in the hands of Calakmul, his accession nevertheless would have been typically flamboyant.

A jade mask would have partly obscured his face, while an intricate wood and jade headdress composed of further mask images and topped with rare green quetzal feathers would have towered above his head. Large jade pendants decorated with intricate floral designs would have hung heavily from his ears, while lying across his bare chest would have been a ten-inch-long rectangular jade ceremonial plaque. Attached to an intricate belt would have been three jade skull masks. And around his middle, above his loincloth, he probably sported a jaguar-pelt skirt, open at the front, while his royal feet would have been clad in leather sandals decorated with small masks and feathers.

The moment of accession would have been symbolized by his accep-tance of the royal scepter—a bizarre sculpture of a god whose long left leg, transformed into a serpent, would have been grasped by the new king in his outstretched hand. The ceremony would have been carried out as Animal Skull sat on a jaguar-fur cushion upon a great stone (or possibly wooden) throne draped with a profusion of puma, deer, and jaguar pelts.

If the scant evidence from other Mesoamerican sites is any indication, the enthronement probably took place at the summit of one of Tikal's major palace platforms. Shielded from the direct heat of the sun by a se-ries of beautifully crafted cotton canopies, the newly enthroned puppet king would have gazed out over a landscape of red-painted palaces, pyra-mid temples, and dazzling white plaster plazas, and beyond it almost endless suburbs stretching as far as the eye could see. Although Tikal's monumental city center covered only a little over one square mile, its often quite densely populated suburbs covered up to fifty times that area.

But it was against this backdrop of urban architectural splendor that the bloody suffering of 562 also took place. For as the boy-king was being enthroned, his predecessor, the fifty-four-year-old King Double Bird, hav-ing presumably been captured by Calakmul's soldiers, was almost cer-tainly offered as a high-grade human sacrifice, quite possibly to Calakmul's cosmic ally, the war god Venus.[2]

The fate of Double Bird and other captured Tikalis would have been gruesome in the extreme. It's likely that the former king of what was then the greatest city of the Maya world had his back broken as his body was bent backward to form a sort of living human wheel, which was then rolled down a small flight of steps into a courtyard used for ritual ball games. It is also likely that he was then taken to the adjoining temple where, if Mesoamerican sacrificial tradition was followed, his heart would have been extracted from his body with a razor-sharp obsidian knife.

It's probable that large numbers of Tikali prisoners were sacrificed at Animal Skull's enthronement. Stripped naked or clad in scraps of tree-bark paper, their traditional Maya gestures of submission—hands in the mouth or across the chest—would not have saved them from painful tor-ture prior to final death. They would have been disemboweled, their fin-gernails would have been ripped out, and their jaws would have been removed before the actual moment of sacrifice itself.

The conduct of Maya power politics, war, and religion were integrally linked, as in so many other parts of the world. Human bloodlust and sadism merged with Maya theology to create a murder machine that was evil by any human standard, yet also theologically just in Maya cosmic belief. For, from the Maya point of view, the gods provided sustenance to mankind, and rightly deserved prompt and appropriate gratitude and payment.

It should be added that it was not only captives who were offered as sacrifices. Members of the religious and political elite often performed painful autosacrifice, with women passing thorn-adorned cords through their tongues, while men mutilated their own private parts. Indeed, it is very likely that such autosacrifice, as well as full human sacrifice, took place on a fairly lavish scale at the installation by Calakmul of the boy-king Animal Skull at Tikal in 562. Venus must have been well satisfied.

It was a change in the geopolitical situation as a whole that had persuaded King Sky Witness of Calakmul to opt for war in the first place. The choice of date might have been up to Venus, but the strategic decision to conquer Tikal was almost certainly prompted by what must have been the increasing weakness of Tikal itself.

The great city had been Teotihuacan's main protégé in the Maya region, and the drought-induced decline in Teotihuacano power in the mid–sixth century (leading very rapidly to complete collapse) had left Tikal without a superpower patron.

From the first half of the fourth century onward, Teotihuacan had maintained a presence—probably a colonial one—in the Maya world. At first, it had been the city of Kaminaljuyu, merely a foothold used to secure sources of vital raw materials: obsidian, jade, copal (incense), cotton, cacao, and bird feathers. Near this first colony in the Maya area were one of the very few sources of obsidian in Mesoamerica and one of the even rarer sources of that most valued of commodities, the pre-Columbian stone of life, jade.

Then, having established a center of influence and probably a military base at Kaminaljuyu, the Teotihuacanos seized political control of at least two more Maya cities, either through conquest or more likely through dynastic marriage and geopolitical pressure. Teotihuacano dynasties were established in Uaxactun (pronounced "washak-toon") and in Tikal itself in January 378—and over the next half century Teotihuacano influence and/or control seems to have been extended from Tikal to several other Maya cities: nearby Yaxha; Becan, in the north; Copan, two hundred miles to the south; and even possibly the great riverside trading city of Yaxchilan, on the Usimacinta River. Some evidence—mainly architectural—suggests that Teotihuacano influence spread even farther in the fifth and early sixth centuries A.D., three hundred miles north of Tikal to the northern Yucatan towns of Dzibilchaltun, Acanceh, Oxkintok, and Uxmal, and to the small but exquisitely rich eastern town of Altun Ha, not far from the Caribbean coast.[3]

The key to this expansion seems to have been heavy Teotihuacano political influence and/or control at Tikal itself. After 378 Tikal appears to have been Teotihuacan's proxy in the Maya world. The man behind the 378 Teotihuacano takeover of Uaxactun and Tikal was a Teotihuacano general called Fire Born, and it was this military figure who then installed as king of Tikal a man called Nun-Yax-Ayin (Mystical Green Alligator), who was the son of a king called Spear Thrower Shield, who was himself almost certainly the ruler of Teotihuacan at the time. Whether the previous Tikali monarch, King Jaguar Paw I, had been violently removed or whether his natural death had caused a dynastic power vacuum is as yet unresolved.

As Teotihuacan's main client/protégé in the Maya area, Tikal had become the linchpin of Maya geopolitics. So when Teotihuacan went into rapid, drought-driven decline in the mid–sixth century, Tikal felt the backdraft a thousand miles to the east. Teotihuacan's cataclysmic collapse had to have had a profoundly unsettling effect on its culture's religious and political credibility. The chaos at the great metropolis had also no doubt paralyzed it militarily.

Economically, the rapid decline of Teotihuacan and its empire must also have had a heavy impact on the Mesoamerican economy. As we have seen in Chapter 23, the great metropolis had been for centuries a massive trading machine, sucking in vast quantities of raw materials and other imports while spewing out substantial quantities of manufactured goods. In the Maya world there would almost certainly have been a drop in external demand for cotton textiles and copal. And the collapse of long-distance trade routes that accompanied the decline of Teotihuacan would also have impacted heavily on Tikal as the dominant Maya power. These reductions in external trade robbed Tikal and its dynasty of tax-in-kind revenue—precisely because as top dog in the Maya world, it would have been milking the trade system more than its not-so-powerful competitors. What is more, any reduction in inbound luxury goods would have deprived Tikal of the very items it needed to maintain its political patronage system.

As Tikal's regional control began to disintegrate, its ability to extract tribute from other cities would have declined, and it would have become more vulnerable to internal dissent and external aggression. And that is precisely what appears to have happened in the fateful year 562.

The long-term significance of the decline and fall of Teotihuacan and the change of regime at Tikal becomes apparent only some three hundred years later, at the time of the final collapse of the major Maya civilizations. For centuries—especially since the mid- to late fourth century—the pace of political and demographic evolution within the Maya world had been to a substantial extent conditioned by the political, religious, and economic influence of Teotihuacan. Then, after the metropolis collapsed in the mid- to late sixth century, the pace of Maya political, economic, and demographic evolution was no longer constrained by Teotihuacan's semicolonial hand.

Teotihuacan had boasted a population of between 125,000 and 200,000—some five to eight times larger than the biggest Maya city of the period. What is more, it directly or indirectly controlled a territory dozens of times bigger than any Maya city. And in religio-cosmic terms, it was the center of the Mesoamerican world. Thus its presence distorted the whole of the rest of Mesoamerican history for much of the first five centuries A.D. Conversely, its rapid disappearance from the scene created a huge political vacuum and freed up the entire Maya world in political and economic terms. Within the Maya sphere, existing cities evolved rapidly into regional powers, chief among them Calakmul, Caracol, and Copan.

Caracol, an ally of Calakmul against Tikal in 562, experienced a huge increase in population—from twenty thousand to anything between forty thousand and a hundred thousand in the late sixth century and the first half of the seventh. During this expansion period, a superb radial road system was constructed within the city, the monumental buildings were refurbished and enlarged, and hundreds of miles of stone agricultural terraces and scores of water reservoirs were built. It became extremely wealthy, and the archaeological evidence suggests that the entire population shared in this prosperity. A large middle class appears to have developed, probably among the first occasions on which this occurred in the Maya world.

Over the same period, Calakmul's population also rose by 200 percent (from around twenty thousand to about sixty thousand). Copan too saw its population begin to increase rapidly in the late sixth century. Even Tikal recovered, and its population rose substantially as well.

It is highly likely that the urban population increases of the late sixth and seventh centuries resulted directly from the freeing up of the political and economic environment following the evaporation of Teotihuacan's semicolonial presence in the mid–sixth century—symbolized by the fall of Tikal in 562. Tragically, however, by the mid–eighth century, population expansion led to land exhaustion, food shortages, and interstate and internal conflict—and ultimately to political and demographic collapse, thus ending the great classic era of Maya civilization.

The sequence of Mesoamerican events had run its course following the Teotihuacano drought of the mid–sixth century. But *north* of Mexico, the climatic catastrophe may have triggered cultural developments that still affect America to this day.

25

NORTH AMERICAN
MYSTERY

The United States' oldest surviving urban culture can be found in the deserts of New Mexico and Arizona, where thirty-seven thousand Pueblo Indians still live in thirty-one exclusively Pueblo towns—the oldest of which was founded nine hundred years ago. Through a combination of strong community values and intense cultural conservatism, they have been more successful than any other American Indian people at preserving their identity.

Their medieval ancestors, now usually called the Anasazi, developed an extraordinary civilization—building towns from A.D. 1000 onward, large dams and reservoirs, up to five hundred miles of thirty-foot-wide roads, and a rapid communications system operated through a complex of signal stations. They were the first Indians north of Mexico to use looms, weaving cotton cloth as early as A.D. 750. But perhaps the most intriguing aspects of the Anasazi civilization's past are the nature and date of its origins, for in that respect, Anasazi history echoes that of so much of the rest of the world.

It's known that the climatic chaos of the mid– to late sixth century did affect what is now the western United States, but the evidence is patchy. The only definitive data comes from tree rings obtained from bristlecone pines growing at relatively high altitude in California and Nevada; low-altitude tree-ring data, including that for New Mexico and Arizona, show no evidence of climatic problems in the years or decades following 535. And yet the archaeological evidence tells a different story—one of relatively sudden cultural change and perhaps even of geopolitical stress.

Prior to the sixth century, the Anasazi did not tend to live in villages, had an economy that was only 40 to 50 percent agricultural, and used spears for hunting. Pottery manufacture was practiced in half of the Anasazi territory but was not commonplace. Stone tool technology was relatively primitive.

Then in the mid- to late sixth century, for no apparent reason, the Anasazi totally changed their economy. They became 80 percent agricultural, and yet (in common with other Indian peoples at the time) they also improved their hunting technology by abandoning spears and adopting the bow and arrow. Settlement sizes began to increase, and the first villages appeared. Sophisticated stone axes (suitable for agricultural use) were developed, and pottery became much more widespread. Within just a few decades the foundations had been laid on which Anasazi urban culture would later develop.

The sudden transformation of Anasazi society—a virtual technological and cultural revolution—is a riddle. But there are four clues as to what might have generated the change.

First, one of the key aspects—the adoption of the bow and arrow— was shared by many other Indian peoples in the sixth century and was therefore part of a wider North American phenomenon. Second, in the northeast fringe of Anasazi territory there is archaeological evidence of mid- to late-sixth-century structures—specifically stockades. Once again this may have been part of a more general sixth-century North American phenomenon, namely, an increase in warfare. Third and most intriguing is that there is ceramic evidence of cultural contact in that period between the Anasazi and another rapidly evolving Indian culture, known as the Late Woodland, seven hundred miles to the east on the other side of the Great Plains, in the Mississippi Valley. The fourth potential clue is that all these took place at a time of increased climatic stress in most areas of the world.

So even if, for local climatic reasons, the Anasazi were not directly hit by severe drought, it is quite possible that they were put under demographic or competitive pressure or threat by peoples in other regions who *were* hit. Certainly the appearance of pottery styles borrowed from seven hundred miles to the east suggests that something unusual was happening in the area in between, that is, on the plains. Either population movement was increasing or trans–Great Plains cultural contact was made possible by a hitherto unsuspected thinning out of Plains Indians populations. Certainly in the Mississippi Valley, the mid– to late sixth century saw the total collapse of the old way of life and the old geopolitical arrangements.

The late-sixth-century Mississippi Valley ceramic connection with the Anasazi is particularly intriguing. The changes the Mississippi Valley experienced came at exactly the same time as the Anasazi were being transformed—and with identical long-term consequences: the bow and arrow replaced the spear, finer pottery was developed, settlement numbers began to increase, and the food economy changed with the introduction of large-scale wild-rice gathering. By 700 monumental earth-mound effigies of sacred birds were being built, and by 1000 the first Mississippi Valley towns were being constructed—at virtually the same time that witnessed the first signs of urbanism far to the west in the Anasazi region. Indeed, both areas reached their urban peaks in the thirteenth century A.D., with populations of three thousand and twenty thousand respectively for the largest Anasazi and Mississippian towns.

Thus North America's two medieval urban cultures north of Mexico had very similar developmental trajectories in technological and chronological terms. Both were born in the tenth and eleventh centuries A.D. but had been conceived in the mid– to late sixth century—the very period that witnessed so much change elsewhere in the world. In other regions of the planet, the changes in the mid– to late sixth century were quite clearly climate-driven in the last analysis. The North American changes probably were, too, but in the absence of any written record, the case there has to remain unproven.

26

FROM ART TO
OBLIVION

Scattered across one of the world's driest and most barren deserts are the largest works of art on earth. Etched on the desert floor in southern Peru are some 1,300 extraordinary drawings—everything from giant birds (some almost a thousand feet long) and killer whales, to abstract designs resembling the spokes of giant wheels and single straight lines, some of which can be up to thirty miles in length.

Discovered by Peruvian airline pilots back in the 1920s, this complex of vast drawings—spread over nearly two hundred square miles of desert—became, in the popular imagination, one of the world's greatest archaeological mysteries. Explanations of their origins and purpose have been almost as numerous as the drawings themselves, and have even included suggestions—from the literary, rather than the archaeological, world—that they were made by aliens from outer space!

There are six main types of drawing: figurative biomorphs (animals, humans, plants, etc.); huge spirals; giant trapezoids; parallel line systems; ray systems; and single straight lines. The available archaeological evidence suggests that nearly all were made between 400 B.C. and A.D. 600 by local people who, up until approximately the time of Christ, are referred to by archaeologists as the Paracas culture and who thereafter are known to the archaeological world as the Nasca culture. Their real names have been long lost in the mists of time.[1]

The fifty nonabstract drawings include a 261-foot capuchin monkey with a long curly tail, a 152-foot spider (possibly a black widow), ten humans, a desert fox, a 1,620-foot lizard, and three killer whales—including one 89-foot specimen holding a severed human head. There are also eighteen birds, including a pelican, a condor, a frigate, two humming-birds, and a huge 947-foot-long marsh bird.

It is possible that the spirals—around thirty of them—may also be biomorphs. Some archaeologists think that these drawings, which range from 30 to 170 feet in length, could be highly stylized images of seashells, some real examples of which appear to have been featured in ancient Nascan rituals and have been found scattered on the desert floor.

The third category of desert drawing, the so-called trapezoids, are by far the most common. There are around a thousand of these usually long wedge-shaped features. Varying between 65 and 5,300 feet in length and 16 and 200 feet in width, they may have been constructed as symbolic representations of valleys.[2] A substantially rarer linear feature, parallel lines, can be even longer—up to 1.5 miles in length and yet only around 23 feet wide.

There are approximately a hundred of the so-called ray systems, and because of their vast size and clarity they tend to dominate much of the Nascan landscape—from the air, that is. Each system consists of between five and twenty-five absolutely straight rays, each up to 2.5 miles long. In virtually all cases, the rays converge on little hills up to 65 feet high that stand out from the largely flat desert floor. Again, archaeologists have sug-gested that the little hills have symbolic topographic significance, this time as proxy mountains.[3]

By far the largest Nasca drawings are the massive single lines. Totally straight, and anything from 30 feet to 30 miles long, they appear to the modern eye to go from absolutely nowhere to absolutely nowhere! In-deed, they appear to be distributed almost randomly.

The mystery of the Nasca drawings has long puzzled scholars. But embedded within them is evidence that not only can shed light on the purpose of the lines but also can help us discover the ultimate fate of the people who built them.

The drawings were almost certainly seen cumulatively as a sort of cosmic map by the ancient Nasca. Every element symbolically represents either a real feature in the Nascan cosmos or a means of getting to it. The little hills, trapezoids, and animals were proxy representatives of, re-spectively, real mountains, real valleys, and possibly, totemic ancestors or animal spirits. The straight lines—either on their own or in the ray systems—were dual-purpose "ducts" through the cosmos. In real life they

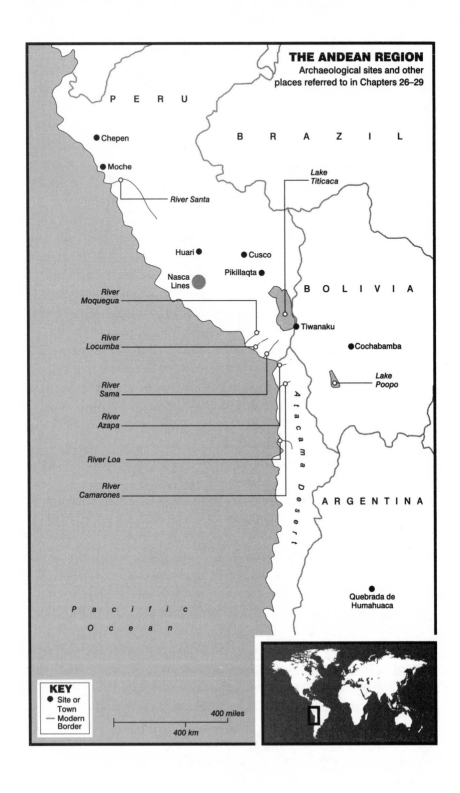

THE ANDEAN REGION
Archaeological sites and other places referred to in Chapters 26–29

P E R U

B R A Z I L

- Chepen
- Moche

River Santa

Lake Titicaca

- Huari
- Cusco
- Pikillaqta

Nasca Lines

B O L I V I A

River Moquegua

River Locumba

- Tiwanaku

- Cochabamba

River Sama

Lake Poopo

River Azapa

A t a c a m a   D e s e r t

River Loa

River Camarones

A R G E N T I N A

- Quebrada de Humahuaca

P a c i f i c   O c e a n

KEY
- Site or Town
— Modern Border

400 miles

400 km

could be used for ritual processions, but in a sense they could also be "flown" along by priests in trance.

Although, of course, none of the ancient Nascan shamans actually ever saw the whole "map" or even bits of it from the air, the shamans would have been able to "fly" along those cosmic ducts in their mind's eye while under the influence of local hallucinogens.

Shamanism was almost certainly the main form that religious belief took in the Americas in pre-Columbian times. In parts of Peru (the north and the east) it still survives today. The hallucinogenic plant used by modern Peruvian shamans to go into trance, the San Pedro cactus, was almost certainly used by Nascan shamans, as that very cactus is one of the plants that feature as motifs on their pottery.

Throughout parts of Asia and in a few places in the Americas (including eastern Peru) shamanic flying (sometimes known as "soul flight") is still an important feature of shamanic religious practice. And anthropologists have collected evidence showing that soul flight in some Amerindian cultures is (and presumably was) seen as being conducted along perfectly straight "flight paths."

The purpose of shamanic flight in Amerindian society today is to maintain contact with long-dead ancestors. Using hallucinogens, the shaman goes into a trance and imagines that his soul (or in some cases also his physical body) is flying through the cosmos from the world of the living to that of the dead, and then back again. In eastern Peru, modern shamans, having actually "seen" the cosmic landscape, have drawn cosmic maps so as to more graphically describe to anthropologists what they have witnessed.

But if ancient Nascan shamans were using the straight desert lines as "flight paths" to reach their long-dead ancestors, we must try to understand why they would wish to do so. The reason lies in the Nascan environment—and in their economy. The terrain is unremittingly dry (less than an inch of water per century in the most arid areas). And the Nascan economy (probably mainly maize cultivation) relied totally upon the water that flowed down from the mountains along ten mainly seasonal river courses. There was no rainfall and there were no natural springs. The water from the Andean peaks, just forty miles away, that flowed down the vital Nascan valleys was the only source of life for the Nasca. Its denial meant famine and death.

Thus it was that shamanic contact with the ancestors or the gods—or both—via soul flight would have been so important. It was a means of direct access to the powers behind their water supply. Interestingly, a much later Inca straight-line ray system was also associated with securing water sources. Dust from the rays was collected and ritually dumped into rivers, which delivered it to the ancestors as a sort of "payment" for water—a form of divine water tax.[4]

There is evidence that the real-life processions along the Nasca straight lines—which would have retraced the shamanic soul flight journeys—featured the playing of panpipes whose sound specifically represented the sound of running water, according to surviving Peruvian folklore. In recent years, several expeditions actually found ancient panpipes on the lines themselves.[5]

Furthermore, on the summits of the small hills—the proxy mountains—at the centers of the ray systems, archaeologists have found evidence of religious ritual activity that was almost certainly designed to secure water from the real mountains forty miles to the east.

Just as the Teotihuacan empire of Mexico was ultimately dependent economically, religiously, and politically on water, so were the Nasca tribal chieftaincies. And just as Teotihuacan declined when drought struck, so did Nasca in the face of the same mid-sixth-century global climatic crisis. Evidence obtained from an ice core extracted from Peru's Quelccaya glacier—just 230 miles east of Nasca—shows that Peru was hit by a massive thirty-year drought that started around 540 and ended around 570 (see Chapter 23).

The exact details of the epic story of how the Nasca waged and ultimately lost their battle to survive will never be known, as the Nasca left no written record. Yet by piecing together the archaeological evidence, it is still possible to reconstruct the probable mechanisms that led to their demise.

Tattooed, resplendent in his great fan-shaped red, blue, and yellow feather headdress, his shoulder-length jet-black hair swirling from side to side, the shaman shuddered and shook to the beat of drums and the rhythmic clatter of rattles.

Trembling, screeching, arms outstretched—as if a bird in flight—the shaman in his mind's eye flew fast as a condor and straight as a dart over the Nasca wasteland, across his people's proxy cosmos, to the ancestors and the spirits in the Andean mountains to the east.

His eyes were glazed, and small streams of mucus oozed from his flared nostrils—a side effect of the herbal drugs that had helped send him into trance. His short-sleeved black-and-white knee-length tunic was heavy with pungent sweat, and his great embroidered cape stretched out on either side of him like wings. A dark pink necklace made of seashells bounced rhythmically up and down upon the checkerboard design of his tunic. The great round eyes of a falcon painted on his face began to smudge and run as beads of sweat trickled from his forehead to his mustache and small goatee.

Around him, as dusk began to fall, people chanted and stared and even collapsed on the floor of the great plaza where the shaman had gone into trance. As it began to clip the horizon, the huge orange sphere of the desert sun bathed the scene—and groups of strange "buildings" around the plaza—in a warm red glow.

This was the Nascan capital, a vast city without citizens, a place reserved for priests, pilgrims, and the Nascan equivalent of prayer—soul-flight communication with the next world. Known to modern archaeologists as Cahuachi (its original name remains a complete mystery), it had an architectural style that was a bizarre blend of natural and man-made elements. Although the city covers 375 acres, technically it had virtually no true buildings, for almost all the forty structures in Cahuachi (all of them step pyramids) were to an extent never actually built. Instead, they were sculpted out of the living rock and then given further shape through the addition of quantities of mud bricks. The largest had six tiers and were some 50 feet high.

In the plaza, the shaman continued to shake and shudder, arms outstretched in trance. His altered state of consciousness was lasting longer, the crowds were bigger, and the mixture of despair and hope etched on people's faces was more intense than normal, for on this occasion the shaman's mission was one of life or death. A great drought had struck the Nasca valleys and brought famine and death in its wake, and the traditional shamanic soul flight journey across the cosmos to secure water was, on that occasion, more crucial than it had ever been before.

The scenes above, or something very like them, probably did occur, although the actual details have had to be re-created from images on Nasca pottery and textiles, from anthropological accounts of the behavior associated with surviving Peruvian shamanic traditions, and from the archaeological evidence that Cahuachi was a city of religious ritual, not of citizens.

But archaeological and ice-core evidence also suggests that the Nascan efforts to secure rain utterly failed, as the drought continued for some thirty years.

Dating in Nasca archaeology is far from being an exact science, but the available evidence suggests that Cahuachi was abandoned as a great ritual center around the very time that the drought started. Certainly, even after just a few years of crop failure and famine, it is likely that the abject failure of established religious practice would have begun to provoke religious and political tensions and change. And according to the archaeological record, that is precisely what seems to have occurred.

The first act in the drama appears to have been the abandonment of Cahuachi and a switch of ritual and religious emphasis away from the city to the open wilderness and its sprawling proxy cosmos—the vast desert drawings.

There seems to have been a decentralization of religious practice, probably with different Nascan clans or tribal subgroups etching very large numbers of new line systems on the desert floor. Dozens of new ray complexes were created, and virtually every hillock worthy of the name was turned into a proxy mountain on which rituals were then carried out in an increasingly desperate bid for water. On their summits, archaeologists have found the still perfectly preserved offerings made almost fifteen hundred years ago to the gods or to the ancestors to coax water from the skies. Maize cobs, the remains of sacrificed llamas and guinea pigs, and quantities of smashed pottery have been discovered lying exactly where they were left back in the sixth century.

Along with the sudden proliferation of ray systems came an intensification of other forms of desert mega-drawing. Giant trapezoids were introduced, and increased numbers of zigzag patterns, some over three hundred feet long, may at this stage have been meticulously etched onto the scorched surface of the Nasca desert.

But it wasn't just the desert drawings that changed and proliferated. The iconography on the Nasca pottery—among the finest in the world—also began to change. The images on the pots became more violent, more jarring. Increasingly they featured spikes, jagged staffs (probably spears), warriors, severed heads, and even killer whales replete with fanged mouths dripping with blood. A key religious icon—a probable deity—evolved from being fairly human into a far more demonic and aggressive monster.

The abandonment of Cahuachi and the orgy of line drawing were followed not only by more aggressive iconography but also by more real conflict. As the long drought continued, not only religious but also political stability seems to have broken down. Competition and raiding for food became the order of the day, and archaeologists have succeeded in uncovering compelling evidence to illustrate the full horror of this increase in warfare.

In 1989, on a hillside overlooking a valley near the modern town of Palpa, archaeologists excavated a cache of forty-eight sixth-century severed heads.[6] Detailed forensic examination of the skulls and associated material revealed that the victims had first had their throats slit.[7] Once dead, their brains, tongues, facial muscles, and skin were removed. Then the skin was refitted and the cheeks and eyeballs were stuffed with cloth. Finally, a hole was punched in each forehead so that the severed head could be suspended from a cord of cotton or human hair. It's likely that the heads originally belonged to warriors killed or captured in battle and were displayed as trophies on some sort of timber scaffold erected by the victors above the very valley in which the victims had been slaughtered.

Increased conflict was an almost inevitable consequence of the growing competition and political chaos that flowed from prolonged drought. The drought-period Nasca fought with weapons that were crude but nonetheless cruelly effective. The pottery and textile iconography and other evidence show that they included five-foot-long spears (for lunging with), wooden clubs, stone axes, slings, and eighteen-inch-long throwing spears launched by wooden spear throwers with whale-ivory handles.

Warriors would have fought wearing short, often sleeveless tunics, probably sometimes reinforced with padded cotton armor. To protect their heads, they would often have sported conical padded cotton helmets, each topped with a fan-shaped crest of brown feathers.

But politico-religious change and warfare were not the only Nascan responses to the great drought. In a few areas the Nasca fought back against natural catastrophe with their own version of high technology—and it must almost have worked, at least until other factors overwhelmed them. The "high-tech" solution was to dig for water deep underground, capture it, and channel it to where it was needed.

Almost certainly while the drought was raging, the Nasca invented and then engineered around fifty such water-extraction systems, with a total length of some thirty miles. Thirty-six systems survive, and some are still in use to this day. They vary from narrow, three-foot-wide tunnels deep underground to large, V-shaped, cobble-faced canals three feet wide at the bottom but ten times that width at the top.

Each system, known as a *puquio*, was a purely local solution and was usually between 1,300 feet and 1.5 miles in length. Their age was for a long time a mystery, but now three types of evidence have combined to tie them to the sixth century. First of all, careful water-level analysis of the *puquios* has revealed that they were built in conditions of extreme drought, much more extreme than even the ultradry conditions that exist in the Nasca desert today. Second, to dig thirty miles of *puquios* requires more than just a few years. Third, radiocarbon and associated pottery dates all point to the sixth century.

But there is one last piece of fascinating and poignant evidence that also links it to the great drought, namely, an extraordinary piece of local folk memory. Local legend has it that the *puquios* were built at a time of great drought to collect the tears wept by the local Indian god as he beheld the suffering of his people. Some linguistic authorities have even suggested that the history of the great drought is preserved, in a sense, in the very name of Nasca itself, for in the local Quechua language the word for pain, *nanay,* is said to have evolved into the name *nanascca,* which has come down to our own times simply as Nasca.

And so it was that the creators of the largest artworks on earth became victims of the mid-sixth-century climatic catastrophe. But they were certainly not the only Peruvian victims of the great drought.

27

THE MUD

OF HADES

Naked, terrified, staggering from blows delivered with wooden mace heads, and prodded with copper-tipped lances, the half-dead gifts to the storm god entered at last the place of their deliverance.

Their suffering at the heart of one of South America's most sacred ancient sites—the now long-deserted city of Moche in northern Peru—formed part of what probably qualifies as the world's most bizarre mass human sacrifice. Many of the victims had their fingers and toes sliced off and inserted into the dead bodies of their colleagues. Other individuals had their fingers crushed with rocks. Still others had their feet pierced by copper lance heads. Most were probably finally dispatched by decapitation or with a blow to the head administered with a heavy wooden mace. Others, however, were almost certainly bled to death.

For their tortured corpses, however, the ordeal was far from over. Some of the bodies were systematically chopped up and ritually re-arranged. In certain cases heads were placed between legs—and bodies were deliberately positioned on top of each other.

But in terms of probable meaning, the most telling aspect of this ghastly ritual deposition was its precise location—buried within a matrix of sacred mud. For the torrents of clinging mud in which the butchered bodies were finally laid to rest were nothing less than the "melted" outer surfaces of a giant adobe temple.

The sacrificial victims' rendezvous with the mud of their mass grave was no coincidence. The utilization of the sacred mud from the elaborately decorated outer surfaces of the temple was a deliberate act that by its very nature had to coincide with an extremely heavy rainstorm. And in and around the north coast of Peru, where the sacrificial site is located, the only occasions on which such intense downpours occur are during the very worst occurrences of the intermittent climatic phenomenon known to the world today as El Niño.

Recent archaeological excavations show that these mass sacrifices took place in association with at least two El Niño events, and that each ritual slaughter involved up to forty victims.[1] The excavations have even revealed the tombs of the executioners—almost certainly warrior-priests of some sort. In one such tomb was found the skeleton of a sixty-year-old man who had been buried together with the macabre tool of his trade—a three-foot-long mace still encrusted with the blood of his victims. Medical analysis of his bones suggest that, even at sixty, he had massive muscles and must have been physically very strong. With him was buried a child—a sixteen-year-old boy, perhaps his personal servant, who was probably put to death in order to accompany him to the next world. A nearby double tomb also housed an adult male, also around sixty, and another young boy, this time just thirteen years old.

The mass sacrifices—and there are probably many more groups that have not yet been discovered—took place at some point between the years A.D. 500 and 700. They illustrate the sort of extreme ritual religious reaction that occurred when Moche society came under climatic threat. In the examples excavated so far, these associated threats were the massive El Niño rainstorms, cataclysmic events that were capable of washing away whole towns, destroying entire irrigation systems, and plunging societies into chaos.

During the mid-sixth-century climatic problems, the Moche civilization was hammered mercilessly by a combination of intense drought and intermittent devastating floods. The evidence for a great drought in the Americas has already been outlined in Chapter 23, but one of the sources for that evidence, the Quelccaya glacier ice core, also revealed the increasing frequency of major El Niño events: in c. 490, c. 526, c. 556, c. 580, c. 590, c. 592, and c. 630. Notice that between 490 and 592, the gaps between really major El Niños decreased from thirty-six years, to thirty, to twenty-four, to ten, and finally to two years (see Chapter 23).

It is almost certain that the great Andean drought (c. 540–570) was part of the mid-sixth-century climatic crisis, but whether that crisis played any part in accelerating the frequency of sixth-century El Niños is less certain. However, the worldwide problems almost certainly made the El Niños substantially more severe than they would otherwise have been.

The Moche reaction to intense drought, just as much as intense flood, would have included attempts to placate their gods with human sacrifice. Like Nasca religion, Moche religion is likely to have been largely shamanic in nature. Contact with ancestors, especially in times of climatic crisis, would have been a vital ingredient—ancestors could intervene with the gods or with the powers of nature to prevent disaster, terminate adversity, or bring prosperity.

Contact with the dead was of real economic and political impact, and a recent archaeological discovery may well be illustrative of just how important it was. Buried within the floor of one of a Moche temple's many rooms were found what appear to have been a set of life-size dancing skeleton puppets—made out of real bones. Detailed examination of the bones revealed that they were deliberately defleshed using butchering instruments and that all the bones were kept in an articulated state.

In Europe, such a concept would be straight out of Dante's *Inferno*, but in a mid-first-millennium Peruvian context, the skeletons need to be seen as elements of rituals designed to breach the barriers between this world and the next. They may even have symbolized the ancestors whose intercession would so desperately have been required in times of climatic crisis.

At the height of its power, probably in the early sixth century A.D., the Moche state controlled up to fifteen thousand square miles of territory between the Piura River in the far north of Peru and the Huarmey, three hundred miles to the south.

The capital covered at least three-quarters of a square mile, had an estimated population of up to ten thousand, and was dominated by two huge buildings, the largest of which was a massive cross-shaped structure with a 160-foot-high pyramid at its southern end. This vast cruciform edifice covered 14 acres and consisted of 2 million cubic yards of mud bricks and other building material—three-quarters of the volume of the Great Pyramid in Egypt! Most of the complex was ultimately destroyed by Spanish treasure hunters, who diverted an entire river in their desperation to wash away the mud bricks in their search for hidden gold.

But it was the second great structure in the city center, a slightly smaller temple, that has revealed most about Moche religion and ritual. It was here that archaeologists found the human mass sacrifices, the tombs

of the executioner priests, the skeleton marionettes, and a series of spectacular wall paintings depicting frightening large-fanged anthropomorphic and zoomorphic beings, probably deities.

The climatic events of the mid–sixth century—the drought and the El
Niños—had the effect of destabilizing the Moche empire. The thirty-year
drought must have led to severe famines, and the c. 556 El Niño flood
would have destroyed irrigation systems, thus making the food supply
situation even more precarious. The population, weakened by starvation,
would then have fallen prey to a range of contagious diseases, much as
the Teotihuacanos of Mexico were succumbing to famine and disease at
exactly the same time.

Although the entire Andean region was hit by the climatic problems,
the already arid coastal plain was almost certainly affected more disas-
trously than the highland areas to the east. In times of drought, lowlands
normally suffer worse than highland areas. Those few rain clouds that are
around will tend to shed their load when they encounter mountain terrain. What is more, the reduced rainfall in the mountains is not sufficient
to sustain the river volumes required to water coastal plains. The water-
starved lowlands would have lost much of their vegetation cover, and the
loss in turn would have reduced water retention, accelerated soil erosion,
and encouraged the encroachment of desert terrain.

Additionally, the large coastal plain populations had only two ecological niches to exploit for food—the flatlands and the sea. By contrast,
highland peoples, with a variety of altitudinal zones at their disposal, had
more options. They could exploit valley bottoms, mountain slopes, high
mountain pastures, and even lakes. Even when the lakes shrank, they
often actually assisted agriculture by revealing new, ultrafertile land. And
of course all mountain peoples were, by definition, closer to key water
sources.

At first the change in geopolitical balance would probably have allowed foothill areas between the coastal plain and the highlands to break
loose from Moche control. This would have made access to their food,
copper, gold, and silver resources, as well as the ritually important drug
crop coca, much more difficult for the Moche and much easier for the
highland peoples, especially the most powerful highland group, the
Huari.

As the economic as well as geopolitical situation increasingly favored
the mountain areas, the north-south highland trading trail would have
become the key commercial highway in Peru—very much at the expense

of the only other major north-south trail, the one that ran along the coast.

Moreover, the coast soon began to suffer the bizarre secondary effects of drought and severe El Niño flooding. During the brief yet severe episodes of such flooding, millions of tons of sand were scoured out of the parched landscape, swept coastward by the El Niño torrents, and dumped immediately offshore. Long-shore drift then spread them out along the coast, while the tides swept them onto the beaches and strong coastal winds formed them into dunes and drove them inland. In classic desert fashion, the dunes marched inland—well after the drought had ended—and destroyed agricultural land and even towns. Indeed, part of the Moche city around the Huaca del Sol was inundated by this tide of sand.[2]

Thus it was that this lethal cocktail of disasters affected the highland and coastal areas to quite different degrees, and the people of the relatively poor mountainous interior almost certainly suffered less than their ostentatiously rich, coastal-plain opposite numbers.[3] Demographically and in terms of social organization and control, the coast no longer had an advantage. The Moche civilization appears to have fragmented politically, probably under pressure from highland peoples, especially the Huari.[4] Moche itself, the pyramid city, survived relatively unscathed, but it lost much of the territory it controlled. In one area eighty-five miles to the north, a new city, Pampa Grande, grew up and eventually adopted a strongly Huari-influenced culture, which probably reflected increasing Huari geopolitical power.[5]

In fact, within a few generations, highland-influenced populations were living in a new town—now a group of ruins known to archaeologists as Galindo, just twenty-three miles northeast of Moche.[6] The ancient city became more and more isolated; Moche survived at least another century, but its glory days were over.

Along with this decline in Moche's power came a marked increase in warfare. A series of massive defensive walls were built by various northern Peruvian coastal cultures, including the Moche. The most spectacularly located was built on the rugged mountain summit near modern Chepen, a hundred miles north of Moche, by the same highland-influenced culture that created Galindo. This now-deserted mountaintop city is surrounded by massive, twelve-foot-wide stone ramparts that even today stand in places to a height of twenty-seven feet. With an estimated population of around five thousand, it boasted large apartment complexes and a probable palace—but, extraordinarily, it appears to have had no water supply! Water probably had to be carried by porters from the valley below and somehow stored. And south of Moche are the ruins of further massive defenses, in the Santa Valley and at Cerro de La Cruz in the Chao Valley, where piles of stones meant to be slung at enemies still lie as mute testimony to the deterioration of security conditions following the climatic problems of the mid–sixth century.

Even near Moche itself, a massive 1,600-foot-long stone and adobe-brick rampart was built, presumably to defend the city, while at Galindo a 13-foot-high wall complete with parapet cut across the valley in a great 1,300-foot curve.

Meanwhile, as the Huari began to expand in central and then northern Peru, a similar or related process was taking place in the extreme south of Peru, in Bolivia, and in northern Chile with the expansion of the highland state of Tiwanaku, again at the expense of the coastal plains—and these Huari and Tiwanaku superstates influenced the long-term future of South America.

28

BIRTH OF AN
EMPIRE

A hundred and fifty miles from the distant ocean, deep in the interior of central Peru, surrounded by sixteen-thousand-foot-high peaks, is one of South America's strangest ancient cities.

Covering almost half a square mile, it consists of a series of twenty great rectangular plazas, each flanked by as many as 150 cell-like rooms, many stacked up to three stories high. Each plaza was separated from the next by massive forty-foot-high stone walls, and the three thousand cells were all built to just half a dozen basic designs.

At first, archaeologists thought the entire complex—at a place called Pikillaqta, near Cusco—must have been a vast ancient prison. Its sheer uniformity, and the military precision with which it was built, certainly seemed to betray an obsession with control and organization. Even now, its precise function remains a mystery, especially as it is merely the largest example of a whole series of these mystery complexes scattered throughout Peru.

They have the same basic layout and they all date from the early phases of the first great pan-Peruvian empire, that of the Huari—an imperial system that started to emerge following the climatically triggered geopolitical dislocation of the mid– to late sixth century.[1] They were almost certainly constructed as visually impressive imperial administrative centers and may well have been used to house officials, some ordinary civilians, and probably substantial military garrisons as well as to store vast quantities of tribute and tax in kind.

The Huari created an empire of some 130,000 square miles—900 miles from north to south and, on average, around 150 miles from east to west. It had a population of several million and a capital city—also called Huari—that covered 1,750 acres and had an estimated thirty thousand citizens. The emergence of their empire profoundly changed subsequent Peruvian—indeed, subsequent South American—history. As the first pan-Peruvian imperial system, it was the prototype that paved the way for the much later Inca empire and then, in a sense, for Spain's Andean empire in the sixteenth to early nineteenth centuries.

It was probably the Huari who developed the large-scale agricultural terracing system that boosted food production, which in turn permitted demographic expansion and so helped enable the highlands (including the later Incas) to dominate the coast for much of the region's subsequent pre-Columbian history. It is conceivable that the agricultural terracing system was developed as a response to the great drought that disrupted the Andean world between A.D. 540 and 570, and that it was this response that helped Huari to expand during and after that thirty-year disaster.

It was also Huari who probably built the vast road system that helped hold subsequent Inca and early Spanish Andean empires together and helped make them economically viable. These people are also thought to have invented the unique Andean record-keeping system, the quipu, which helped facilitate the running of their empire and of subsequent Andean imperial systems. Consisting of a set of cords in which knots denote numerical values, the quipu would have been used to maintain records of tax and tribute payments and the performance of labor obligations.

Prior to the Huari empire, Andean states had been fundamentally monocultural and relatively small. The largest, the Moche, covered no more than fifteen thousand square miles. The Huari, by contrast, controlled directly or through client relationships an area of around 130,000 square miles (the size of Britain, Ireland, and Holland combined), and therefore automatically had to accommodate dozens of different cultures and belief systems. Again, the concept of a pan-Andean empire resurfaced in Inca times, and continued in Spanish colonial and even postcolonial times.

The cultural diversity of the Huari empire meant that a central state religion had to be developed to provide a unifying factor. Thus it was that a particular solar deity—probably associated with the imperial family— was elevated to the level of a supergod. This deity—a male holding two staffs, possibly weapons—was not designed to replace local deities within the multicultural empire, but was intended to act as an elite addition to the various pantheons; in a sense, it was a common apex shared by them all. The emperor no doubt saw himself as the earthly reflection of this cosmic arrangement: as in heaven, so on earth.

In Inca times, the same superimposition occurred with the Inca sun god, and in Spanish colonial times and even today, the unifying religion, Christianity, is still only the top layer of a multilayered religious cake.

In linguistic terms, too, the Huari empire probably changed Peru. Some scholars believe that it led to the spread of early Quechua, perhaps initially as a lingua franca and then as the dominant pre-Columbian language. Most observers have always attributed the spread of Quechua to the Inca, but in fact the Huari may well deserve a large share of the credit.

In terms of historical continuity, the Inca empire was not the direct successor to that of the Huari. There was actually a five-hundred-year gap between the two imperial systems. However, it was the economic and communications infrastructure (especially the agricultural terracing and the road network) established by the Huari that helped highland Andean imperialism to reemerge under the Incas.

There may also have been some political continuity. Although the Inca empire itself only came into existence in c. A.D. 1300, it probably grew out of the merger of two small but locally powerful states—the Killke and the Huari-derived Lucre, a polity that seems to have started off life as the most militarized and politically strategic province of the Huari empire. The administrative capital of that Huari province had been no less a place than the mystery city of Pikillaqta itself, with its three thousand cells and militaristic ambience.

And just as Pikillaqta had been the key military base of the Huari, so a nearby settlement, Cusco, became the hub of a reborn and highly militaristic Andean empire—that of the Inca. And when, in 1530, the Spanish conquistadors arrived in Peru, they did not immediately proceed to build their own empire, but simply took over the Inca one for a short intermediate period. For three years the Spanish ruled their new acquisition through a puppet Inca emperor, and the Inca capital, Cusco, became the first official Spanish municipality in South America. Moreover, the Spanish took over the Inca (and probably former Huari) forced labor system and used it to underpin their new colonial economy.

The borders of the Inca empire became, by and large, the borders of the Spanish viceroyalty and therefore indirectly helped determine many of the borders of modern Ecuador, Peru, and Chile. So it was that out of the climatic events of the sixth century, an imperial tradition grew that survived even the coming of the Europeans and which has helped in no small way to shape the South America of today.

29

GLORY AT THE HEART
OF THE COSMOS

Long, long ago, according to an ancient Andean myth, God sent a terrible flood that destroyed all living things except for one man and one woman. This couple—the sole remnants of original creation—floated on the waters in a boat, and as the flood began to recede they were finally blown by the wind to a high plateau between the eastern and western sierras of the Andes.

The place the winds blew them to was called Tiwanaku, and it was there that God gave them their destiny. From the caves, rivers, and springs of the sacred landscape of creation, they were to call forth people over whom they would rule as the representatives of God.

But humanity was not yet fully obedient to the will of the Divine, so God decided to create the cosmos to give order to the chaotic mind of man. Thus it was that, on the high windswept plateau of Tiwanaku, the constellations, the moon, and the sun were brought into existence to eternally perform their preordained journeys across the sky—to help keep humanity similarly obedient to God.

In Andean religious belief, Tiwanaku—the place on the plateau—was the crucible of creation. And around this holy place, a sacred city took root. The city's name, in the local Aymara language, was Taypikala, meaning "the stone at the center (of the cosmos)."[1]

Initially, Tiwanaku/Taypikala—located just south of South America's largest lake, Titicaca—may simply have been a local place of pilgrimage.

But in the middle of the first millennium A.D. it became not just the spiritual heart of the cosmos but one of its political hearts as well.

It grew from being a locally important town of perhaps five thousand to ten thousand inhabitants to being the fifty-thousand-strong hub of an Andean superpower, with an immediate hinterland supporting a population of up to a million. As cosmic heart and political center, it became the South American equivalent of Mexico's great metropolis, Teotihuacan.

In a sense, the expansion of Tiwanaku was the central Andean equivalent of the Huari expansion in the northern Andes. They were part of the same geopolitical phenomenon. Both were highland states that rose in the late sixth and seventh centuries to become imperial systems at the expense of coastal plain cultures. Like Huari, Tiwanaku rose to imperial glory following the dislocation of the Andean political system, which occurred at the time of the great mid-sixth-century drought. Although Tiwanaku had probably established a few isolated client relationships with remote areas in the fourth and fifth centuries, its major drive for empire took place in the latter part of the sixth century and then the seventh century and was accompanied by massive population expansion, monument building, and ritual activity in the imperial capital.[2]

This late-sixth-century takeoff was almost certainly facilitated by the demographic, economic, and military imbalance caused by the differential effects of the drought on highland Tiwanaku and the already arid coastal zone. Not only did Tiwanaku, like Huari, have a number of ecological zones to exploit economically in times of climatic stress, it also had South America's greatest single resource of still fresh water, the 3,200-square-mile Lake Titicaca. And because it survived the drought better than the coastal cultures, it was also able to prosper and expand more rapidly once the long drought was over.

Thus, because it was less disadvantaged than its coastal or even highland competitors, it probably started to expand during the middle of the sixth century. It is also possible that the city's obsession with monumental architecture started then. The drought itself may well have led to the creation or expansion of Tiwanaku's largest temple—constructed, in all probability, as a large-scale attempt to propitiate the rain god.

Built as a vast cross-shaped, seven-stepped pyramid, 650 feet wide and 55 feet high, the temple was designed as a replica of a sacred mountain located three miles to the south of the city. Besides its symbolic shape, the pyramid replicated aspects of the southern mountain in two more specifically water-related ways. The summit of the temple was actually made, in part, of layers of distinctive bluish green (water-colored) gravel obtained from the slopes of the mountains to the south. The edifice also had a sophisticated hydraulic system that the temple priests manipulated to send cascades of water pouring down the stepped sides of the pyramid in a manner strikingly similar to the way water cascaded down the real mountain under good climatic conditions.[3] Water was stored in a large reservoir sunk into the summit of the pyramid. Containing up to 1.8 million gallons of water, the reservoir—and the replica waterfalls—were probably manipulated by a series of plugs or sluice gates.

If the pyramid was built during the lengthy drought, rainfall obviously could not have been used to fill the reservoir. (What would be the point of propitiating the rain god if rain was already tumbling from the skies in adequate quantities?) Even in normal times, rainfall would probably not be sufficient to fill it to a level capable of creating a proper waterfall effect. It is likely that in time of drought, lake or river water, stored in animal-skin bottles, was laboriously carried up to the summit by human toil or on the backs of llamas.

The propitiation of the rain god would have been accompanied by sympathetic magic in which the imported water-colored gravel and the replica waterfalls were expected to help produce real rainfall.

The great temple, known as the Acapana (literally, "the place of the dawn")—was the single largest structure in Tiwanaku and likely was decorated with textiles, metal plaques, and possibly carved and painted anthropomorphic and zoomorphic images. The temple priests—who were also possibly the city's rulers—appear, at least at the end, to have lived in houses located on some of the terraces. Somewhere on the Acapana— perhaps in front of the sunken reservoir on its summit—stood a series of twenty-foot-tall statues (perhaps of deified rulers), tiny stone fragments of which have survived.

Just as Tiwanaku's political power increased vis-à-vis its coastal competitors during the great drought, so its population also expanded. Political power increased its commercial, religious, and demographic importance. And so in the years immediately after the drought (or possibly during its latter stages) population pressure and the need for more food combined to force the Tiwanakans to develop new ways of increasing agricultural production.

Vast networks of artificially raised fields irrigated by thousands of miles of canals were created. The new systems were dependent not on direct rainfall but on underground springs and groundwater in the vicinity of Lake Titicaca. The Tiwanakans knew that growing a root crop—potatoes—on relatively low-lying land required them to marginally raise the ground level so that groundwater would not rot the all-important tubers. Whether the new irrigation system was forced on Tiwanaku by the drought or merely by the population increase in the immediate post-drought era, or by both, is not known. Whatever was responsible for jump-starting the system, it soon allowed the Tiwanaku area to increase its population from well under forty thousand to perhaps more than half a million.

Modern experimental archaeology has shown that such raised fields—between 13 and 33 feet wide and up to 660 feet long—were normally at least three times more efficient than conventional nonirrigated direct-rainfall-dependent agriculture in the area; in occasional cold conditions, the irrigated agriculture would have been a staggering nineteen times more efficient than the conventional systems.[4] More than a quarter of a million such plots were ultimately created within a vast network of some fourteen thousand miles of ditch-sized canals.

Although the Tiwanakans could not possibly have understood exactly why their drought adaptation—the raised fields—worked so spectacularly, today's science has succeeded in discovering why. Recent studies designed to adapt this long-forgotten agricultural technology to modern agriculture have shown that raised fields lose soil nutrients more slowly than ordinary fields,[5] enhance nitrogen fixation,[6] and may well reduce soil salinity levels.[7] The use of earth from canal excavations to create a raised growing platform guaranteed that the soil would be highly aerated and not compacted—two qualities that are essential in enabling plants to retain water and to absorb vital water-soluble nutrients.[8]

The canals were also an inexhaustible source of easily accessible natural fertilizer, in that they were quickly colonized by a vast number of aquatic plants, including azolla and other nitrogen-fixers. When this aquatic vegetation, with its ability to fix atmospheric nitrogen, was removed from the water and dumped on the raised fields, it greatly increased the nutrient value of the soil.[9]

Research has also demonstrated that the raised-field system retains heat much more effectively than conventional agriculture, thus protecting crops from destruction by frost. Experiments showed that less than 10 percent of crops planted in raised fields were badly damaged by frost, compared with 70 to 90 percent in conventional fields.[10] The mechanism through which this was achieved was simple yet effective. The canals soaked up solar heat during the day, achieving temperatures up to twenty degrees Fahrenheit higher than the surrounding air temperature. At night—the very time when crops are at risk from frost—the canal retained its warmth and surrounded the growing platforms with a "heat envelope."[11] Heat from the canal radiated upward into the cold night air, preventing air temperatures around and over the raised fields from dropping below freezing. The warmed water was also, through capillary action, drawn through the sides of the canal into the raised crop-growing platform itself, thereby warming the ground in which the crop was growing. The Tiwanakans' life-giving potatoes were thus cosseted by heat from above *and* below.

The demographic consequences of this agricultural practice were spectacular in the extreme—especially when combined with other key religious and social changes directly or indirectly generated by the great drought and the agricultural boom that followed it. The population increased further, both as a result of improved nutrition and infant survival rates and also probably through immigration. Agricultural prosperity may also have enabled Tiwanaku to extend its political power by supplying food and alcohol for both daily consumption and ceremonial use to existing and potential future client tribes.

The Acapana temple to the rain/sky god was not the only great monument in Tiwanaku's ceremonial city center. A second great pyramid, now called the Puma Punku (literally, "the gateway of the puma"), was roughly six hundred feet square but only twenty or twenty-five feet high; like the Acapana, it was fitted with a hydraulic system designed to produce replica waterfalls. Adjacent to the Acapana itself stood a 185,000-square-foot palatial complex that probably served as a temple dedicated to ancestor worship.[12] Surrounded by massive ashlar and sandstone walls and entered through a monumental staircase and gateway, the complex may have been a sort of palace of the dead. Some of its rooms appear to have been decorated with a series of sculptures, probably individual portraits of high-status Tiwanaku men—perhaps past rulers and dynastic ancestors. The rooms may even have been used as a last resting place for the mummified bodies of the rulers themselves.[13] Certainly mummified ancestors would have been important in ancient Tiwanaku, as they were in many other Andean civilizations, including that of the Inca, who used to "invite" their ancestral mummies to attend key state occasions and banquets. Occasionally, the living even arranged for the mummies to "visit" each other socially.

As in all religious and political systems, symbolism was a vital ingredient in the practice of power. The ancestors conferred power, as did affinity with the gods. But the symbolic presence of conquered or client peoples in a subservient position in the sacred heart of a city also conferred substantial power on its elite.

That is precisely what appears to have happened in a large sunken courtyard virtually at the foot of the ancestor temple's entrance staircase. The internal walls of this sunken plaza were (and still are) decorated with hundreds of stone heads, all of different sizes and different styles—probably ancestral portraits belonging to conquered or client people who were subject to Tiwanaku.[14]

The precise date of this probable "gallery of empire" is not known, but it is likely to be either roughly contemporaneous with or later than the Acapana—probably late sixth or seventh century A.D. It may well be associated with the period of colonial expansion (or later imperial consolidation) that accompanied or swiftly followed the growth of the city and the construction of its great ceremonial core.

In a limited sense, just as Europe's initial colonial escapades in the sixteenth century were driven by a desire for exotic goods rather than land or conquest, so too were Tiwanaku's first steps toward empire, but whereas sixteenth-century Europeans wanted to find spices and gold for commercial gain, late-sixth- and seventh-century Tiwanakans needed maize for making beer and coca for use as a drug. Both were vital elements in Tiwanakan religious rituals and in cementing political relationships through the giving of largesse, usually in feast form. Distant colonies were therefore established to obtain the coca and maize, as well as shells, minerals, and exotic fruits and other foodstuffs. Maize may also have been used as a form of currency. Archaeologist Alan Kolata in his book *The Tiwanaku: Portrait of an Andean Civilization* suggests that maize provided "a storable, high value, state-controlled medium of exchange that could be used by the elite to 'purchase' labor from commoners."

Among the first areas to be colonized in the late sixth and early seventh centuries by the newly predominant Tiwanakans was the two-hundred-mile stretch of coastal plain between the river Tambo in southern Peru and the river Loa in northern Chile. Settlements were established in at least eight river valleys in that coastal zone.[15] The largest colony in that region so far discovered by archaeologists—a settlement of up to two thousand people—was built in the valley of the river Moquegua in the deep south of Peru around A.D. 600.

The possession of these coastal colonies, 150 miles west and southwest of Tiwanaku, shows that the metropolis exercised at least some control—direct or indirect—over the intervening territory. Had it not, trading and other contact with its own colonies would have been nearly impossible.

Likewise, 150 miles east of Tiwanaku—in what is now Bolivia's Cochabamba area—dozens of colonies were established in humid valleys among the forest-clad mountains in order to grow maize, coca, peppers, and tropical fruits. Thousands of Tiwanaku-style graves have been unearthed in the area. Again, the intervening territory must have been under Tiwanakan control in one way or another.

Three hundred miles south of the metropolis, near the banks of Lake Poopo, South American's largest lake after Titicaca, settlements were established to control and exploit sources of salt, sulfur, edible clays—and above all basalt, which was used to make high-quality stone artifacts, everything from mundane farm implements to monumental sculptures. In order to obtain large quantities of the best rock, Tiwanakan engineers and miners had to create several miles of spectacular underground galleries. It's not clear whether the mines (at Qeremita, fifteen miles west of the lake) were started by Tiwanakan colonists or by local tribes before the colonists arrived, but it is certain that the gallery system was at the very least massively extended and expanded by Tiwanaku. Today the Lake Poopo and Lake Titicaca/Tiwanaku areas are linked by the Pan-American Highway. But in the first millennium A.D., mining-derived products— tools and sculptures (some weighing up to half a ton)—would have had to be transported 250 miles along the Desaquadero River.

The mining complex is probably South America's least-known major archaeological site. Indeed, the scale of its association with Tiwanaku was discovered only in the 1960s by Bolivian archaeologist Carlos Ponce. More recently scientists, using a high-tech method called neutron activation analysis, have matched basalt objects from Tiwanaku with rocks from Qeremita.[16]

Qeremita was already 250 miles south-southwest of Tiwanaku, but the city's most distant colonies were established—probably as trading stations—hundreds of miles beyond even these remote mines. Some 570 miles south-southwest of the metropolis, a Tiwanakan presence of some sort was established in what is now Argentina at Quebrada de Humahuaca, the heart of a region rich in agricultural and mineral resources including copper, silver, gold, obsidian, and basalt. And 350 miles west of Quebrada—in the middle of one of the driest deserts on earth, the Atacama—a trading-station colony was established to exploit and/or trade in such exotic goods as lapis lazuli, crystals, and turquoise.

The Tiwanakan empire lasted for at least six hundred years, ultimately collapsing in circumstances that were in some ways not dissimilar to those in which it was born. Climatic problems again changed Andean history in the eleventh and twelfth centuries A.D., when a particularly lengthy dry period (lasting around 250 years) destabilized the region's geopolitics and humbled Tiwanaku.

The "Stone at the Center of the Cosmos" may have had a diminished political influence by that time, but in religious terms it was far from being unimportant. The site retained its spiritual significance, and its traditions and gods continued to affect subsequent Andean history, including, in many ways, the much-later Inca empire.

Just as Huari tradition had helped shape military and administrative aspects of the Inca empire (see Chapter 28), so Tiwanaku's religious legacy helped shape the Incas' ideological inheritance. Indeed, beneath the veneer of Christianity, ancient Andean religion still survives to a considerable extent among the sixteen million Indians of Peru and Bolivia.

THE CONSEQUENCES OF A.D. 535 FOR SOUTH AMERICA

A.D. 535 Event and possible secondary event in A.D. 541

Climatic problems (exacerbated El Niño floods and long Andean drought)

Droughts and other climatic problems weaken Moche and probably lead to political fragmentation of their state and the area it controlled.
Between major droughts, floods hit northern Peru (Including Moche "capital") and wash sand into rivers, which deposit it in the sea. Long-shore drift then increases, leading to increased coastal sand dune formation. Sand dunes then advance inland, destroying agricultural land and some towns

Nasca culture hit by famine

Religious and political unrest and changes

Nasca "capital" abandoned and changes in "ground art"

Increase in war, head hunting, and violent art

Decline of Nasca culture

Drought triggers expansion of highland irrigation systems

Highland survival and recovery better than in lowlands

Highland peoples including the Huari take advantage of Moche weakness. Further fragmentation of Moche-controlled territory under Huari pressure. Much former Moche territory comes under Huari influence

Emergence of highland-based Huari empire in central Andes

Expansion of highland-based Tiwanaku empire in south-central Andes

Consolidation and survival of highland-based imperial infrastructure (roads, "fiscal" systems, etc.)

Inca empire

Brief puppet Inca empire run by Spaniards

Spain's Andean empire

Modern nations of Andean South America

PART NINE

THE REASONS WHY

30

IN SEARCH OF
A CULPRIT

"There was a sign from the sun, the like of which had never been seen and reported before. The sun became dark and its darkness lasted for 18 months. Each day, it shone for about four hours, and still this light was only a feeble shadow. Everyone declared that the sun would never recover its full light again."[1]

A sixth-century historian and prominent church leader, John of Ephesus, wrote these words describing the apparent fate of our planet's star in the years 535 and 536. And, as already mentioned at the very beginning of this book, the Roman historian Procopius also described the apparently bizarre behavior of the sun at this exact time. He regarded it as a very bad omen indeed—a sentiment that was to prove only too correct. "And it came about during this year that a most dread portent took place," he wrote. "For the sun gave forth its light without brightness like the moon during this whole year, and it seemed exceedingly like the sun in eclipse, for the beams it shed were not clear, nor such as it is accustomed to shed."[2]

Other, similar accounts were provided by writers across the globe: in the Mediterranean region, in East Asia, in western Europe. And as we have seen in much detail in the preceding chapters, tree-ring, ice-core, and archaeological data all confirm that the mid–sixth century was a time of extraordinarily adverse climatic conditions. But what caused it?

The suddenness with which climatic catastrophe overtook both hemispheres of the world in this period and the apparent dimming of the sun in the initial stages of the disaster point inexorably toward a causal event that hurled vast quantities of pollution into the atmosphere. In effect, the mid-sixth-century climatic experience was the natural equivalent of what scientists fear would befall the world's climate in the event of nuclear war—the so-called nuclear winter, when nuclear-weapon explosions would force vast quantities of pulverized debris, dust, and temporarily vaporized earth up into the atmosphere. There this material would form a barrier preventing much of the sun's light and heat from reaching the ground. Temperatures would fall, the world's climate system would be thrown into chaos, and famine, followed by epidemics, would begin to rage.

There are three possible natural causes of this type of phenomenon: an asteroid impact, a comet impact, or a volcanic eruption.[3]

OPTION ONE:
AN ASTEROID IMPACT

The climatic effects produced by the 535–536 event—including the apparent dimming of the sun—are, in theory at least, consistent with a collision between the earth and a small asteroid of around 2.5 miles in diameter. On average, asteroid impacts of that scale occur on earth every fifty million years or so.

The last known occasion on which a cosmic object of this approximate size is known to have hit the earth was fifty-two million years ago—and the only reason the scientific world knows about it is because the crater still survives, buried beneath 1,600 feet of later sedimentary rocks and more than 300 feet of ocean. Located off the coast of Nova Scotia, the crater is just over 25 miles in diameter, and an estimated 1,650 feet deep from the crater's lip to its lowest point.

Of course, no humans were around at the time to write down accounts of the experience. However, using modern knowledge of astronomy and physics, it is possible to reconstruct what happened then—and what would also have happened in 535 if indeed the worldwide catastrophe was caused by an asteroid impact.

There are in the solar system literally tens of millions of asteroids—including about a million that are more than a half mile in diameter.[4] Contrary to popular belief, they are not the sad remnants of some broken-up planet but are instead left-over building blocks from which planets were never formed. Once, 4.5 billion years ago, the entire solar system consisted of billions of asteroids; by 3.5 billion years ago, most of them had coalesced, through gravity, to form the major planets. Asteroids with a diameter of 2.5 miles are therefore really protoplanets.

Most asteroids circle the sun in elliptical orbits that usually stay between the orbits of the planets Mars and Jupiter. Occasionally, however, a sizable asteroid crosses the earth's orbit; even more rarely, one actually hits our planet.

There exist around 60 asteroids with diameters of approximately 2.5 miles that cross the orbit of planet Earth. Fifty-two million years ago (and potentially, therefore, in 535 A.D.) a notional skilled observer would first have been able to sight the approaching asteroid some fifty-four hours before impact. But at 1.5 million miles from the earth, it would have been nothing more than a barely noticeable speck of light in the night sky.

Only an hour before impact would our observer have noticed anything strange. By then, at thirty thousand miles' distance, its shape would have been just discernible as more than simply a point of light. Half an hour later, barely thirty minutes before impact, the asteroid, now just fifteen thousand miles away, would have been the brightest object in the night sky, apart from the moon, and would even have been visible in daylight. At that stage it would have been brighter than Venus.

Then, six minutes before impact—still twenty-seven hundred miles away—it would have been thirty times brighter than Venus and would have appeared to be a tenth of the moon's diameter.

Now, with the asteroid plunging toward Earth, its apparent brightness would have increased almost ninefold within four minutes, so that two minutes before zero hour, it would have been 250 times brighter than Venus, with an apparent diameter equivalent to a quarter of the moon's.

Then, just eight seconds from impact, this invader from outer space would have hit the earth's atmosphere—and for the first time would have produced its own light both directly and indirectly.

For just a few seconds prior to collision it would have become the brightest object in the sky. Observers three hundred miles away would have seen a fireball as bright as the sun. Observers thirty miles away would have witnessed a brief aerial light show a hundred times brighter than the sun.

Most likely coming in at an angle of between 30 and 60 degrees, and at a speed of forty thousand miles per hour (having been accelerated some 25 percent by Earth's gravity), the asteroid's surface would have been hotter than the surface of the sun (nearly 11,000 degrees Fahrenheit).

But that would not have been the main source of the light. Most of that would have been generated by the trillions of air molecules through which the asteroid passed. Through friction, some of the vast kinetic energy of the asteroid would have heated the air molecules to a blistering 45,000–55,000 degrees Fahrenheit!

If the 535 event was caused by an asteroid, it would certainly have had to be a deep-ocean impact. First of all, a land impact would have created an enormous crater, which, because it would have been formed relatively recently, would be known to the geological world. No recent craters of such large dimensions exist on land.

What's more, in order for the dimming of the sun to have lasted twelve to eighteen months and for the climatic events to have lasted so many years, something finer than normal dust had to have been hurled into the atmosphere. Most ordinary dust would have fallen out of the sky too quickly to generate such medium- and longer-term effects. Volcanoes can achieve this by forcing huge quantities of sulfur into the stratosphere, which become sulfuric acid aerosols, capable of staying aloft and directly changing weather for several years.

But asteroids don't generate much sulfur. So what could such an impact do to the atmosphere that would produce those long-lasting sun-dimming and other climatic phenomena? The answer lies not in the asteroid itself but in the medium it lands in. If it hit ocean, huge quantities of water—both vaporized and in liquid form—would have been injected directly into the stratosphere. This water would have formed rapidly into high-altitude stratospheric clouds of tiny ice crystals, which would in turn have restricted and scattered the sun's beams, creating an apparently dimmed sun, a drop in temperature, and a lot of climatic repercussions over a considerable period.

If the 535 event *was* asteroid-caused, with an ocean impact, the cosmic rock—all hundred billion tons of it—would have vaporized within a quarter of a second on impact with the water and the ocean floor. Perhaps 10 percent of the asteroid's kinetic energy—around twenty quadrillion joules' worth of it (equivalent to a five-million-megaton nuclear explosion)—would then have been transferred to the surrounding ocean in the form of heat and water movement. (Five million megatons is equivalent to a hundred thousand of the largest nuclear bombs.)

One hundred cubic miles of water would have been vaporized almost instantly, generating 140,000 cubic miles of water vapor, which would have exploded skyward at more than twenty thousand miles per hour, rapidly penetrating the stratosphere. And around the vaporized impact site, a huge wave—between fifteen and twenty miles in height—would have reared up out of the ocean, driven by the shock wave created by the impact. Like the high-speed vapor stream, the top part of the wave would have penetrated the stratosphere.

Moving outward at around a thousand miles per hour, the wave would have gradually lost height, so that five hundred miles from the impact site, it would have been only two hundred feet high.

OPTION TWO:
A COMET IMPACT

Just as an asteroid collision with Earth would have produced mid-sixth-century-style climatic mayhem, a comet would have had much the same effect. But because comets are less dense than asteroids, yet normally travel faster, an equivalent energy release on impact would have required a comet nucleus with a diameter of about four miles. And although there are millions more comets traveling around the sun than there are asteroids, comets hit the earth ten times less often than asteroids do, mainly because comets normally come nowhere near our planet.

Indeed, the most remote of them have solar orbits that take them 750 times farther out into space than Pluto, the most distant of the sun's planets. Out of the ten thousand billion comets estimated to be orbiting the sun, only a few thousand come within even three hundred million miles of the earth—or the sun!

Very, very few ever actually hit our planet. It's estimated that a comet of the size required to generate mid-sixth-century-style climatic chaos collides with the earth on average only once every five hundred million years. But although comet impacts may be extraordinarily rare, they still have to be considered as theoretically possible culprits for the 535 catastrophe.

Comets are 70 percent frozen water, 15 percent frozen carbon monoxide and other gases, and 15 percent dust, stones, and possibly even boulders. Most comets are simply frozen lumps of ice and dust with temperatures as low as minus 454 degrees Fahrenheit. But a tiny number of them come briefly close enough to the sun to begin to "melt" (technically, they sublimate). Three hundred million miles out in space they then begin to form atmospheres—derived from their "melting" frozen-gas bodies. By the time the comet is 250 million miles from the sun, elements of that atmosphere and the freed-up dust within it begin to be pushed out to produce one (or sometimes two) "tails," which can be up to 100 million miles long. It is the physical pressure of light (photons) on tiny dust particles that, quite literally, pushes the dust outward to form a tail. The gas molecules making up the atmosphere form the rest of the tail system by being given an electric charge and then by being carried along by ionized atomic particles shot out by the sun (the so-called solar wind).

The only comet impact ever actually witnessed and recorded by scientists was the collision of the comet Shoemaker-Levy 9 with Jupiter in 1994. In that event, a 2.5-mile-diameter comet nucleus broke up while temporarily orbiting the giant planet, and the twenty-one resultant fragments plunged at 2,200 miles per hour into Jupiter's atmosphere. There was then a huge explosion that created a nuclear-style mushroom cloud extending two thousand miles above the cloud tops, billowing spectacularly into outer space, way outside the Jovian atmosphere. This massive cloud was caused by simply the largest fragment—a lump of ice and dust just half a mile across.

If it was a four-mile-diameter comet that caused the A.D. 535 event, the explosion would have been twenty times as great as the one on Jupiter in terms of energy release!

Although the comet or asteroid scenarios would explain the size and nature of the sixth-century catastrophe, there are a number of serious objections to either of these explanations.

First of all, an asteroid (or comet) impact, by definition, releases virtually all its energy in less than a second. The explosion caused by a large asteroid or comet hitting the ocean at high speed would have caused a vast circular wave, consisting of hundreds of cubic miles of water, to rear up around the impact site, penetrating deep into the stratosphere. The impact itself and the collapsing wall of water would then have sent a series of huge tidal waves hurtling across the ocean. Ninety-nine percent of each wave structure would have been deep below the ocean surface—stretching up to 3 miles down. Each visible wave would have been merely the surface symptom of a massive movement of subsurface water. Thus, at any one time, the wave motion would have involved thousands of cubic miles of water. On the surface, well away from the impact site, say two thousand miles, the tidal wave would probably have been only fifty feet high.

But as the wave approached land and entered shallower water, the percentage of the wave structure above sea level would have massively increased. Indeed, by the time the largest tidal wave reached the thousands of miles of coastline surrounding the ocean, it would have been perhaps three hundred to nine hundred feet high, enough to devastate hundreds of thousands of square miles of coastal land. Only where high cliffs or coastal mountains blocked the tidal wave's path would the devastation have been limited. But where coastal plains were low-lying or where deep river valleys stretched inland through coastal mountains, the destruction would have been total, with the tidal wave penetrating dozens or even hundreds of miles inland in some areas.

The problem is that it would be nearly impossible for such a coastal catastrophe to have gone unnoticed by modern archaeologists, geologists, and historians. A tidal wave of such proportions would have rivaled Noah's flood in any legend, would have been recorded in horrified terms by any literate societies affected, and would have been detected by archaeologists and geologists on any archaeological and geological site anywhere along thousands of miles of the relevant ocean's coastline.

It is virtually unthinkable that an impact event of that magnitude only fifteen hundred years ago could be unknown to science today.

OPTION THREE:
A MASSIVE VOLCANIC ERUPTION

Another clinching piece of evidence that points away from a cosmic impact explanation and toward the third option—a volcanic one—is this: Buried up to sixteen hundred feet below the surface of the Greenland and Antarctic ice caps is a telltale layer of ice contaminated by sulfuric acid of volcanic origin that was almost certainly associated with the twelve- to eighteen-month-long sun-dimming event of 535–536 and the subsequent climatic chaos.

Back in 1978, a joint Danish-Swiss-U.S. scientific team landed on the south Greenland ice cap in several large freight aircraft specially fitted with giant skis. The planes carried massive quantities of equipment, including generators, refrigeration units, prefabricated living quarters, and a huge drill.

This latter piece of hardware was used to extract more than a mile of ice core in about six-foot lengths. Working in temperatures as low as minus 22 degrees Fahrenheit, engineers and scientists drilled in three shifts, twenty-four hours a day, going deeper and deeper into the ice cap at roughly 400 feet per week.

Then, early in the second year of the operation, after just a few weeks of drilling, the team extracted some lengths of core covering the second quarter of the sixth century A.D. Back in a laboratory at Copenhagen University, chemical analysis of this sample revealed that there had been two substantial volcanic eruptions. These same eruptions were then detected in a second core drilled in summer 1990 in central Greenland.

Because the dating of Greenland ice cores at that time depth is only roughly accurate (say, to within five or eight years, depending on the core concerned), the two cores each gave slightly different dates for the same sulfuric acid layer. Dates are determined by simply counting back annual layers of snow—so unusually high precipitation can sometimes appear to add extra years, making an acid layer seem marginally older than it is.

The annual layers of snow (which under many tons of pressure turn into ice) are detected by measuring the normally regular annual variations in the percentage of snow consisting of so-called heavy water. Most water molecules, in liquid or frozen state, consist of two atoms of hydrogen and one oxygen atom with an atomic weight of 16. However, around 0.2 percent of water consists of molecules made up of two hydrogen atoms plus one oxygen atom of atomic weight 18. But the actual percentage of heavy water being precipitated onto a given point on the earth's surface at any given time depends upon the weather. The proportion goes down to around 1,960 parts per million in very cold conditions and up to 2,000 parts per million in very warm conditions. In a polar environment the amount ranges from 1,960 parts per million in winter up to 1,975 parts per million in summer. Thus, by studying the regular (normally annual) rise and fall of heavy-water content in ice cores, scientists can construct an ice-core chronology and obtain dates for volcanically derived acid concentrations detected in the core. The system is accurate to within a few years, but unseasonable temperature fluctuations or substantially reduced levels of precipitation can distort the dating, especially at relatively large time depths.

For eruption one, the high-altitude GRIP core gave an apparent date of 527, while the lower-altitude DYE 3 core (three hundred miles to the south) yielded an apparent date of 530. The volcanic explosion must have been very substantial, as evidence from the GRIP core shows that acid-rich snow was falling at the GRIP site in Greenland for more than two years and at the DYE 3 site for at least a year.

For eruption two, the high-altitude GRIP core provided an apparent date of 532, with acid snow falling on the site for just over a year. For this same eruption, the DYE 3 core yielded an apparent date of 534 and evidence of acid snowfalls of around four months.

The final evidence, however, comes from ice cores drilled ten thousand miles to the south, from deep inside the Antarctic ice cap. There, 660 feet below the windswept surface, scientists discovered evidence of a truly massive volcanic eruption.[5] The ice-core material revealed that acid snow had cascaded down on the Antarctic for at least four years running. From the Antarctic ice cores at that time depth there are no accurate dates available—only rough, fifty-year-long ranges of dates. All that can be said is that the four-year-long acid snow episode recorded in the core occurred sometime between 490 and 540.

But by examining the acid traces left by other first-millennium A.D. eruptions it is possible, through a process of elimination, to conclude that the four-year acid episode must have been associated with the climatic catastrophe and probably with the 535 eruption. This is because the two chronologically adjacent Antarctic acid episodes were, respectively, in the fifty-year brackets 231–281 and 614–664—and because the four-year event that occurred in the 490–540 bracket is by far the biggest event recorded in Antarctica for the whole of the first millennium A.D.

It is very likely, therefore, that the Greenland and Antarctic ice cores signal the same atmosphere-polluting climate-changing event recorded historically and in tree-ring terms for 535–536.

Alternatively, though much less likely, the four-year Antarctic event could record a second, totally separate (or, indeed, connected) volcanic eruption destabilizing Southern Hemisphere climate in around 540—and helping to further destabilize Northern Hemisphere weather, already thrown into chaos by the big 535 event. The second Greenland acid signal (532–534 +/− 5–8 years) could conceivably, in this alternative though less likely scenario, have been generated by such a 540 second eruption.

But where did the 535 eruption take place? Which volcano was the culprit?[6]

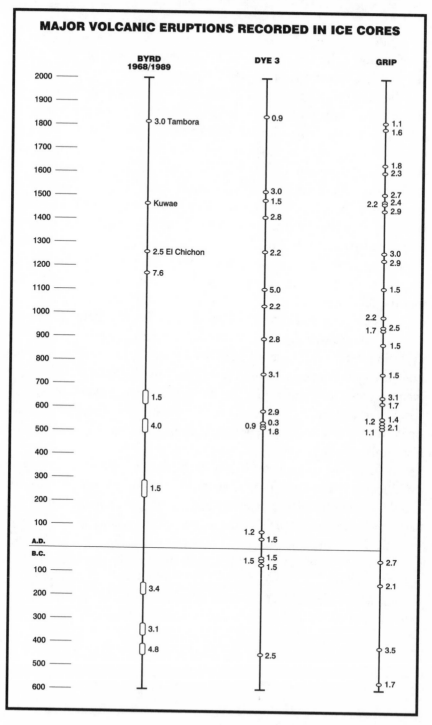

Numbers indicate years of volcanic-originating acid precipitation. Source of data: C. U. Hammer et al., *Climatic Change*, volume 35, 1997; and H. Clausen et al., *Journal of Geophysical Research*, volume 102/C12, 1997.

31

THE BIG BANG

The first clue as to the location of the 535 eruption is the fact that the event is probably recorded in both the Greenland and the Antarctic ice cores. This double record indicates that the eruption must have been within the tropics; otherwise it would not have shown up as an acid spike at opposite ends of the world. It shows that acid snow was falling on both ice caps and had to have been delivered there by the two totally separate high-altitude wind systems that operate in the Northern and Southern Hemispheres, respectively. Only a tropical eruption could have achieved this to any substantial extent. However, the fact that acid-snow deposition took place for at least twice as long in Antarctica as in Greenland suggests that the eruption occurred in the southern rather than the northern tropics.

Luckily, there are only a limited number of active volcanic areas in the southern tropics: East Africa (including the Comoros Islands), the central Andes, the Galápagos Islands, and the huge chain of volcanoes stretching five thousand miles from the tiny Pacific island of Samoa to the large Southeast Asian island of Sumatra.

Judging by the massive climatic effects and the longevity of the acid spike in Antarctica, the eruption must have been absolutely enormous—bigger, probably substantially bigger, than the 1815 Tambora eruption on the Indonesian island of Sumbawa, which created a caldera over three and a half miles in diameter.

In East Africa, South America, and the Samoa-Sumatra chain, there are

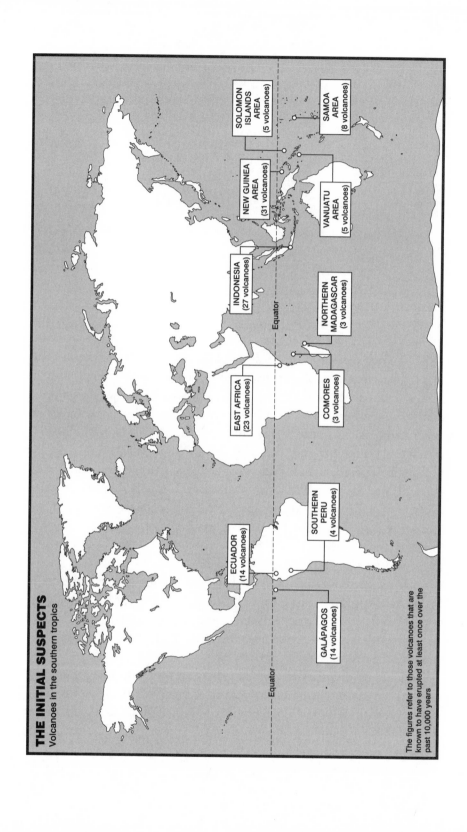

THE INITIAL SUSPECTS
Volcanoes in the southern tropics

SOLOMON ISLANDS AREA (5 volcanoes)

SAMOA AREA (8 volcanoes)

NEW GUINEA AREA (31 volcanoes)

VANUATU AREA (5 volcanoes)

INDONESIA (27 volcanoes)

NORTHERN MADAGASCAR (3 volcanoes)

EAST AFRICA (23 volcanoes)

COMORES (3 volcanoes)

Equator

SOUTHERN PERU (4 volcanoes)

ECUADOR (14 volcanoes)

GALÁPAGOS (14 volcanoes)

Equator

The figures refer to those volcanoes that are known to have erupted at least once over the past 10,000 years fewer than twenty known calderas that are big enough to be candidates—and fourteen of these are in the Samoa-Sumatra complex. However, the eruption dates of five of these are known not to have been in the sixth century.

The search can be further narrowed down by carefully examining the chronology and details of the climatic effects. Of those areas where records were made, the Far East was hit first and worst. That information—together with the fact that 70 percent of the candidate volcanoes lie in the Samoa-Sumatra complex—strongly suggests that the culprit erupted somewhere in that chain. By pure good luck, the suspects can be narrowed down still further, for buried deep in the Chinese *History of the Southern Dynasties* is a reference to what appears to have been a vast explosion in February 535.

The actual text says that "there twice was the sound of thunder." Nothing very extraordinary about that, you might think. However, the entry becomes potentially significant because it is one of only three references to "thunder" in the whole of the first half of the sixth century—and is the only reference that does not describe the "thunder" as part of a massive storm or as being associated with lightning. In any fifty-year period, the Chinese chroniclers would have been able to record thousands of thunderclaps—but they didn't. Only the very severest thunderstorms or those thunderclaps that were unexplainable or mysterious would have been recorded.

It is also the only one of the three thunder incidents in which the chroniclers specifically noted that it was a double event—that the sound was heard twice. Again, this is potentially significant.

Of course, the mere fact that the explosion appears to have been heard in China does not, on its own, pinpoint any particular volcano. But, fortunately, the brief Chinese account also reported that the two bangs came from the southwest. The chronicle was written by scribes based in the south Chinese imperial capital, Nanjing. So if the Chinese account is to be believed, and if the two bangs were indeed volcanically generated, the culprit volcano must have erupted somewhere southwest of Nanjing.

At first sight, that appears to present a problem, because the nearest suitably sized calderas in that direction are located twenty-eight hundred miles away, in the Sumatra/western Java area—presumably too far away to be within earshot. However, volcanic explosions can indeed be heard for thousands of miles. In 1883 Krakatoa was heard four thousand miles away. In the 1815 Tambora volcanic explosion, the sound traveled at least two thousand miles.

The sound of a volcanic explosion is actually transmitted by being bent and bounced through the atmosphere up to twenty times. Those parts of the sound-wave front that travel straight up from the volcano disappear into the far outer atmosphere and are lost. But most parts of the wave move out from the explosion at angles less than the vertical. As wind speed increases with height and because, starting at around seven miles altitude, air temperature also increases, sound waves are bent in much the same way that light is when it passes through a prism.

The bending process is often so pronounced that after some 150 to 200 miles the waves have been refracted to such an extent that they hit the earth's surface, either the land or the ocean. The low-frequency sound then simply bounces off the surface like a huge echo and heads back into the atmosphere, which bends it a second time. The process is then repeated again and again until finally the energy of the sound wave is dissipated into the ocean, the ground, or the air.

For the sound to travel the twenty-eight hundred miles from a volcano in the Sumatra/western Java area to Nanjing would have taken around four hours, and not all the audible sound would have been lost. In fact, there are several factors that could have substantially strengthened it.

First of all, large volcanic eruptions produce unusually high percentages of low-frequency (i.e., long-wavelength) noise, which is absorbed less well by the atmosphere than is high-frequency (short-wavelength) noise.

And second, because of the refractive effect of the atmosphere, the different parts of the wave front would have traveled along different paths and been accelerated by different wind speeds. The short though very loud sound of a volcanic explosion would therefore have been lengthened into a sound lasting several minutes. However, because so many atmospherically bent sound waves would be echoing off so many parts of the earth's surface, some waves would reconverge at various points, thus reinforcing each other to produce a plural number of sound peaks within a less audible lengthened-sound phenomenon.

So, if the Chinese chroniclers' mystery double bang emanated from a volcanic eruption thousands of miles to the southwest, which volcano could it have been?

*   *   *

Bearing in mind that the eruption had to have occurred in the southern tropics, the area pinpointed by the Chinese account narrows the field down to the southern Sumatra/western Java part of the Samoa-Sumatra volcanic chain.

Significantly, there is only one known caldera of appropriate size and vintage in that relatively small (six-hundred-mile-long) area. It surrounds the site of no less notorious a volcano than Krakatoa, the island mountain that brought death and destruction to Java and Sumatra in the 1880s. Could an earlier, bigger eruption of Krakatoa have been responsible for the catastrophe that tormented the world in the mid–sixth century A.D. and changed its history forever?

Here the evidence takes a fascinating turn. For buried deep in a little-known and normally ignored Indonesian chronicle is an extraordinary passage that may well describe the 535 supereruption itself.

Describing a huge volcanic event in the Sunda Straits area (between Sumatra and Java), where Krakatoa is located, the chronicle says that a "mighty roar of thunder" came out of a local mountain (Mount Batuwara, now called Pulosari).

"There was a furious shaking of the earth, total darkness, thunder and lightning.

"Then came forth a furious gale together with torrential rain and a deadly storm darkened the entire world."

The chronicle—known as the *Pustaka Raja Purwa*, or *The Book of Ancient Kings*, goes on to state that "a great flood then came from Mount Batuwara and flowed eastwards to Mount Kamula [now called Mount Gede]." It then claims that the eruption was so massive that large areas of land sank below sea level, creating the straits that currently separate Sumatra and Java.

Claiming to describe the dramatic course of events, the chronicle says that "when the waters subsided it could be seen that the island of Java had been split in two, thus creating the island of Sumatra."

The earliest surviving manuscript of this chronicle dates from 1869.[1] A second, slightly different manuscript of the same chronicle, dating from the mid- to late 1880s, purports to provide a more detailed description of the event, although some extra information in this second manuscript may be additions inspired by observations of the 1883 eruption of Krakatoa and extrapolated to the earlier event.

This 1880s edition of the chronicle—some of which was potentially contaminated by observations of the 1883 eruption—says that "a great glaring fire which reached to the sky came out of the mountain."[2]

"The whole world was greatly shaken, and violent thundering accompanied by heavy rains and storms took place.

"But not only did this heavy rain not extinguish the eruption of fire, but it made it worse. The noise was fearful. At last the mountain burst into two pieces with a tremendous roar and sank into the deepest of the earth.

"The country to the east of the mountain called Batuwara [now called Pulosari] to the Mountain Kamula [now called Gede] and westward to the Mountain Rajabasa [in southern Sumatra] was inundated by the sea.

"The inhabitants of the northern part of the Sunda country to the mountain Rajabasa were drowned and swept away with all their property.

"After the water subsided the mountain [which had burst into pieces] and the surrounding land became sea and the [single] island [of Java/Sumatra] divided into two parts. This [event] was the origin of the separation of Sumatra and Java."

The event described in both editions fits the bill superbly. Its apparent size would have been more than sufficient to produce all the climatic and other effects of 535. And, what is more, it is in *exactly* the right place—a southern tropical location far to the southwest of Nanjing. And yes, the eruption could have been heard in the south Chinese capital, 2,800 miles away.

However, there are two apparent problems with the evidence as related by *The Book of Ancient Kings*. First of all, the surviving manuscript texts were written in the nineteenth century—thirteen centuries after the events described. And the eruption is described as having taken place in the 338th year of the Shaka calendrical era, which in Western terms equates only to the year A.D. 416, not 535.

Very few academics have ever studied the Javanese *Book of Ancient Kings* in any detail. There has never been a proper detailed analysis of its contents from a historical point of view. The chronicle (part of the six-million-word *Book of Kings*, one of the longest books in the world) has been looked at purely as a work of nineteenth-century Javanese literature, written at a time of evolving anticolonial consciousness. It is normally seen solely as an attempt by a Javanese intellectual, Ranggawarsita III, to create a national history.[3] Scholars of Javanese literature of this period all too often consider the information in *The Book of Ancient Kings* to be completely fictitious, the product of what they claim to be Ranggawarsita's vivid imagination.

However, other experts—especially those specializing in earlier Javanese texts (medieval and sixteenth- or seventeenth-century material)—take a slightly different view. There are only a handful of such specialists worldwide, but they tend to take a more sympathetic view of *The Book of Ancient Kings*.

Rather than characterizing it as fictitious, they suggest that it is based on four main types of evidence. First, there is, they suspect, some material in the chronicle that was gleaned by Ranggawarsita from Javanese or Sumatran folklore, drama, and oral traditions. Second, perhaps information was obtained from Western, likely Dutch, intellectuals whom Ranggawarsita knew in Java. Third, there may be material Ranggawarsita had a hunch about or simply wanted to have happened, and which was therefore just concocted by him. But fourth, there is information that may well have come from ancient Javanese manuscripts written on palm leaves found by Ranggawarsita III or his contacts, or passed on to him through his family.

At least ten thousand of these Javanese palm-leaf manuscripts still survive—half in Indonesia and half in Europe and Australia. Although most of the known examples have been seen by scholars, very few have ever been properly read. All the manuscripts date from the seventeenth century through the nineteenth century, but about half are texts first written during that period, while the rest are copies of texts written as early as the ninth century. The oldest surviving texts are, typically, Javanese versions of Hindu religious epics. Javanese medieval historical chronicles are very rare, and at present just two of recognized historicity are known: the mid-fourteenth-century *Nagarakreta-gama*, and the sixteenth-century *Serat Pararaton* (Book of Kings), which chronicles Javanese history from 1200 to 1500.

The thousands of texts are in various different scripts, a fact that severely limits the number of scholars who can read them. At least four hundred are in so-called mountain script, which fewer than half a dozen scholars worldwide can now read. However, Ranggawarsita was able to read several of the scripts—including Javanese, Balinese, and mountain—so he would have been able to transcribe and understand most of the palm-leaf manuscripts he had access to. His father, grandfather, and great-grandfather had also been able to read the old scripts. And hermits living in remote mountain areas were able to read them as well and could have assisted him.

It is therefore possible that Ranggawarsita III had access to historical chronicles that have since been lost. Because *The Book of Ancient Kings* has never been studied from a historical perspective, it is not possible to know how much internal evidence in it might prove or disprove its claims to historicity.

However, some internal evidence within *The Book of Ancient Kings* does suggest at least two earlier occasions on which the eruption account was recopied or edited.

It is said to have been written down under a medieval Javanese king called Jayabaya and then copied (or presumably recopied from an intermediate fifteenth- or sixteenth-century version) in 1745 by a group of Javanese literati led by Ranggawarsita III's great-great-grandfather, Padmanagara. According to *The Book of Ancient Kings*, this group succeeded in gathering together large quantities of palm-leaf manuscripts and notes, which they used to write a now-lost account of the early history of Java.

The King Jayabaya who is said by *The Book of Ancient Kings* to have overseen the writing down of the eruption account, probably lived in the twelfth century—a historically attested king of that name reigned from A.D. 1134 to 1157. But it is possible that an earlier, otherwise unknown king of the same name was responsible. Certainly *The Book of Ancient Kings* gives a date that suggests this Jayabaya ruled in the tenth century A.D.

However, whether the Jayabaya in question was a tenth- or twelfth-century monarch, *The Book of Ancient Kings* gives no real historical indication as to where he got the account from, saying merely that he received it from the Hindu god Naraddha, who came down from heaven and told him to stop wasting his royal time researching foreign (Indian) history and to concentrate on Javanese history instead. Naraddha is said to have arranged to come down from heaven—along with a secretarial assistant— every forty days so as to dictate an account of Javanese history to the king's scribes.

Up till Ranggawarsita III's time, almost all accounts of Javanese history had been written in poetic form. Ranggawarsita is thought to have been the first to produce an extended prose version—*The Book of Ancient Kings* as it exists today. However, it is possible that Ranggawarsita merely edited and developed a work that may have been done at least partially by his father, Ranggawarsita II. The younger Ranggawarsita would have had good reason to keep secret his father's role in the work, for Ranggawarsita II had been arrested and probably murdered by the Dutch earlier in the century, and Ranggawarsita III, who worked for a pro–Dutch collaborationist Javanese king, was almost certainly very keen to distance himself from his father's memory.

Like Ranggawarsita III, Ranggawarsita II had been a leading literary figure at the Javanese royal court. Born in around 1780, he became head of the royal secretariat, became a protonationalist rebel against Dutch imperial rule, was captured in 1828 during an anti-Dutch revolution, and likely was executed extrajudicially the following year. He was highly intelligent, but many of his writings were destroyed by the Dutch and his name was virtually erased from history.

Ranggawarsita III had access not only to any surviving writings of his father, but also probably to those of earlier generations of his family. Ranggawarsita III's grandfather (1756–1844) had been the Javanese royal poet, and his name, Yosodipuro II, alias Sastranagara, actually described his literary job, translating as "creator in the palace," alias "literature of the realm."

Ranggawarsita III's great-grandfather, Yosodipuro I (1729–1803), had been royal poet too, and was a historian of some renown, having written large numbers of Islamic religious tracts and reworked Hindu classics and Javanese histories. What's more, Yosodipuro I's father, Padmanagara—Ranggawarsita III's great-great-grandfather—had also been a prominent poet and royal courtier. Indeed, Ranggawarsita III's family had been a powerful element within Javanese society for at least three hundred years, having been descended from a sixteenth-century central Javanese ruler named Hadiwijaya, the sultan of Pajang.

Quite apart from the chronicle's claim to a medieval pedigree for the eruption account, three features of the eruption entry of *The Book of Ancient Kings* do lend it added credibility.

One key piece of evidence is that volcanologists who have read the eruption account in the 1869 manuscript of *The Book of Ancient Kings* say that it is a very good description of the type of eruption that almost certainly did occur in the Sunda Straits between Java and Sumatra. They believe that neither Western scientists nor Javanese scholars in the 1850s or 1860s would have had the geological data to reconstruct the probable sequence of events and geography of a Sunda Straits eruption occurring in the first millennium A.D.[4] So Ranggawarsita's description had to have been based either on a virtually impossible degree of guesswork or on a real and now long-lost historical account.

The second thing to note is that great natural catastrophes such as the 535 eruption often induce political instability, administrative dislocation, and the consequent collapse of regular record keeping in affected societies. Thus perhaps it is significant that a collapse of record keeping is precisely what appears to have been recorded in *The Book of Ancient Kings* after the eruption. Looking at the century as a whole, in the thirty-seven-year period before the eruption, 75 percent of all years have chronicle entries. Then, in the eighteen years after the eruption, only 18 percent have entries, while in the following forty-two years, 63 percent have entries.

Thus the evidence suggests that Ranggawarsita may have obtained his description from information contained in now unknown or lost palm-leaf manuscripts, and that the account of the great eruption in the Krakatoa area as written in *The Book of Ancient Kings* is therefore probably at least substantially true.

The second problem with the Ranggawarsita account is the date he attributes to the event. Writing in the 1850s, he says that it took place in the 338th year of the Shaka calendar, which is A.D. 416 of our calendar. The first question that must be answered is therefore whether there was in fact an eruption of the described proportions in that year. The only way to check that is to examine the ice cores for that period—especially those for the Antarctic, as Java is in the southern tropics.

Even allowing for the very broadest of error rates (plus or minus twenty-five years), there were *no* major volcanic eruptions around A.D. 416 in the Southern Hemisphere. It must therefore be concluded that the 416 date is wrong. But that should come as no great surprise, because in many of the world's older quasi-historical texts, individual dates are often among the major elements that are incorrect.

In the *Book of Ancient Kings* eruption account, as in other quasi-historical texts from around the world, this chronological error may have been due to a medieval or later misinterpretation of a poorly understood earlier dating system, or to a later exaggeration of reign lengths. Alternatively, the error may have occurred in the initial oral transmission of the information.

It is also possible that the apparent eighteen-year period of poor record keeping (suggesting administrative collapse) after the eruption may in reality have been a good deal longer. The admittedly scanty archaeological record does suggest a major political and administrative hiatus after the eruption.

The archaeological evidence shows that a substantial civilization flourished in the fifth and possibly very early sixth century in western Java. According to Chinese sources, this civilized state appears to have been called Holotan (the southern Chinese pronunciation of the name). According to the archaeological record, its best-known king was a man called Purnavarman. Royal inscriptions, the probable site of a canal, and the brick foundations of what may be Purnavarman-period Hindu temples and Buddhist shrines have been found. A few fifth-century statues of the Hindu god Vishnu have also been discovered, as have ceramics of the first few centuries A.D. But after the early sixth century, all datable archaeologically detectable or historically recorded activity appears to cease and does not reemerge until the mid– to late seventh century—and then only in central, not western, Java.

In terms of Javanese history, the 535 eruption was a pivotal event, causing a cultural and political discontinuity in which ancient (west Javanese) civilization collapsed after flourishing for up to five centuries. But it was this very disaster—the destruction of west Javanese political/ cultural predominance—that seems to have cleared the way for the rise of central Javanese political and cultural power in the seventh and eighth centuries A.D.

While western Java remained a backwater for at least eight hundred years, the seventh century saw the emergence of several important new states in central Java. By 640 Chinese sources were remarking upon the power of a central Javanese kingdom called Holing. A second central Javanese kingdom, by the name of Mataram, also flourished and had taken over Holing by 720. By 900 this merged central Javanese polity had succeeded in uniting much of Java into a single state. Meanwhile, by the late eighth century in another part of central Java, another kingdom—ruled by the Shailendra dynasty—flourished and produced spectacular monumental architecture. One particularly notable temple, that of Borobodur, still covers half a square mile.

But then, in the tenth century A.D., another volcanic catastrophe (Mount Merapi, c. 928) hit Java. This time it was the central portion of the island that was devastated. Borobodur was partially buried under volcanic ash (and fully reexposed only in our own century, a thousand years later), and the rulers of Mataram were forced to relocate their capital from

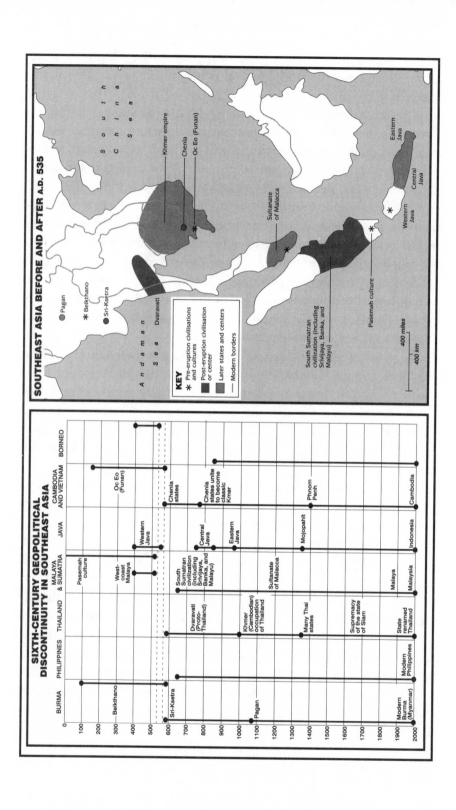

SOUTHEAST ASIA BEFORE AND AFTER A.D. 535

South China Sea

Andaman Sea

● Pagan
✱ Beikthano
● Sri-Ksetra

Dvaravati

Khmer empire
Chenla
Oc Eo (Funan)

Sultanate of Malacca

South Sumatran civilization (including Srivijaya, Banka, and Malayu)

Pasemah culture

Western Java
Central Java
Eastern Java

KEY
✱ Pre-eruption civilisations and cultures
▓ Post-eruption civilisation or center
▒ Later states and centers
— Modern borders

400 miles
400 km

SIXTH-CENTURY GEOPOLITICAL DISCONTINUITY IN SOUTHEAST ASIA

BURMA | PHILIPPINES | THAILAND | MALAYA & SUMATRA | JAVA | CAMBODIA AND VIETNAM | BORNEO

0
100 — Beikthano
200
300
400
500
600 — Sri-Ksetra
700
800
900
1000
1100 — Pagan
1200
1300
1400
1500
1600
1700
1800
1900 — Modern Burma (Myanmar)
2000

Oc Eo (Funan)

Western Java

Pasemah culture

West-coast Malaya

South Sumatran civilization (including Srivijaya, Banka, and Malayu)

Chenla states

Central Java

Eastern Java

Chenla states unite to become classic Kmer

Dvaravati (Proto-Thailand)

Khmer (Cambodian) occupation of Thailand

Sultanate of Malacca

Many Thai states

Mojopahit

Phnom Penh

Supremacy of the state of Siam

State renamed Thailand

Modern Philippines

Malaya

Malaysia

Indonesia

Cambodia

central Java to the eastern periphery of their state—probably near the Surabaya area of eastern Java.

The Surabaya area quickly became the most powerful political center not only of Java, but of the Indonesian archipelago as a whole. Indeed, by the fourteenth and fifteenth centuries, the area had grown into the epicenter of a great empire, known—after its capital—as Mojopahit. Ruling over Java, Bali, eastern Sumatra, and southern Borneo, it was, in truth, a proto-Indonesia. But its distant early medieval origins were in central rather than eastern Java. And that original central Javanese civilization had probably been able to flourish only because ancient western Javanese power had been extinguished by the catastrophe of 535.

Thus modern Indonesia can be seen ultimately as the end product of a political process triggered by the disaster of the mid–sixth century.

It can be argued that most of the other countries that make up Southeast Asia also seem to owe their genesis to the eruption of 535. Throughout the region there was a marked geopolitical and cultural hiatus in the mid- to late sixth century, immediately following the catastrophe. Both the direct effects of the volcanic eruption and the consequent climatic problems must have hit agriculture and trade, and this in turn seems to have created economic and political imbalances between polities— imbalances that went on to produce fundamental changes across the region.

Proto-Thailand—the Kingdom of Dvaravati—came into existence in c. A.D. 580. Proto-Cambodia (the Kingdom of Chenla) was born at virtually the same time, following the demise of the ancient Mekong Delta civilization of Oc Eo (Funan) sometime in the mid–sixth century. Proto-Malaya (the medieval Sultanate of Malacca) evolved out of a civilization in southern Sumatra that first emerged in the form of the Kingdom of Srivijaya in the middle of the seventh century, following the demise (probably as a result of the eruption) of the fierce prehistoric megalith-building warrior culture known to archaeologists as the Pasemah. And farther north, proto-Burma (the Kingdom of Sri-Ksetra) came to prominence around A.D. 600 following the demise of its apparently more ancient rival, the Kingdom of Beikthano.

Thus, in its own way, Southeast Asia too fits the wider pattern of planetwide sixth-century destruction and subsequent political reformation, which helped destroy the ancient world and ushered in the proto-modern one.

32

RECONSTRUCTING
THE ERUPTION

Reconstructing the immediate sequence of events associated with a volcanic eruption that occurred fifteen hundred years ago is a daunting task—but not an impossible one. Using historical, tree-ring, ice-core, and other data, it is possible to compare the event and its climatic consequences with more recent eruptions of known size and effect.

Using the quasi-historical account in the Javanese *Book of Ancient Kings*, it is possible, assuming the account to be at least part genuine, to gain an insight into specific aspects of the eruption itself. And using geological and volcanological knowledge of the area and records of more recent large eruptions, it is possible to reconstruct what probably happened.

Between 530 and 535, there would almost certainly have been a long series of earthquakes in what is now western Java, southern Sumatra, and the neighboring seas. These earthquakes and accompanying seismically triggered tidal waves may well have seriously disrupted life in the region. Typically, volcanic eruptions are preceded by increasingly frequent and violent tremors. Often the larger the eruption, the longer the seismic run-up to it will be.

In the case of the 530s catastrophe, the run-up to the eruption may even have included several earthquakes of level 6 on the Richter scale. Throughout the second half of 534, earthquakes would have struck the region at the rate of one or two per day. In the weeks immediately before the eruption, the rate would have accelerated to a peak of fifty quakes per hour in the final twenty-four hours, mainly in the range of 1 to 3 on the Richter scale.

Although it is a controversial proposal, it is geologically possible that Sumatra and Java were one island prior to the 535 supereruption—exactly as the Javanese *Book of Ancient Kings* describes.[1] The 535 eruption would therefore have burst forth from a volcanic mountain located on fairly low-lying ground where the shallow Sunda Straits between Java and Sumatra are today. For several years, a huge mass of molten magma would have been moving closer and closer to the surface—probably at the rate of up to thirty feet per month. This would have caused the land surface above to bulge upward into a low dome, increasing in height at up to three feet per year over perhaps a five-year period.

Then suddenly the pressure of the magma, two or three miles below the ground, would have proved too great; a crack would have opened up, and the first phase of the eruption would have started. A vast cloud of ash would have billowed forth, followed by a column of red-hot magma that would have shot out of the mountain like a fountain. A week or two later, as the magma came yet nearer to the surface, one of the earthquakes accompanying the eruption probably fractured the rock above the magma chamber, allowing the sea to rush into the wide tubes through which the magma was rising from the chamber to the surface. The second phase began with a vast explosive event that shot even larger quantities of molten magma into the air at up to 1,500 miles per hour, reaching heights of perhaps thirty miles. The sound from this explosion would have broken the eardrums of most humans and animals living within a fifteen-mile radius.

The shock wave from the explosion would have moved outward at 750–1,500 miles per hour, devastating everything in its path for up to twenty miles. Houses, bridges, temples, and every single tree would have been leveled like so many matchsticks. And within an estimated ten-mile radius there would also have been massive fire damage as the shock wave compressed the air, heating it to very high temperatures and causing combustible material to simply burst into flames.

Most of the molten magma fountain would have broken up into fragments ranging in size from less than a thousandth of an inch to a yard or more in diameter and would have partially solidified at an altitude of two or three miles. The larger fragments—along with car-sized chunks of the mountain itself—would have fallen back to earth within a radius of three to seven miles. The microfragments, however, would have been carried skyward by powerful convection currents.

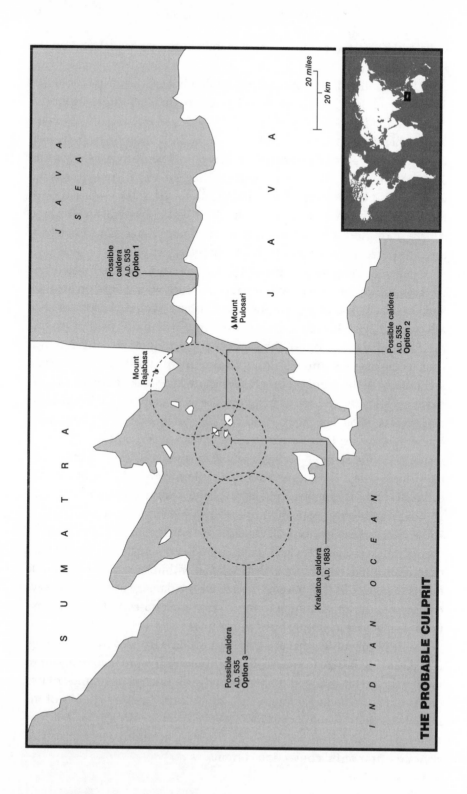

THE PROBABLE CULPRIT

As the second phase of the eruption continued, a vast mushroom cloud of ash and debris would have penetrated far into the stratosphere, reaching altitudes of up to thirty miles and carried aloft by extremely strong, high-temperature convection currents, moving at hurricane-force speeds.

In the center of the volcano, temperatures would have reached 1,650 degrees Fahrenheit, generating the heat that forced the ash cloud heavenward. As the mushroom cloud increasingly blotted out the light of the sun and day was turned into night, ash would have rained down on forests and fields alike up to a thousand miles away, and houses would have been shaken by the eruption at similar distances. The sea for dozens of miles around would have been covered with a six-foot-thick floating carpet of pumice, and ships at sea would have become terminally stranded in this volcanic quagmire.

Stupendous amounts of magma, vaporized seawater, and ultrafine hydrovolcanic ash (generated by magma-seawater interaction) would by now have been hurled into the sky, and a substantial percentage of it would have entered the upper part of the earth's atmosphere, the stratosphere. As it spread sideways at high altitude, away from the immediate area of the eruption, the material cooled and the water-vapor component would have then condensed directly into vast clouds of tiny ice crystals. It is estimated that the entire eruption may have generated up to 25 cubic miles of ice crystals; spread out in a thin layer in the stratosphere, these would have caused sunlight diffraction and cooling over vast areas of the globe. Superfine hydrovolcanic ash and huge quantities of sulfur and carbon dioxide gas would have had similar effects. Unlike ordinary volcanic ash, which falls to earth within a few months, hydrovolcanic ash, high-altitude ice-crystal clouds, and sulfuric acid and carbon dioxide aerosols (minute drops) can stay in the stratosphere for years, forming a long-term barrier to normal sunlight and solar heat transmission.

Within hours after the start of the second phase of the eruption, part of the huge mushroom cloud above the volcano would have become too heavy with ash to stay aloft. This part would have collapsed back to the ground, spreading horizontally over land and sea in all directions away from the volcano in what is called a pyroclastic flow,[2] but thousands of times larger than similar flows that partly destroyed the island of Montserrat in the Caribbean in 1997–98.

This horizontally moving cloud would have swept across the ground (and the sea) like a boiling-hot tidal wave of steam, sulfur, air, carbon dioxide, carbon monoxide, ash, and rocks. This hot, poisonous wall of destruction, more than a thousand feet high, would have moved outward perhaps as much as forty miles from the volcano at up to 250 miles per hour, killing anything in its path.

Then, as the eruption progressed further, the third phase would have begun. Because the huge magma chamber beneath the surface was now partially empty, its roof would have been unable to support the weight of the rock above it. As a result, it would have fallen inward, causing a sudden catastrophic drop of between three hundred and a thousand feet in the level of the land above. As the land surface sank below the level of the adjacent sea, the sea itself would have surged in to cover the former land. Seawater would have again come into direct contact with some of the remaining molten magma, and there would have been a series of immense explosions, producing even larger pyroclastic flows.

After the catastrophic pyroclastic flow, eruption, and caldera collapse, the fourth and final phase of the eruption would have begun. The explosions would have started to subside over a period of weeks or even months, during which quiet episodes might have persisted for several days or more, punctuated by eruptive bursts of dwindling power. The caldera probably left small island vents that continued to periodically belch steam and ash several miles into the sky for years to come as the residual magma deep below the caldera gradually was quenched.

Comparing this scientific account with the description in the Javanese *Book of Ancient Kings*, we can see that the whole event appears to have been recorded with some accuracy: "At last, the mountain burst into pieces with a tremendous roar and sank into the deepest of the earth. The water of the sea rose and inundated the land. The land became sea and the island [of Java/Sumatra] divided into two parts."

In the past, virtually all geologists thought that the fall in land level could have been caused only by gradual tectonic forces. But a reanalysis of the available geological evidence carried out by volcanologists as part of the research for this book shows that that view is incorrect.[3] The crucial land-level reduction that caused the formation of the Straits of Sunda *could* have occurred as a result of a volcanic caldera eruption. This geological evidence, when combined with the Chinese historical, Javanese quasi-historical, ice-core, and other evidence, makes the Sunda Straits caldera, proto-Krakatoa, the most likely site of the 535 supereruption.

33

THE ENDGAME

The 535 eruption was, as near as can be determined, one of the largest volcanic events of the past fifty thousand years. Whether looked at in terms of short- and medium-term climatic effects, caldera size (assuming proto-Krakatoa was the culprit), or ice-core evidence, the eruption was of truly mammoth proportions. Climatologically, the tree-ring evidence shows that it was the worst worldwide event in the tree-ring record. Looking at the ice cores, we see that it may well have been the largest event to show up in both northern and southern ice caps for the past two thousand years.

And in terms of caldera size—again assuming that proto-Krakatoa was the culprit—the eruption resulted in one of the half dozen largest calderas known anywhere in the world. Up to ninety-six thousand cubic miles of gas, water vapor, magma, and rock were hurled into the atmosphere.

Most of the heavier material—rocks and larger ash fragments—and water vapor would have fallen straight back to earth as muddy rain. But much (perhaps 50 percent) of the water vapor, the other gases, and the hydrovolcanic ash penetrated the stratosphere and was light enough to stay aloft for years.

Some water vapor mixed with sulfur gas to form tiny drops of sulfuric acid. Most of the water vapor, however, condensed into tiny ice crystals, like frozen fog. And the hydrovolcanic ash dispersed widely in the stratosphere, forming a dust veil over the globe. All three materials would have formed single or multiple stratospheric layers cloaking most of the planet, conceivably with different or sometimes overlapping geographic distributions.

Depending on the number of layers involved, the thickness of each layer, their stratospheric distribution, and the material involved (ice, sulfuric acid, or hydrovolcanic ash), the amount of sunlight and solar heat penetrating these layers would have been reduced differentially in different parts of the world. In some areas where material was dispersing sunlight very effectively, the sun would have appeared to have lost much of its shine. In all areas, temperatures would have dropped. As the air cooled, the water vapor in it would have turned into water and would have fallen to the ground as rain. But the colder weather also meant there was less evaporation from the oceans and the land. So the sky would have run out of rain, and major droughts would have set in worldwide.

This is, of course, exactly what actually happened—in China, Japan, Mongolia, parts of Europe, Arabia, East Africa, Mexico, South America, and no doubt many other areas for which we have no direct information.

In the Northern Hemisphere, the summer monsoons would have weakened and become drier, while the winter monsoons would have become stronger but, once again, also drier. Of particular importance would have been the abnormally small amount of rain, probably over two or three years, produced by the northeast monsoon blowing from India to East Africa. It was this failure that caused bubonic plague to break out of its naturally immune wild-rodent pool and spread to the Mediterranean and Europe, changing the region's history forever. The weakened summer southwest and southeast monsoons failed to bring rain to Mongolia and thus altered the political balance there in a way that was also to change world history.

In a "flip-over" phenomenon that is as yet poorly understood, long droughts frequently end spectacularly in large storms and massive floods. Because of the chaotic climate, these often feature giant hailstones the size of golf balls. If storms and floods had followed drought in East Africa in the sixth century, the plague's breakout would have been even more spectacular than if only following a drought. The scale of the plague's impact around this time strongly suggests that this drought/flood phenomenon was what actually occurred.

In the Southern Hemisphere, the cooling not only caused massive droughts but also interacted with the larger El Niño storms that periodically hit Peru. This interaction would have substantially intensified the El Niños, with devastating consequences.

Throughout the world, levels of pollution in the lower atmosphere (the troposphere) would have increased dramatically at various times of the year, as massive dust storms and forest fires broke out. Both are typical phenomena associated with drought conditions. The "yellow dust" that fell like snow in China and the dust layers detected in the Quelccaya glacier ice cores from Peru testify to the giant dust storms that must have engulfed many areas of the world.

The immediate effects of the 535 eruption and a possible second eruption from a different (and as yet unlocated) volcano in c. 540 lasted five to seven years in the Northern Hemisphere and even longer in the Southern Hemisphere. However, poorly understood climatic feedback systems were almost certainly responsible for years of further climatic instability (including subsequent droughts) in the Northern Hemisphere (up till c. 560) and in the Southern Hemisphere (up till the 580s). The eruption(s), directly and/or through feedback, altered the world climate for decades, and in some regions for up to half a century.

The explosion and climatic changes destabilized human geopolitics and culture, either directly or through the medium of ecological disruption and disease. And because the event, through its climatic consequences, impacted on the whole world, it had the effect of resynchronizing world history.

For the people who lived then, it was a catastrophe of unparalleled proportions. Procopius, referring to the darkened sun, later wrote that "from the time this thing happened, men were not free from war, nor pestilence nor anything leading to death." However, for us today, the sixth-century catastrophe and the swirling tide of interacting events that flowed from it shed new light on the origins of our modern world, on the processes of history, and—perhaps most alarmingly—on the ultimate fragility of our planet's human culture and geopolitical structure.

PART TEN

THE FUTURE

34

BEYOND
TOMORROW

B rooding an estimated six miles beneath the scenic wonderland of America's Yellowstone National Park is a vast liquid time bomb the size of Lake Michigan or the Irish Sea. Made of molten rock, this ultrahot subterranean reservoir of volcanic magma will almost certainly one day burst forth upon the world, changing our planet's history just as proto-Krakatoa did fifteen centuries ago. For Yellowstone is host to the world's largest dormant volcano—a huge caldera covering around fifteen hundred square miles.

It appears to erupt roughly once every 600,000 to 700,000 years— and the last eruption was 630,000 years ago. What's more, the last decade or so of the twentieth century has seen a substantial increase in potential pre-eruption activity there.

Since 1988, upward pressure exerted by the magma reservoir and by magma-heated water vapor (around thirty-five thousand pounds per square inch) has forced hundreds of square miles of land to rise by approximately three feet. Moreover, the pattern of geyser activity at the park has begun to change.

Yellowstone is known to have erupted cataclysmically on three occasions in the past: 2 million years ago, when it spewed out nearly 600 cubic miles of magma; 1.3 million years ago, when it ejected "just" 70 cubic miles of the stuff; and 630,000 years ago, when it generated about 250 cubic miles of magma.

Of course, no one knows when Yellowstone will erupt again. But it's a pretty safe bet that one day it will.

Another potential catastrophe in North America is a currently dormant supervolcano in Long Valley, California. Over the past twenty years this too appears to have become progressively less stable. Since 1980 some 18 million cubic feet of carbon dioxide gas has been ejected from volcanic-related vents, killing off dozens of square miles of local forest. What's more, earthquake clusters are becoming much more intensive, with up to 1,600 tremors (each up to 3.5 on the Richter scale) per cluster. Local hot-spring behavior is also changing. The only known major eruption of Long Valley's 212-square-mile caldera occurred seven hundred thousand years ago, and because records have been kept over only the past fifty years, no one knows whether the volcano's current restlessness presages a massive eruption or merely the resumption of calm and tranquility.

When Long Valley last erupted, it produced 125 cubic miles of magma and generated a pyroclastic flow of such vast proportions that when the wave settled it added 350 feet to the surface height over several hundred square miles.

Half a world away in Europe, another vast caldera is beginning to flex its volcanic muscles. Just three miles beneath the western suburbs of Naples is a huge magma reservoir containing between 70 and 250 cubic miles of molten rock. Since 1969 pressure from this magma has caused land to rise and fall twice—by about six feet. In the early 1980s it generated up to three hundred small earthquakes per week (each up to 4.2 on the Richter scale). There is no doubt that this caldera, known as the Campanian/Campi Flegrei complex, is becoming increasingly restless.

So far, it is known to have erupted cataclysmically twice—once thirty-seven thousand years ago, when it ejected 20 cubic miles of magma, and once twelve thousand years ago, in an explosion about a sixth of the size of the earlier one. In the first eruption the pyroclastic flow—the wave of superheated dust and gas surging along the ground—was so deep that it engulfed three-thousand-foot-high ridges thirty-five miles away.

The Campanian/Campi Flegrei caldera complex[1] is about 150 times as large as the crater area of the more famous nearby volcano of Vesuvius, which in A.D. 79 produced less than half a cubic mile of magma when it erupted. Again, no one knows when the Italian caldera will explode again on a truly massive scale but, like Yellowstone and Long Valley, it is virtually certain to do so one day—perhaps, in this European example, sooner rather than later.[2]

The fourth major volcanic caldera currently displaying ominous signs of increasing restlessness is that of Rabaul in Papua New Guinea. Since 1910 the number of minor eruptions *appears* to have increased (it may simply be that records have been better kept this century than last). Minor eruptions and earthquakes have occurred in twenty-two of the past ninety years, compared to only two recorded in the previous ninety years. What's more, earthquakes also seem to have increased—there have been up to thirteen thousand tremors per year since the early 1980s. Rabaul is known to have erupted cataclysmically twice so far—3,500 and 1,250 years ago.[3] In the later eruption, the 48-square-mile crater produced about 2.4 cubic miles of magma.

Along with these four, there are five other large and potentially active caldera volcanoes in the Alaskan Aleutian Islands and Mexico. These nine restless craters represent a significant threat to the world's future economic and political well-being. If any one of them was to explode, world climate would be plunged into chaos, precisely as it was in the sixth century. But with world population at forty times its sixth-century level, the death toll would almost certainly run into the hundreds of millions. And just as history was resynchronized fourteen and a half centuries ago, a future caldera eruption, through its climatic impact, would almost certainly destabilize the economic and geopolitical status quo, leading to a second resynchronization of history.

Tracking down what really happened in the distant past is difficult enough, but working out what might happen in the future is even more of a challenge. Nevertheless, the two tasks are integrally linked. Futurology, that most problematic of disciplines, relies almost entirely on learning from the past in order to predict the future—or at least to offer options as to what might happen.

Given the experience of the sixth-century eruption and its consequences, yet taking into account the more integrated nature of the modern world, I believe that a similar catastrophe today would ultimately shift the balance of geopolitical power away from the West and in favor of the Third World.

Any major nontropical Northern Hemisphere eruption would disrupt climate throughout North America, Eurasia, and Africa. An eruption of the caldera of Rabaul would almost certainly also affect climate in South America and Australia, as it would distort the wind circulation and ocean current systems in both the Northern and Southern Hemispheres.

In the Third World, the dust, sulfuric acid aerosols, and ice-crystal clouds spewed into the air would possibly lead to drought and massive crop failure—exactly as it did in the sixth century. China, India, Africa, and (depending on the latitude of the eruption) Brazil would be hit hardest. Outside the Third World, Russia would also be very badly affected. Historically, these areas have always been the most vulnerable to famine. Indeed, on a number of occasions, natural oscillations in world climate have produced multiregion crop failures without volcanic factors playing any part at all.

The last such catastrophe—largely ignored by the history books—was back in 1876–1878, when fifteen to twenty million people died in droughts in north China, central India, Morocco, and northeast Brazil. In China nine and a half million people perished in four provinces. In the worst hit, Shanxi, just over a third of the population (six million out of fifteen million) died, while the death tolls in the other three provinces (Zhieli, Henan, and Shandong) were two and a half million, one million, and half a million, respectively. So desperate was the situation that many had to resort to cannibalism or eating the thatch from the roofs of their houses to survive. To avoid death by starvation, destitute farmers had to sell their daughters into prostitution and their sons into slavery.

At the same time, at least five million died in India, with particularly severe suffering in the provinces of Madras, Bombay, and Mysore. In the Madras region alone three and a half million people died from starvation and cholera. The cities were packed with refugees from the drought-stricken countryside. In Bombay, quite apart from cholera, tens of thousands of the inhabitants—weakened by lack of food—died in a devastating smallpox epidemic.

Farther west, in the northern half of Africa, Morocco and Ethiopia were also hit by famine, while in South America, half a million people died in northeast Brazil in a catastrophic drought. Up to 50 percent of the population was killed in some areas.

A similar multiregional famine also struck in 1789–1792 and seems to have contributed to the French Revolution. In those years, crops failed in France, the northern United States, northeast Brazil, and most appallingly in India, where the resultant mass starvation—known as the

"Skull Famine"—caused so many deaths that it was impossible to keep count of the bodies. Bombay, Hyderabad, Gujarat, Orissa, and North Madras were devastated.

In neither the 1790s nor the 1870s catastrophe was there any volcanic causation—and it must be noted that these disasters were on nothing like the scale of the mid-sixth-century holocaust, which *was* proportionately volcanically triggered. Nevertheless, the eighteenth- and nineteenth-century disruptions do vividly illustrate precisely which areas of the globe would be most vulnerable to a modern-day volcanically induced famine.

A major caldera eruption could quite easily disrupt climate to such an extent that hundreds of millions of people would die. If by some awful coincidence the event struck at the same time as a natural downturn (such as occurred in the 1790s and 1870s), the death toll from starvation and associated epidemics could well top a billion, or even two billion.

In a virtually planetwide disaster of this scale, political administration would rapidly disintegrate in many areas. Banditry would increase, huge refugee flows would develop, epidemics would break out, and the medical infrastructure would be totally overwhelmed. Cholera, measles, typhus, and dysentery epidemics would occur on a massive scale. And, as in the sixth century, it is even conceivable that bubonic plague could again devastate substantial areas.

Contrary to popular belief, plague is still alive and well in a number of locations on four continents. Over the past ten years at least twenty thousand individuals have contracted the disease. Four thousand have actually died from it in such places as Peru, Vietnam, China, India, southern Africa, and Madagascar.

Millions of wild rodents in central Asia, southwest China, East Africa, the central Andes, the western United States, Brazil, and central India still carry the plague bacillus. Climatic chaos could still lead to the disease breaking out of its wild-rodent reservoir into the human world on a substantial scale in Asia, Africa, and South America if the medical infrastructure collapsed there.

Refugee flows would serve to further spread disease and provoke conflict. In many areas, refugees would be seen by local populations as competition for scarce resources and might well be slaughtered in substantial numbers. Although most refugee flows would be within the Third World itself, some would also penetrate the First World.

Mexican refugee pressure on the mile-long U.S. frontier would almost certainly be beyond the U.S. government's ability to contain. Even now, in totally normal climatic circumstances, undetected illegal economic migration from Mexico totals an estimated 230,000 individuals per year.[4] And the Mediterranean would almost certainly prove no obstacle to desperate groups of refugees seeking to enter Europe from northern Africa.

While much of the Third World would be suffering from famine, epidemics, and administrative collapse, western Europe, the United States, and Canada would suffer from massive food shortages—but probably not from starvation. The West's higher-yield crops and more sophisticated and entrenched governmental machines and transport systems would almost certainly ensure that absolutely basic food needs were met and that emergency measures were introduced to ensure proper allocation and distribution. Rationing would no doubt have to be in force for several years.

Of course, wherever the eruption took place, substantial numbers of people would die as a direct result of the explosion and subsequent devastation. A full-blown eruption of the Italian caldera would kill up to several million people within a few days. Dozens of towns and cities in and near the Campanian area of southern Italy, including Naples and Salerno, would be utterly destroyed by fire caused by the initial shock wave and the huge pyroclastic flow that would roll out from the crater. A thousand square miles of southern Italy would virtually cease to exist. Nearby Pompeii and Herculaneum (two Roman towns destroyed by Vesuvius in A.D. 79) would simply be reburied along with two thousand years of subsequent southern Italian history. Scientists monitoring the Campanian/Campi Flegrei caldera would probably be able to give only a few days' notice of the timing and expected scale of any impending eruption. To evacuate at least four million people from a thousand square miles of territory in such a short time would probably prove impossible.

In the United States, neither the Yellowstone nor the Long Valley caldera is located anywhere near a large population center, and evacuation would probably prove easier—although Las Vegas and Phoenix would almost certainly be thrown into chaos by ash falls from any major Long Valley explosion. Both cities would be covered in a three-foot-thick blanket of volcanic dust.

In the West as a whole, the main immediate consequence of any large calderic explosion anywhere in the Northern Hemisphere or the tropics would be economic and political. Much of western Europe's and North

America's wealth depends on worldwide trade and international invest-ments that also involve the Third World. If much of Asia and Africa was plunged into demographic, agricultural, and political chaos, the West would quickly feel the draft. This would almost certainly lead to a down-turn in western economies, already likely to be enduring food and gasoline rationing, and a slump would obviously create substantial unemployment.

Not all countries in Europe would be hit equally—and this in itself would impose major political strains within the European Community.

Inevitable U.S. and European attempts to use their wealth to import scarce food from a famine-hit Third World, the West's inability to deliver effective aid, and inevitable fury over Western attempts to repel refugees would combine to inflame Third World public opinion against the West. The event would have the long-term effect of reducing Western involve-ment in, and power over, the Third World. Europe, North America, and potentially Australia would probably develop a siege mentality and be-come increasingly isolated.

Significantly, this would have the related long-term effect of freeing up the Third World, removing superpower influence over it. Its debt bur-den would simply vanish. The disaster would no doubt allow some Third World countries to dominate others in a way that Western economic, po-litical, and military influence has prevented up till now. And the famines and epidemics might well also lead to the strengthening of fundamental-ist religious movements.

In the long term, the catastrophe would, I believe, have the effect of reducing the geopolitical imbalance between the West and the Third World. Although Asia, Africa, and possibly South America would lose hundreds of millions of their inhabitants to famine and disease, they would in the end emerge stronger rather than weaker vis-à-vis the West. Just as the eruption of 535 changed world history and brought the ancient world to a close, so any future supereruption would potentially end our Western-dominated era and usher in—in embryonic form—the geopolitical shape of the distant future.

As the evidence in this book has demonstrated, climate has the potential to change history—not just on a short-term basis but in the long term as well. Volcanic activity is merely one of the triggers that can change climate and wield such power. Global warming (due to increased atmospheric pollution), sunspot activity, meteor or comet impacts, periodic small changes in the shape of the earth's orbit, and minor changes in the earth's axis of rotation are all capable of triggering dramatic changes in climate— and human history.[5]

However, only the future will tell which of these factors, or combinations of them, will determine the direction and nature of our destiny.

APPENDIX

THE CLIMATIC EVENTS OF THE MID-SIXTH CENTURY: A FINAL SURVEY AND ADDITIONAL PROOF

For reasons of narrative style, some historical evidence, scientific data and graphs were not included in the main body of this work. For academic reasons, they are added or expanded on here.

From the Mediterranean region there are five historical sources for the A.D. 535/536 event. A sixth-century historian and prominent church leader, John of Ephesus, wrote that "there was a sign from the sun, the like of which had never been seen and reported before. The sun became dark and its darkness lasted for eighteen months. Each day, it shone for about four hours, and still this light was only a feeble shadow. Everyone declared that the sun would never recover its full light again."[1] This apocalyptic description was set down in the second volume of his greatest historical work, the *Historiae Ecclesiasticae (Church Histories)*. Sadly, only the third volume has survived fully intact, but luckily, the description of the apparent near-demise of the sun and other fragments of the preceding tome were plagiarized by a much later historian, a patriarch of Antioch called Michael the Syrian, who wrote six centuries later.

As already mentioned at the very beginning of this book, the Roman historian Procopius also described the apparently bizarre behavior of the sun at this exact time. He regarded it as a very bad omen indeed—a sentiment that was to prove only too correct. "And it came about during this year that a most dread portent took place," he wrote. "For the sun gave forth its light without brightness like the moon during this whole year, and it seemed exceedingly like the sun in eclipse, for the beams it shed

were not clear, nor such as it is accustomed to shed," said the historian—
a top Palestinian-born government and military official.[2]

Another sixth-century writer, Zacharias of Mytilene, was the author of
a chronicle containing a third account of the 535 and 536 "Dark Sun"
event. "The sun began to be darkened by day and the moon by night," he
recorded.[3]

A fourth account was written by a Roman official and academic of
Anatolian origin known as John the Lydian, who reported that "the sun
became dim for nearly the whole year."[4]

All these reports were compiled by eyewitnesses in the Roman imperial capital, Constantinople. But in Italy, a very senior local civil servant
also recorded the solar phenomenon. "The sun seems to have lost its
wonted light, and appears of a bluish color. We marvel to see no shadows
of our bodies at noon, to feel the mighty vigor of the sun's heat wasted
into feebleness, and the phenomena which accompany a transitory eclipse
prolonged through almost a whole year," wrote Cassiodorus Senator in
late summer 536. "The moon too, even when its orb is full, is empty of its
natural splendor," he added.[5]

It wasn't just the sun's light that appeared to be reduced. Its heat
seemed weakened as well. Unseasonable frosts disrupted agriculture. "We
have had a spring without mildness and a summer without heat," wrote
Cassiodorus. "The months which should have been maturing the crops
have been chilled by north winds. Rain is denied and the reaper fears new
frosts."

In normally warm Mesopotamia, the winter was "a severe one, so
much so that from the large and unwonted quantity of snow, the birds
perished," and there was "distress among men," says the chronicle written
by Zacharias of Mytilene.

John of Ephesus (reported through Michael the Syrian) said that "the
fruits did not ripen and the wine tasted like sour grapes," while John the
Lydian noted that "the fruits were killed at an unseasonable time."

On the other side of the planet, the abnormal weather was also being
recorded. As mentioned in Chapter 22, the Japanese great king is reported
in the ancient chronicle of Japan (the *Nihon shoki*) to have issued an edict
lamenting hunger and cold: "Food is the basis of the empire. Yellow gold
and ten thousand strings of cash cannot cure hunger. What avails a thousand boxes of pearls to him who is starving of cold?" said the king.

*   *   *

In China, as already noted in Chapter 19, the disaster is chronicled in greater detail. In 535, there was a massive drought in the north of the country. The *Bei Shi* (the north Chinese chronicle) says, in an entry for late April/early May, that "because of drought, there was an imperial edict which ordered that in the capital [Chang' An], in all provinces, commanderies and districts, one should bury the corpses."

By the fifth month, the situation had deteriorated to such an extent that in the capital itself the government "was forced to provide water" for the population "at the city gates."

Soon the drought had become so intense that hundreds of thousands of square miles of normally fertile or semifertile land became totally arid. The evidence suggests that huge dust storms began to rage.

Between 11 November and 9 December 535, the capital of south China, Nanjing, was deluged by dust falling from the sky. As already mentioned in Chapter 19, "yellow dust rained down like snow." The time of year, the color, and the apparent quantity strongly suggests that this dust from the sky was, in fact, a yellow-colored fine sand called loess, which had been carried by the wind from the interior of China. In normal conditions, loess dust comes only from the Gobi Desert and other inland arid areas—and storms only affect areas hundreds of miles north and west of Nanjing. But in extreme drought conditions, when unusually large areas become arid, much wider areas can be inundated by the dust.

As the drought worsened in 536, the *Bei shi* says, in the central Chinese province of Xi'an, seven or eight out of every ten people died. Survivors were forced to eat the corpses of the dead.

As the months rolled on, the climate became increasingly bizarre. The *Bei shi* reports that in some areas of north China (Bian, Si, Zhuo, and Jian) hail fell in September 536—but there was still "a great famine." Between 29 November and 27 December 536 and again in February 537, in the south Chinese capital Nanjing, even greater dust storms covered the city in a saffron-colored blanket: "Yellow dust rained down like snow. It could be scooped up in handfuls," said the *Nan shi (History of the Southern Dynasties)*.

In early 537 in nine provinces of north China, the drought continued but was increasingly interrupted by hail. Then finally, in 538, the drought ended, but the climatological chaos continued—there were now huge floods. In the summer of that year, the toads and frogs were said to be "croaking from the trees," so torrential was the rain. The instability continued into the 540s with major droughts in 544, 548, 549, and 550.

*   *   *

In Korea, 535–542 had the worst climate recorded for the peninsula for any time in the ninety-year period 510–600, and 535–536 was the worst twenty-four months in that nine-decade time span.

As described in previous chapters, the mid-sixth-century climatic disaster also struck the Americas, the steppes of Russia, western Europe, and other regions. But many of those areas left no written records. It is a plethora of nonwritten sources that must, therefore, provide the evidence for the climatic situations in these regions.

The most accurate records of climate change are those hidden inside the trunks of trees. The growth rings of many species preserve an indelible annual record of climatic history. Tree-ring specialists (dendrochronologists) can attempt to reconstruct past climate by studying two telltale sets of data. One is the width of each annual growth ring, which reveals the exact amount of growth in a given year (indeed in a given growing season, usually spring and summer). A drought or unseasonable frost that restricts growth will therefore produce narrow rings. The second, the density of each ring in conifers in cool climates, yields information about temperature. The colder the weather the less dense was the timber growing at that time.

Continuous tree-ring chronologies, going back to the sixth century A.D. and beyond, now exist for Finland, Sweden, the British Isles, central Europe, the Aegean, Siberia, North America, Chile, Argentina, and Tasmania. In a substantial percentage of all the tree-ring chronologies covering the sixth century that have been constructed so far, the period 535–550 (and sometimes even till 560 or beyond) stands out as a time of unusually low tree-ring growth. In several key chronologies, that twenty-five-to-thirty-five-year period contains many of the narrowest ring sequences known for the past 2,000 years.

The narrow widths and low densities of rings for 536 found in Scots pines from northwest Sweden, for instance,[6] indicate the second-coldest summer for the past 1,500 years.

The tree rings for the year 539 found in bristlecone pines in California are among the five narrowest in the A.D. 400–600 period for that location.[7]

Narrow foxtail pine rings from the Sierra Nevada mountains in California show that 535, 536, and 541 were the second, third, and fourth coldest years there in the past 2,000 years.[8]

In southern South America, temperatures declined from 535 to 537, marginally recovered in 538, and then plummeted in 540 to the coldest summer temperatures experienced there in the past 1,600 years. The main tree-ring evidence for this is from *Fitzroya cupressoides* conifers from Chile[9]—but new evidence from Argentina[10] also suggests unusually low temperatures in 540.

In Tasmania, a tree-growth decline (huon pines) between 546 and 552 culminated in the coldest temperatures of that century.[11]

At Khatanga in the north-central Siberia region of Russia, a twenty-year decline in tree growth in the 530s and 540s was the most serious of the past 1,900 years![12]

And further west, in Poland, Germany, and the British Isles, oak growth massively slowed down in 539–542. Over the past 2,000 years, one of the European oak master chronology's lowest growth years was 540.[13]

An analysis of tree rings around the world yields clues as to the actual sequence of events that followed the initial major deterioration in the 530s. Many reveal that there was already a minor decline in tree growth occurring in 533 and 534. Then, as the sun became partially obscured in 535 and 536, tree-ring growth rates in parts of western North America, in Europe, Scandinavia, the Russian steppes, and Australia (Tasmania) plummeted. In some areas (e.g., western North America, western Europe, and Scandinavia), there was then a small temporary recovery for a year or two.

But from 538 or, in many places, 540, there was an almost universal massive decline lasting between two and eight years. Often this was followed by between ten and thirty years of recurrent low and/or cold growth episodes. This was particularly marked in the southern hemisphere where, in Chile[14] and Tasmania, for example, full recovery was not achieved until the 580s and the 570s respectively.

Other less chronologically refined evidence of a mid-sixth-century climatic disaster is provided by studies of river flood and lake levels–and by archaeology. One particularly dramatic set of data from the Lower San Jorge Basin of Colombia has revealed that over the past 3,500 years the lowest floodwater levels were in the mid–sixth century A.D.[15]

And, as described in Chapter 23, human skeletal material from Teotihuacan in Mexico strongly suggests that a massive famine struck the city just prior to its demise in the mid– to late sixth century A.D.

In Peru, purely archaeological evidence also points to a sixth-century catastrophe with the Nasca desperately constructing their underground water-management system (see Chapter 26). Hydrological studies have revealed that these subterranean "canals" were built when underground water levels were at a virtual all-time low.

Important glacial ice-core evidence comes from the mountain fastnesses of western South America. The 18,700-foot-high Quelccaya glacier—a vast "carpet" of ice on top of part of the central Andes—has provided scientists with data that suggest drought-induced dust storms were raging in Peru from around 540 to around 570. Scientists from Ohio State University climbed to the top of the glacier in 1983 and, using solar power, sank a drill deep into the ice. With this equipment they succeeded in extracting two roughly 530-foot-long ice cores, the water from which was then studied in detail under laboratory conditions. The raw data showed that the ice, between 563 and 594 (+/– twenty-five years), was riddled with drought-induced dust, suggesting a thirty-year-long drought—the most sudden and intense in Andean and possibly South American history. But glacial ice cores are often inaccurate in terms of chronology, especially at substantial time depth. Compression of the ice can lead to some layers (perhaps as much as one or two years per century) not being counted. Up to twenty-five years can potentially, therefore, be added to the date of the drought, thus pushing it back to 530 or 540.[16] Significantly, the abrupt cooling revealed by Chilean and Argentine tree rings[17] can be precisely dated to exactly 540. It is therefore possible that the Peruvian ice-core dust and the Chilean and Argentinian cooling are both manifestations of the same sixth-century climatic catastrophe.

While drought was a common manifestation of the mid-sixth-century climatic disaster, the chaos often expressed itself in quite different ways.

In the Arabian Peninsula an inscription found by archaeologists in Yemen has revealed that a vast dam was destroyed by a massive flood in the 540s (see Chapter 8).

In Africa, too, there is evidence—albeit circumstantial—of climatic catastrophe. As described in Chapter 2, the plague almost certainly originated in east Africa in the 530s. Both drought and flood, or, most devastating of all, a combination of both, would almost certainly have been required to cause the disease to break out of its natural pool of immune wild rodents.

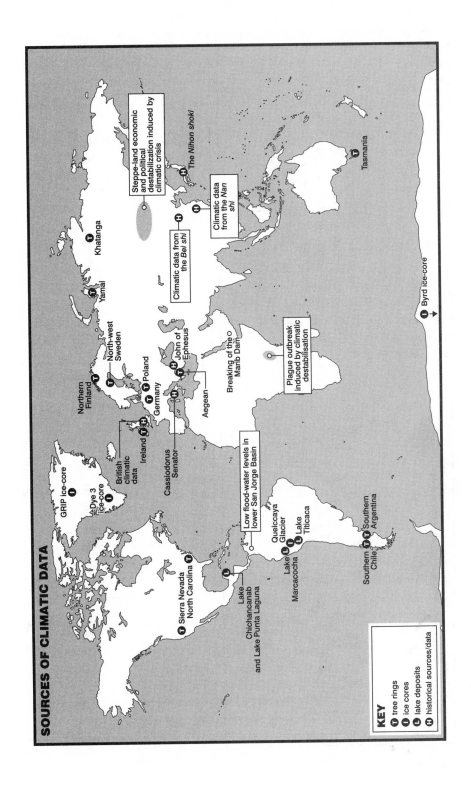

SOURCES OF CLIMATIC DATA

Steppe-land economic and political destabilization induced by climatic crisis

The *Nihon shoki*

Climatic data from the *Nan shi*

Khatanga

Climatic data from the *Bei shi*

Yamal

Tasmania

North-west Sweden

Byrd ice-core

Poland

John of Ephesus

Northern Finland

Germany

Aegean

Breaking of the Marib Dam

GRIP ice-core

Ireland

Plague outbreak induced by climatic destabilisation

British climatic data

Dye 3 ice-core

Cassiodorus Senator

Low flood-water levels in lower San Jorge Basin

Quelccaya Glacier

Lake Titicaca

Sierra Nevada North Carolina

Southern Chile

Southern Argentina

Lake Marcacocha

Lake Chichancanab and Lake Punta Laguna

KEY

T tree rings
I ice cores
L lake deposits
H historical sources/data

This graph shows how in A.D. 536 temperatures were the coldest for the past 2,000 years. It also suggests that the sudden climatic downturn occurred in the middle of a roughly eighty-year-long cold spell. The mid-530s event seems to have transformed a relatively poor, though not exceptional, climatic situation into a climatic disaster—unparalleled in the past two millennia. This graph was produced by Keith Briffa of the Climatic Research Unit of the University of East Anglia, using data provided by H. Grudd, R. Hantemirov, and M. Naurzbaev.

INFERRED SUMMER TEMPERATURE GRAPH FOR WESTERN SIBERIA AND
NORTHERN SCANDINAVIA DERIVED FROM TREE-RING DATA A.D. 1–1997

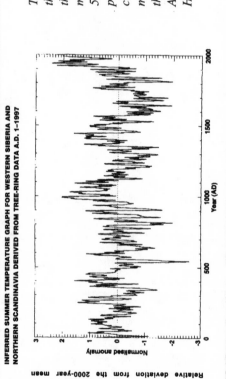

This graph—produced by Stepan Shiyatov and Rashit Hantemirov of Ekaterinburg Institute of Plant and Animal Ecology, Russia—also shows how in the mid–sixth century temperatures were the coldest in almost 2,000 years.

TEMPERATURE GRAPH FOR KHATANGA, NORTH-CENTRAL SIBERIA, DERIVED FROM PINE TREE
GROWTH RING DATA, A.D. 100–A.D. 1998

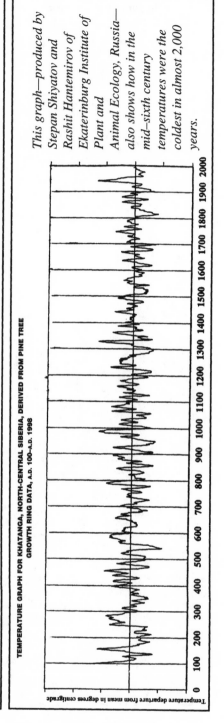

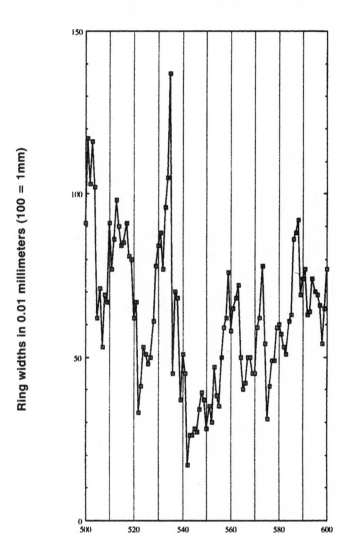

This graph—based on data from Pentti Zetterberg of the University of Joensuu, Finland—illustrates how the temperature appears to have dropped abruptly in 536 and fell again in 539 and again in 541, reaching a low point in 542—the coldest year of the past one and half millennia.

EUROPEAN OAK GROWTH IN THE SIXTH CENTURY A.D.

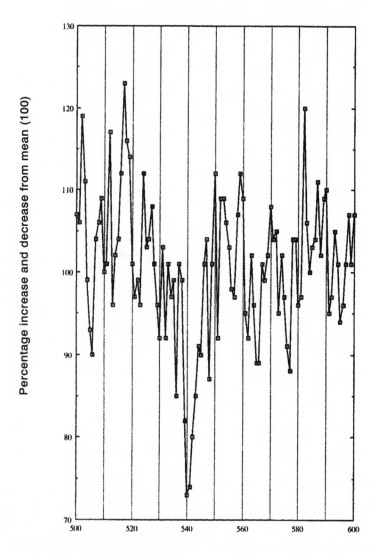

This graph, compiled by Mike Baillie of Queen's University, Belfast, is derived from data provided by dendrochronologists in many different parts of Europe (from Ireland in the west to Poland in the east). It shows a substantial dip in 536 and an even greater decline in tree growth in 539 and 540. The ring width in A.D. 540 represents one of the three lowest growth years of the past fifteen centuries. In some of the tree-ring chronologies used to create this master graph, tree growth in 539 was the lowest in 1,500 years.

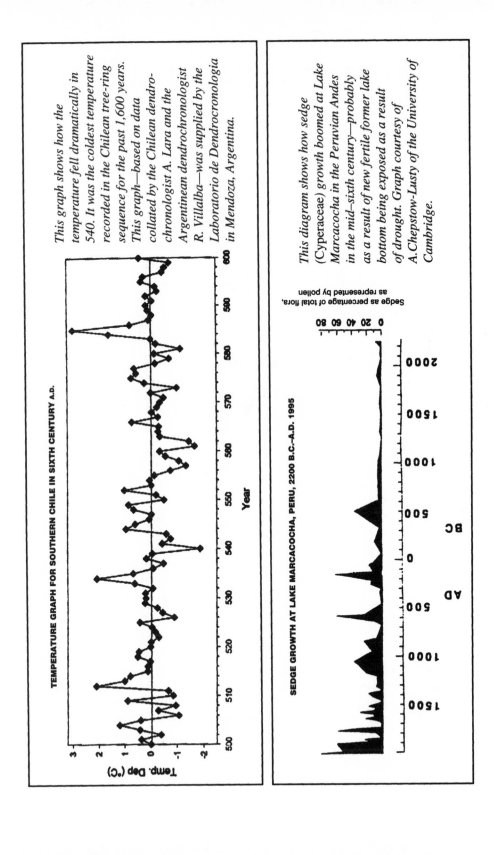

TEMPERATURE GRAPH FOR SOUTHERN CHILE IN SIXTH CENTURY A.D.

This graph shows how the temperature fell dramatically in 540. It was the coldest temperature recorded in the Chilean tree-ring sequence for the past 1,600 years. This graph—based on data collated by the Chilean dendro-chronologist A. Lara and the Argentinean dendrochronologist R. Villalba—was supplied by the Laboratorio de Dendrocronologia in Mendoza, Argentina.

Temp. Dep (°C)

Year

SEDGE GROWTH AT LAKE MARCACOCHA, PERU, 2200 B.C.–A.D. 1995

Sedge as percentage of total flora, as represented by pollen

This diagram shows how sedge (Cyperaceae) growth boomed at Lake Marcacocha in the Peruvian Andes in the mid–sixth century—probably as a result of new fertile former lake bottom being exposed as a result of drought. Graph courtesy of A. Chepstow-Lusty of the University of Cambridge.

WESTERN AMERICAN FOXTAIL AND BRISTLECONE PINE GROWTH, SIXTH CENTURY A.D.

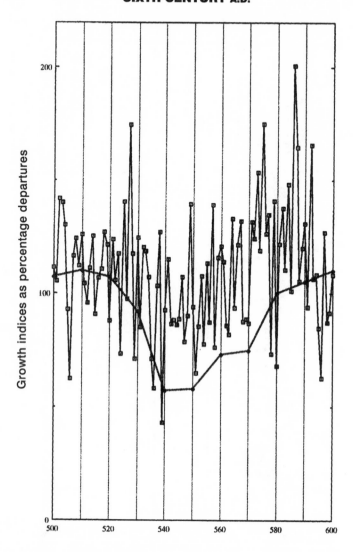

This graph shows bristlecone pine ring widths (small squares) and ten-year average growth indices for foxtail pine (small black circles) and illustrates how temperatures fell in the mid–sixth century. They are based respectively on data produced by Wes Ferguson and Val LaMarche, University of Arizona, and Louis Scuderi at the University of Boston.

NOTES

CHAPTER 1

1. From the account written by the sixth-century cleric Evagrius, translated from the original Greek by the Oxford University scholar Peter Sarris, but unpublished. However, a new translation, by Michael Whitby, is being published in the year 2000.

2. The "at least 50 percent" estimate was made by Cyril Mango on page 51 of his *Le Développement Urbain de Constantinople (IV–VII Siècles)*, Paris, 1985.

3. From the account of the plague in Constantinople by John of Ephesus, as preserved in the *Chronicle of Pseudo-Dionysius of Tel-Mahre*, part III, edited and translated by W. Wittakowski, Liverpool University Press, 1996, pages 74–98. Subsequent quotations from John of Ephesus are also from this source, unless otherwise stated.

4. Particularly such scholars as P. Allen and Lawrence Conrad.

5. This agricultural abandonment has already been referred to briefly on page 10–11. There I quoted an eyewitness of the epidemic catastrophe, John of Ephesus, as describing how he saw grain fields that had nobody to reap them, "cattle abandoned" and "flocks of sheep," etc., who had "forgotten [life in] a cultivated land." No doubt each major outbreak of the plague wrought similar havoc. Yet there are relatively few extant eyewitness historical accounts describing the rural wilderness that must so often have resulted from plague devastation. There is, however, a second type of evidence—but only for the most severe episodes of abandonment. It is provided by those ancient chroniclers and historians who included major outbreaks of locust infestation in their works. One of the worst periods of the plague pandemic

(especially in terms of geographical spread) was in the late sixth century—in the 570s and 580s—and it is from precisely that period that we get the only known locust invasions of the Mediterranean basin and the Middle East prior to the 670s. According to *Invasions des Acridiens Sauterelles en Algerie* (2 volumes, by J. Kunckel d'Herculais, Alger-Mustapha, 1893–1905), locust swarms attacked Syria and Iraq (Mesopotamia) in A.D. 576. And in exactly the same period, Gregory of Tours (in book VI, 33, of *The History of the Franks*) says that locust swarms arrived (in 578) in Spain and devastated the area around the capital, Toledo. "Not a single tree remained, not a vine, not a patch of woodland," he wrote. "There was no fruit of the earth, no green thing which these insects had not destroyed." (From page 364 of *The History of the Franks* by Gregory of Tours, translated by L. Thorpe, Penguin, London, 1974.) The devastation was almost certainly wider than that, but information was obviously easier to obtain from the capital than from more remote areas. Gregory (book VI, 44) says that the locust swarms ravaged the Toledo region for five years and then spread out along the line of a major road and "invaded" another province. He tells us that the swarm was 100 miles in length and 50 miles across. I believe that locust infestation in areas not normally affected seriously by them should be regarded as a marker for agricultural abandonment. This is because locust swarms are particularly attracted to large tracts of abandoned agricultural land. For the attraction to work, all the land has to have been abandoned at roughly the same time, as would occur during and after a severe epidemic. The locusts prefer land with an abnormally wide variety of plant species—and abandoned agricultural land provides exactly that phenomenon. Under cultivation, the number of species is obviously kept deliberately very low—and under normal long-term wild conditions, interspecies competitive pressures ensure that the level of diversity is also relatively low. However, after agricultural land has been abandoned, a huge variety of different wild plant species flourishes for around five years until the natural competitive pressures start to substantially decrease that number. That gives a massive window of opportunity to locusts. What's more, if vast areas of land were in this recently abandoned (fallow) condition simultaneously, then overall locust numbers would increase dramatically because the additional nourishment would boost reproduction, thus making movement into new areas even more likely. Two other factors would also boost reproduction. First, locust egg pods survive better in fallow than in cultivated terrain, because plowing exposes the pods to sunlight, which kills them. Second, previously uninfested terrain is relatively free of those parasites that attach themselves to, and finally kill, locust eggs. A locust swarm such as that covering 5,000 square miles in Spain would have consisted of around 770 billion insects and would have devoured some 1.5 million tons of plant and tree cover per day.

6. During the plague pandemic of the sixth and seventh centuries, large numbers of towns and villages must have become partially or fully depopulated. Even at the beginning of the pandemic, John of Ephesus wrote of "desolate" villages, and later in the sixth century, Evagrius wrote that some cities were "rendered empty of almost all their inhabitants." Today, however, it is difficult for archaeology to determine exactly which towns and villages—or which parts of them—were abandoned specifically as a result of plague rather than war or general economic decline. However, by working out when particular cities or other settlements experienced particularly steep declines, it is possible to suggest which archaeological sites were abandoned or substantially abandoned as a result of the plague. Prime candidates for substantial abandonment include Anamur, Anavarza, Canbazli, Corycus, Dag Pazari, and Kamlidivane (all in southern Turkey); El Bara, Sinhar, Deir Sim'an, Sergilla, and Kfer (all in northern Syria); and Dion at the foot of Mount Olympus in Greece. Candidates for partial (and in some cases perhaps final) abandonment as a result of plague include a clutch of sites in Tunisia: Dougga, Sbeitla, Thuburbo Majus, and the northern part of Carthage itself. Depopulation evidence has also come from rural areas. Surveys carried out in the Tunisian countryside have revealed that population densities fell by 50 percent between 550 and 650 around Carthage and by 70 percent between 550 and c. 600 around Dougga.

CHAPTER 2

1. Rhapta was the name the Greek sailors gave to this city. It simply means "sewn boats" in ancient Greek and probably refers to the sewn boats presumably used by the inhabitants.
2. Claudius Ptolemy, *The Geography*, translated and edited by E. L. Stevenson, published by New York Public Library, 1932, and republished by Dover Publications, Mineola, New York, 1991, page 38.
3. *The Periplus Maris Erythraei*, text with introduction, translation, and commentary by L. Casson, Princeton University Press, 1989, page 61.
4. From Ptolemy.
5. From *The Periplus*.
6. More detail on this change to pastoralism is provided later in this chapter.
7. The plague organism is called *Yersinia pestis*, formerly *Pasteurella pestis*.
8. The sixth- to seventh-century plague was the world's first firmly attested outbreak of this disease. However, there must surely have been earlier major pandemics that history has not recorded, or that modern historians have not definitively attributed to plague. The Dark Age pandemic came to an end in c. 750 and the known world was not afflicted again until the Black Death of the fourteenth century. Occasional plague epidemics struck various parts of Eu-

rope in the fifteenth and sixteenth centuries, and also ravaged Britain, mainland Europe, and the Middle East in the second half of the seventeenth century. A third great pandemic broke out in the mid–nineteenth century, this
time in China. Between 1894 and 1923 the disease spread from China
throughout the world—especially India—and tens of millions of people died.

9. The first clear exposition of the African rather than Asian origin of the sixth-
to seventh-century plague pandemic is contained in "The Justinianic
Plague—Probable Origins, Possible Effects," an unpublished paper by Peter
Sarris, prepared for a seminar held at Oxford University in May 1993.

10. According to a Yemeni inscription. For further details, see Chapter 8.

11. Prior to the mid–sixth century there is no sure evidence for any other plague
epidemics affecting the Middle Eastern and Mediterranean world, although
there certainly must have been at some stage in antiquity.

12. After a flea has become infected, it takes some five to fourteen days for its gut
to become blocked. However, the blockage can take place only if the temperature has fallen below 27.5° centigrade—exactly the sort of cooling effect
that would have occurred in East and Central Africa during the 535/536
event. At above 27.5° plague bacteria release an anti–blood clotting enzyme
that is designed to assist rapid spread of the disease within the host animal.
Below 27.5° the anti-clotting agent is not released and clots form in the flea's
gut. In those regions of Africa some areas would have experienced such comparatively low temperatures for parts of the year in normal times, but in the
mid–530s, the reduction in solar heat (and quite possibly consequent climatic phenomena) would have meant that much larger areas experienced
temperatures of less than 27.5° for larger amounts of time. This would have
played a key role in the spread of plague. Cooler temperatures would
have also increased adult flea life span and population levels. The research on
clot formation at 27.5° was published in an article by D. C. Kavanaugh on
pages 264–273 in the *American Journal of Tropical Medicine and Hygiene*, volume 20, 1971.

13. The disease is passed on because the gut-blocked flea regurgitates its blood
meal—it cannot keep its meal down.

14. Virtually all mammals are vulnerable to plague to one extent or another. Humans, cats, and some rodents are very susceptible, while others, including
dogs, are more resistant.

15. The Bantu—today Africa's largest linguistic group—came originally from
central-west Africa, started expanding outward from that area in around 500
B.C., and took over large tracts of East Africa and other areas between A.D. 1
and 500. Their economy has always been based on farming, especially of root
crops. The Cushites were—and still are—a large, mainly pastoral African linguistic group that originated in Ethiopia in prehistoric times. At their largest

extent, some two thousand years ago, they inhabited large swaths of what is now Tanzania, Kenya, Uganda, Somalia, Ethiopia, Sudan, and eastern Egypt.

16. Each tusk would have weighed between 11 and 22 pounds and most would have been obtained by killing large solitary adult males. Today there are 500,000 elephants in Africa; twenty years ago there were 1.2 million, and 1,500 years ago there were probably several million—so the killing of up to 5,000 per year would not have appreciably affected population levels. A site on the island of Zanzibar—Unguja-ukuu—has produced evidence for east African trade with the Roman Empire in the form of imported Roman north African pottery dated by radio carbon tests and ceramic style to around the mid–sixth century A.D. Even more remarkably, the excavations recovered a *Rattus rattus* bone in similarly dated levels, as well as bones of large rodents that the inhabitants were apparently catching and eating for food. Here existed a fatal combination for the transmission of plague to Europe.

CHAPTER 3

1. The main historical source is the history of the Chinese Zhou Dynasty, the *Zhou shu*, written in the early seventh century A.D. The Avars were known to the Chinese as the *"rou ran"* or the *"ruan ruan"*—literally, the "wriggly worms."

2. Originally Turkic nomads from northern Mongolia and southern Siberia, the Uighurs dominated Mongolia for many generations until 840, when they were defeated by the Kyrgyz and subsequently became farmers. Today there are six million Uighurs in China and Kazakhstan, and since 1921 they have experienced a national and cultural revival.

3. The Kyrgyz are a Turkic-speaking people, originally from the Yenisey region and of Turkic and possible paleo-Siberian origin. Since late medieval times they have lived in what is now called Kyrgyzstan.

4. The tree-ring data are from Khatanga, in northern Siberia, and were compiled by Stepan Shiyatov and Rashit Hantemirov of the University of Ekaterinburg.

5. It is known from the *Zhou shu* that the Turks were at this stage involved in metalworking and that their leading element—the Asina people—had had a farming background, almost certainly involving, among other things, cattle rearing. Some central Asian Turkic peoples keep large herds of cattle to this day.

6. To dominate and rule, the Avars (like all ruling nomadic steppeland elites) needed mobility and military clout. In order to attain these two objectives they required horses—indeed many horses per warrior male. But that dependence on mobility and horses substantially restricted the breadth of their economy to highly mobile livestock (chief among which were, of course, horses) and that made them more vulnerable to climatic crises when they occurred (especially given what we now know of horse vulnerability to severe

climatic problems). But such climatic crises were very rare. The day-to-day, year-in-year-out maintenance of political and military power—and its horse- and mobility-oriented requirements—inevitably therefore took precedence over economic diversity and the ability to survive rare climatic crises.

7. Also spelled A-Na-Kuei.

8. The Turks' practice of keeping slaves is mentioned in eighth-century inscriptions referring to earlier periods, and in Roman sources.

9. Some also fled to China, according to the *Bei shi* (the *History of the Northern Dynasties*). There they were seized, bound, and handed over to the Turks. Every man over sixteen—some 3,000 in all—was beheaded. Those under sixteen were enslaved.

10. Horse numbers may well have recovered to some extent in the decade after the worst of the drought—but not in time or in sufficient numbers to reverse the political damage the Avars had suffered.

11. The Kutrigurs were first attacked by the Avars in the mid-550s. They therefore fled west and invaded Roman territory, causing mayhem in 558–559 (for more detail see page 34). These Kutrigurs then retreated and were subsequently attacked again, and finally conquered, by the Avars in the 560s.

CHAPTER 4

1. The description is from *Maurice's Strategikon*, written by Emperor Maurice in the 590s, probably revised by Emperor Heraclius in the 620s, and translated by George T. Dennis, University of Pennsylvania Press, 1984. As I have already said, the Avar hordes also included large numbers of other steppeland people.

2. According to Procopius.

3. From Procopius (*Wars* VII), translated by H. B. Dewing, Loeb Classical Library, published by Harvard University Press and Heinemann.

4. From an unpublished English translation by Peter Llewellyn, University of Wales, retired.

5. *The Emperor Maurice and His Historian*, Michael Whitby, Oxford University Press, 1988.

6. Maurice's campaign against the Avars lasted seasonally from 591 to 602. It was his first long-lasting, and indeed his first offensive, campaign against them. Previous anti-Avar operations in 587 and 589 had been mainly defensive and had each been limited to a single fighting season.

CHAPTER 5

1. His youngest boy, whose name is thought to have been Justinian.

2. From *The Chronicle of Theophanes*, written in c. 813 and partly based on now substantially lost works by the seventh-century historian Theophylact, adapted

by Michael Whitby especially for this book from Harry Turtledove's translation, University of Pennsylvania Press, 1982.

3. Theophanes.

4. Theophanes.

5. The supporters of one of the empire's two main chariot-racing organizations, which had green as its emblematic color.

6. The praetorian prefect, Constantine Lardys.

7. Theophanes.

8. Tiberias, Peter, Paul, Justin, and Justinian, but not his eldest son, Theodosius.

9. Anastasia, Theoctiste, and Cleopatra.

10. Constantine Lardys was the imperial official who was in charge of taxation and financial administration. The fate of Theodosius is still somewhat of a mystery. Some sources say he was captured and executed, as recounted here. Others maintain he escaped to Persia and was crowned there by the Persian emperor, Chosroes II, as "Roman emperor in exile," but many historians believe that the "exiled emperor" was an impostor.

11. From an unpublished translation by Peter Llewellyn, University of Wales, retired, of the *Chronicon Paschale*, written by anonymous clerics in Constantinople during the first half of the seventh century. There is a published translation of the *Chronicon Paschale* by Michael and Mary Whitby, Liverpool University Press, 1989.

12. Maurice had helped reinstate the Persian king, Chosroes II, in 591 after a Persian coup d'etat in 590 had temporarily ousted his family from power.

13. According to the late-seventh-century Egyptian bishop and chronicler, John of Nikiu, C.103.

14. Theophanes.

15. *John of Nikiu*, C.105, R. H. Charles, London, 1916.

16. *The Miracles of St. Demetrius.*

17. *Chronicon Paschale.*

18. Theophanes.

CHAPTER 6

1. In late antiquity and medieval times the Adriatic town we now call Split was known variously as Aspalathos, Spalaton, Palatium, or Spalato.

2. From *The Miracles of St. Demetrius.*

3. Vasmer's work, published in 1941, is controversial, particularly in Greece—but the general pattern his place-name survey reveals is probably a fairly accurate one, reflecting a substantial Slav influx into Greece in the sixth and seventh centuries and undoubtedly on several occasions since then.

4. Many of these Slav place-names have been changed to new Greek ones in recent decades.

5. Vasmer, 1941.

6. *The Miracles of St. Demetrius,* the second miracle of the second collection.

7. From the book *On the Capture of Jerusalem,* written around 620 by a monk called Antiochus Strategus, translated by F. C. Conybeare, *English Historical Review,* volume 25, 1910, pages 502–517.

8. Antiochus Strategus.

9. Antiochus Strategus.

10. From the *Chronicon Paschale.*

11. From the *Chronicon Paschale.*

CHAPTER 7

1. Towns were often net consumers of wealth rather than net contributors—thus the difference between 33 percent and 10–15 percent.

2. By Justinian, according to Procopius and John Lydus.

3. There were literally fewer citizens to man the same circumference of city walls.

4. See Chapter 4.

5. *Islam* actually means "submission," referring to the necessity of human obedience to God.

CHAPTER 8

1. Surah 34, verse 16. All material from the Koran in this book is according to the translation by Muhammad Marmaduke Pickthall, published by Harper-Collins, London.

2. The dam burst sometime between 541 and 548, most probably in 542 or 547, depending on the precise modern interpretation of the ancient Yemeni dating system. The breaking of the dam (and subsequent dam bursts at Marib) has also been identified geomorphologically by a Swiss scholar, Ueli Brunner, who published his findings in *Die Erforshung der Antiken Oase von Marib Mit Hilse Geomorphologischen unter Suchungs Methoden* (volume 2 of *Archaeologische Berichte aus Dem Yemen*) published by Philipp von Zabern, Mainz, 1983. Other irrigation systems in Yemen may also have been damaged or abandoned at roughly the same time. In the Wadi Markhah in central Yemen, Brunner has identified, since 1992, at least half a dozen settlements, including four small towns that appear to have become deserted in the sixth or seventh century. Abandonment is even recorded in Arab tradition, which maintains that many people left Wadi Markhah to take part in the early Islamic expansion. One group that, according to local tradition, did *not* leave is still known today as the al-Nisiyin—the forgotten people. Another area, Wadi Jawf, in northern Yemen, has at least a dozen deserted settlements, most of which were also probably abandoned in the sixth or seventh century.

3. The eighth-century Arab historian Ibn Hisham, as published in notes ap-

pended to *The Life of Muhammed—a Translation of Ibn Ishaq's Sirat Rasul Allah*, by A. Guillaume, 1955/1967/1996.

4. From page 17 of volume VI of *The History of al-Tabari*, translated and annotated by W. Montgomery Watt and M. V. McDonald, State University of New York Press, 1998.

5. From page 16 of volume VI of *The History of al-Tabari*.

6. From page 27 of *The Life of Muhammad—a Translation of Ibn Ishaq's Sirat Rasul Allah*, translated by A. Guillaume, Oxford University Press, Karachi, 1967.

7. Paraphrased quote from Theophalact Simoccata. The exact words, as translated by Michael Whitby, read: "The day without evening will dwell among mortals and the expected fate will achieve power when the forces of destruction will be handed over to dissolution and those of the better life hold sway." The "day without evening" and the "expected fate" refer to the millennium of divine rule and peace which Christians expected would precede the apocalypse. It was to be a millennium-long Sabbath, which would follow six millennia of world history, as the peaceful holy Sabbath day, the Christian Sunday, follows the six secular days of the week. The "forces of destruction" represented Satan.

8. As the Jews did not accept the Christian claim that Jesus was the Jewish Messiah, they were still waiting for the Messiah to arrive.

9. *Doctrina Iacobi Nuperbaptizati*, the doctrine of the newly baptized Jacob. From page 317 of *The Later Roman Empire 284–602: A Social, Economic and Administrative Survey* by A. H. M. Jones, Blackwell, Oxford, 1964, 1990.

10. *Doctrina Iacobi Nuperbaptizati*.

11. The Koran, the holy book of Islam, is seen by Muslims as the word of God, as revealed to Muhammad in a series of divine encounters between 600 and 632.

12. Surah 30, verses 2 and 7.

13. Surah 30, verse 10.

14. Surah 20, verse 102.

15. Surah 20, verse 24.

16. Surah 20, verses 124 and 127.

17. Attributed to Mughira ibn Shu'ba in the *Kitab al-Kharaj*, by Abu Yusef Yaqub ibn Ibrahim.

18. Surah 8, verse 52.

19. Surah 8, verse 55.

20. Surah 8, verse 65.

21. Surah 8, verses 12 and 13.

22. Surah 8, verse 15.

23. Surah 8, verse 16.

24. Surah 8, verse 67.

25. From the eighth-century Arab historian Ibn Hisham, as quoted on page 242

of *Meccan Trade and the Rise of Islam*, by P. Crone, 1987. Reprinted by permission of Princeton University Press.

26. From Abid ibn al-Abras IV, 14:17 as translated by C. J. Lyall in *The Diwans of 'Abid ibn al-Abras* as quoted in *Meccan Trade and the Rise of Islam* by P. Crone.

27. The etymology of *mashrafi* is unclear. Various interpretations have been made suggesting either a south Syrian or alternatively Yemeni origin for the weapon—or that it was made by a famous blacksmith of that name.

28. Ibn Hisham, as translated by A. Guillaume and quoted in *Meccan Trade and the Rise of Islam*, by P. Crone, page 244.

29. From *Meccan Trade and the Rise of Islam*.

CHAPTER 9

1. This image is in a fifteenth-century illuminated manuscript edition—now in the Bodleian Library, Oxford—of an eleventh-century Islamic work, the *Book of Kings* by the Persian poet Firdausi. However, the earliest known reference to the concept of Alexander having paid homage at the Kaba is contained in an eighth-century Arabic romance, *The Book of the Crowns of the Kings of Himyar*, by the Arab writer Wahb ibn Munabbih.

2. The Kaba, the most sacred building in the Muslim world, was a holy place even in pre-Islamic times. Although partially rebuilt on several occasions, it has maintained its ancient design. It contains a single chamber 43 feet long, 36 feet wide, and 53 feet high, with a cube-shaped masonry structure of only slightly larger proportions. In the northeast external corner of the building is a large black meteorite, and the entire structure is covered in black silk. The site has been sacred to Islam since Muhammad captured Mecca and cleared pagan idols out of the Kaba in A.D. 630.

3. For more detailed information, see Chapter 7.

4. This is the first time that Christian soldiers on active service were declared martyrs (the procedure which was, several centuries later, formalized into canonization) by the Church following their deaths at the hands of an enemy. The Church was actually quite reluctant to declare them martyrs, but was forced to do so by the Emperor Heraclius. Up until then, the Church had always resisted permitting moral approval to be used for military benefit.

CHAPTER 10

1. Theophanes.

2. Sayf ibn Umar.

3. Eutychius, *Annals*, Breydy 129 text, 109 translation.

4. *Doctrina Iacobi Nuperbaptizati.*

CHAPTER 11

1. The *Zhou shu*.
2. Again, according to the *Zhou shu*.
3. The Samanids were members of an Iranian Islamic dynasty that ruled what is now eastern Iran, western Afghanistan, and parts of Uzbekistan and Turkmenistan on behalf of the caliphate from the early ninth century to 1005.
4. The Qarluqs were probably the main ruling element within the Ghaznavid state.
5. The Seljuks were a very warlike Shiite Muslim Iranian mountain people whose power base was in Iran.
6. The Battle of Manzikert took place near Lake Van in what is now eastern Turkey.
7. The Muslim Ottomans were employed as mercenary allies by one of the factions in a Roman dynastic struggle.

CHAPTER 12

1. *The Thirteenth Tribe: The Khazar Empire and its Heritage*, by Arthur Koestler, Hutchinson, 1976. Reprinted by permission of the Peters Fraser & Dunlop Group Ltd. The correspondence is published in full in *Jewish Letters through the Ages* by Adolph Kober.
2. He was in fact the head of the caliph's household and performed the role of chief minister, handling foreign and domestic affairs of state. He was arguably even more important than the official "prime minister," the caliph's vizier.
3. Hasdai ibn Shaprut had heard about the existence of the Jewish kingdom through Roman diplomats.
4. See Chapters 3 and 11.
5. The Umayyad and then the Abbasid caliphates.
6. The Khazar court was based in the Khazar capital Itil (or Atil, the Turkic name for the Volga) in the great river's delta. Its exact location has never been found. Some scholars suspect it now lies under the Caspian Sea—a sort of steppe Atlantis, having been engulfed by rising sea levels. Others believe it still awaits discovery by archaeologists on land, somewhere near the modern Russian city of Astrakhan.
7. From the *Book of Kingdoms and Roads*, as quoted in *The Thirteenth Tribe*.
8. *The Thirteenth Tribe* by Arthur Koestler, Hutchinson, 1976.
9. There are only a few thousand Karaites worldwide today, mainly in Israel, eastern Europe, Egypt, Russia, and the United States.
10. From a tenth-century letter written by King Joseph to Hasdai ibn Shaprut of Spain, quoted in *The Thirteenth Tribe*.
11. The rest of the population of the Khazar empire were other mainly Turkic groups (Bulgars, etc.), plus groups of Slavs and probably some Goths and Iranians, among others.
12. The rulers of the pre-Ottoman Seljuk empire of Turkey.

13. Qazwini.
14. Suggestion by D. M. Dunlop.
15. According to Arthur Koestler's book *The Thirteenth Tribe*, quoting the Russian scholar M. I. Artamonov.
16. The Pecheneg Turks, a nomadic steppe people living between the Ural and Volga rivers, were driven westward by other tribes in the late eighth and ninth centuries. As a result they collided with the Magyars (Hungarians) and forced them to move westward into what was to become Hungary.
17. Pressburg Ecclesiastical Council, 1309.
18. The tenth-century letter is published in *Khazarian Hebrew Documents of the 10th Century*, by Golb and Pritsak, Cornell University Press, 1982.
19. In later medieval times, these centers also attracted substantial Karaite populations.
20. If the Khazar empire had remained pagan, it would have been much more likely to convert eventually to Islam—but once it had adopted another form of monotheism (in this case, Judaism), conversion to Islam became inherently less likely.
21. This DNA data was published in *Nature*, volume 394, 9 July 1998, pages 138–139, in a chart in an article by M. G. Thomas et al., entitled "Origins of Old Testament Priests."
22. The text of the tenth-century letter is reproduced in *Khazarian Hebrew Documents of the 10th Century*, by Golb and Pritsak, Cornell University Press, 1982.

CHAPTER 13

1. For more details of this, see Chapter 15.
2. I examined all sixty British and near Continental weather entries for the 480–650 period in the Meteorological Office, Geophysical Memoirs number 70, *Meteorological Chronology to A.D. 1450* by C. E. Britton, HMSO, 1937. Britton compiled his chronology by using information contained in large numbers of medieval and later chronicles and surveys. For this period, his main source was a survey compiled in the eighteenth century (published in two volumes in London in 1749) by Dr. Thomas Short. Known as *A General Chronological History of the Air, Weather, Seasons, Meteors, Etc.*, the work appears to make use of many medieval sources, some of which are presumably now lost. On balance, I suspect that the sixth-century entries derived from Short's work are genuine, because many of them are concentrated around the 535–555 period—the precise time when world climate is known to have been in an unstable condition. Britton, however, unaware of the wider international evidence, naturally thought they must be fictitious. In the introduction to his chronology, Britton says that Short spent fifteen years researching and that "his labour in hunting down obscure sources must have been prodigious." In

this period, the key Short-derived entries (referred to on page 105 above) from Britton's *Meteorological Chronology* are for the years 536, 540, 548, 550, and 555. The 545 entry in Britton's work is derived from *Natural Phenomena: And Chronology of the Seasons* by Edward J. Lowe (London, 1870). The 554 entry derives from Roger of Wendover. Another key entry, from the reign of the Kentish King Ochte, derives from *The History of England* by John Seller (London, 1696), who presumably was quoting from a now lost medieval source.

3. They were written by Welsh monks in the tenth century, utilizing older, now unknown sources.
4. Directed by Jacqueline Nowakowski of the Cornwall Archaeological Unit.
5. In the Irish kingdom of Raithliu.
6. Excavated in 1966–1990 by Philip Barker, University of Birmingham.
7. A site that until around A.D. 300 had been the exercise hall of the city's public baths complex.
8. The interpretation of events at Wroxeter is based on archaeological evidence provided by, and discussions with, Roger White of the University of Birmingham, who has made an in-depth study of the structural history of the site. The north wall of this ancient chapel is now known as the Old Work, the only piece of imposing masonry surviving at Wroxeter.
9. The only fairly well documented medieval plague epidemic in England was the Black Death. In the peak eighteen-month mortality period in the late 1340s, 47 or 48 percent of the population is thought to have died (estimate in *The Black Death*, translated and edited by Rosemary Horrox). That, however, is an average figure. In some areas much higher percentages perished. Indeed, Horrox says that the most common contemporary claim—presumably derived from severe local experiences—was that scarcely a tenth of the population survived.

CHAPTER 14

1. Up till now, virtually all academics have taken the view that the concept of the "Waste Land" in the Arthurian romances was pure literary invention or at best inspired by myths.
2. Sometimes referred to, erroneously, as the *Mabinogion*.
3. The name *Annals of Ulster* is the English translation of the Latin name *Annales Ultoniensis*—the title arbitrarily given by the English in the seventeenth century to a late-sixteenth-century chronicle called the *Annale Senait*. The work consists of material copied from at least two earlier manuscripts—the probably tenth-century *Liber Cuanach* and a probably eighth- or ninth-century chronicle of unknown name, neither of which are now extant. Those manuscripts were derived in turn from long-lost annals written by Irish monks on the Scottish island of Iona between 550 and 740 and then by later monks in Kells in Ireland between 740 and 1000.

4. *The Old French Arthurian Vulgate and Post-Vulgate in Translation,* edited by Norris J. Lacy, published by Garland, 1993/96, volume 4, page 65.

5. From *The Mabinogion,* translated by Jeffrey Gantz, Penguin, 1976.

6. As implied in the twelfth-century *Story of the Grail,* by Chrétien de Troyes.

7. Dyfed in the *Mabinogi.*

8. First mentioned in the *History of the Kings of Britain,* it originally may have referred to the west Midlands.

9. *The History of the Kings of Britain,* by Geoffrey of Monmouth, translated by Lewis Thorpe, published by Penguin, 1996.

10. From page 87 of *The Story of the Grail—The Contes del Graal or Perceval,* translated by William W. Kibler, and published by Garland, 1990.

11. From *The High Book of the Grail: A Translation of the 13th-Century Romance of Perlesvaus,* translated by Nigel Bryant, and published by D. S. Brewer/Rowman and Littlefield, 1978, page 90.

12. From *The Elucidation,* translated by Sebastian Evans in *Sources of the Grail,* selected and introduced by John Matthews.

13. From page 65 of *The Lancelot-Grail in Translation,* volume 4, translated by E. Jane-Burns and published by Garland, 1995.

14. From pages 212–214 of *The Post-Vulgate in Translation,* volume 4, translated by Martha Asher, published by Garland, 1995.

15. The identification of Waste Land material from the Arthurian romances in this chapter is based on research carried out for this book by a specialist in medieval Arthurian romance, Elspeth Kennedy of Oxford University.

CHAPTER 15

1. Translation as published in *The Age of Arthur,* by John Morris, 1973. The name Cynddylan is pronounced "Kinthullen."

2. Certainly the settlement discontinuity phenomenon that hit the southwest in the mid–sixth century did not affect the Anglo-Saxon east until sometime in the first half of the seventh century.

3. From *Gildas: Arthurian Period Sources,* volume 7, translated by M. Winterbottom, Phillimore, 1978.

4. The *Anglo-Saxon Chronicle* text covering this period was written in the ninth century, utilizing earlier sources that are now lost.

5. Translation as published in *The Age of Arthur,* by John Morris. The river name Dwyryw is pronounced "Dwiry-oo."

6. Translation as published in *The Age of Arthur,* by John Morris. The place name Catraeth is pronounced "Katrithe." Mynydawc is pronounced "Minoothog."

7. Translation as published in *The Age of Arthur,* by John Morris.

8. Contrary to common assumption, the word *Bretwalda* has nothing to do with the word *Britain.* It was derived from the title Brytenwalda, meaning "wide

ruler." It was only later misspelled and therefore misinterpreted as Bretwalda, that is, "ruler of the Britons." However, as "wide ruler," the Brytenwalda was indeed "ruler of Britain"!

CHAPTER 16

1. From *The Annals of Ulster*, edited by Seán Mac Airt and Gearóid Mac Niocaill and published by the Dublin Institute for Advanced Studies, 1983.
2. The Irish tree-ring record for this period is described by Mike Baillie on pages 212–217 of the journal *Holocene*, volume 4, 1994.
3. The Irish chronicle called the *Cronicum Scotorum* is a seventeenth-century copy of an original of unknown name written sometime between the eleventh and fourteenth centuries. That is in turn derived from annals written down by Irish monks on the Scottish island of Iona between 550 and 740, and then by later monks in Kells in Ireland between 740 and 1000.
4. Because dates in the various Irish annals often conflict with each other and events in some annals even appear twice or three times under different dates, I have used the annals-derived synchronized chronology recently worked out by the Irish chronologist Dan McCarthy of Trinity College, Dublin, and published by him on the Internet at: http://www.cs.tcd.ie/Dan.McCarthy/ Chronology/synchronisms/annals-chron.htm. His analysis of Irish chronological data appeared in an article entitled "The Chronology of the Irish Annals" in the *Proceedings of the Royal Irish Academy*, section C (1998), pages 203–255.
5. Estimated by Matthew Stout, author of *The Irish Ringfort*, published by Four Courts Press, Dublin. Ring forts were not the only defensive structures built at this time. Many communities built fortified artificial islands in the middle of lakes. Known as crannogs, these manmade island fortresses must have been virtually impregnable. Of the hundreds of Irish crannogs that survive, only around fourteen have ever been precisely dated (using dendrochronology)—and nine were built in the period 550–620. The dates for seven of these were published in *Tree Ring Dating and Archaeology*, by M. Baillie, Croom Helm, London, 1982.

CHAPTER 17

1. From *The History of the Franks*, by Gregory of Tours, translated by Lewis Thorpe and published by Penguin, 1974.
2. See Chapter 2.
3. See Chapters 13 and 19, respectively.

CHAPTER 18

1. The Romans had long referred to the Iberian Peninsula as a whole as Hispania, but that had been a purely geographical term. This is the first time that a name derived from it is given to a Roman political unit.

2. The Suevic kingdom had been Arian for some eighty years, having converted to that heresy from Catholicism in the 470s.

3. Reccopolis, now just ruins, is located near the village of Zorita de Los Canes, thirty miles southeast of Guadalajara.

4. Victoriacum has never been located by archaeologists, but it was situated in northern Spain near the border with the Basque country.

5. Often referred to as Hispano-Romans.

6. An alternative account of Hermenegild's career maintains that he converted to Catholicism only after he had revolted against his father, and that his reason for converting was to more easily obtain Roman imperial military backing. Whichever sequence of events is correct, the conversion illustrates the catalytic impact of the Roman conquest of Spain's far south.

7. Quoted in *The Goths in Spain*, by E. A. Thompson, Oxford University Press, 1969.

8. It is known from historical sources that Spain was hit by the plague at least three times—in 542/543 (according to the *Chronicle of Saragossa*) and in 580 and 588 (according to *The History of the Franks*, by Gregory of Tours).

CHAPTER 19

1. The *Bei shi* actually says that the edict was issued in the "third month" of the Chinese calendar for the year 535, which in Western terms corresponded to 18 April to 17 May.

2. From the *Bei shi*.

3. The Emperor Wu of the Liang Dynasty.

4. There had been peasant revolts before, but with the climatic chaos and famines of the mid–sixth century, the frequency and scale of them seems to have increased.

5. From *The Lament for the South* by Yu Xin, translated by William T. Graham and published by Cambridge University Press, 1980.

6. Emperor Jianwen, which translated means, literally, "the frugal and cultured one."

7. Undoubtedly both north and south China suffered terribly from the climatic problems of the mid–sixth century. But politically, the disaster harmed the south much more than the north. In 534 (the year before the climatic chaos started), the north Chinese state (united for the previous ninety-four years) split into rival western and eastern halves. In keeping with previous northern tradition, both northern states (northwest and northeast) developed highly centralized administrative systems despite the climatic problems. This was much easier to achieve in the north than in the south for two reasons. First, the northern economy and social system was much less complex than its southern counterpart and could be centralized more easily. And second, the

northern ruling dynasties were non-Chinese—Mongolian—in origin and derived their political power from soldiers drawn from a military caste (of Mongolian origin) that was not dependent on agriculture or tax-derived pay. By contrast, the southern state had to depend on mercenary troops who had a comparatively lowly social status and who had to be paid out of tax-derived revenues. In the north, centralized government was developed by introducing innovations in famine relief, tax collection, land reform, and the securing of military loyalty. Then, in 577, the northwest Chinese state conquered its northeast rival, thus forming a united northern Chinese empire that was soon to invade and conquer the south, whose more complex economy and society had been much more vulnerable to dislocation during the climatic chaos of the mid–sixth century.

CHAPTER 20

1. Condensed adaptation of the lengthy, twenty-point letter of accusation written by the emperor of northern China to his southern opposite number.
2. The details of the military campaign are from the Sui Dynasty annals, the *Sui shu*.
3. Lake Tai.
4. The *Sui shu*.
5. Quoted in *The Sui Dynasty*, by Arthur Wright, published by Alfred A. Knopf, New York, 1978.

CHAPTER 21

1. The *Samguk sagi*, or *The Histories of the Three Kingdoms*, compiled in the mid–twelfth century A.D. and based on now mainly lost sources.
2. For more detail on Japan, see Chapter 22.
3. 535 is the date proposed by the prominent Korean historian Ki-Baik Lee in his *New History of Korea*, page 59.

CHAPTER 22

1. From page 34 of the *Nihongi: Chronicles of Japan from the Earliest Times to A.D. 697*, translated into English by W. G. Aston, and published by Charles E. Tuttle, Rutland, Vermont.
2. Also sometimes called the *Nihongi*. The *Nihon shoki* was compiled in the eighth century, based on records that are now lost and which even then were probably incomplete. The words may be being put into the mouth of the king by the eighth-century compilers, or they may be "borrowed" from now-lost Chinese texts referring to events in China, or they may be a genuine approximation of what was said. However, because of the date, the adjacent events, and the virtual certainty that Japan was hit by drought and famine

along with China, Korea, and other regions in the mid-530s, the 536 *Nihon shoki* entry should be seen, at the very least, as reflecting an all-too-real event in Japan at that time in which nothing could "cure hunger" and where people really were "starving of cold." The *Nihon shoki* for this early period is often regarded as being of doubtful historical value, but the apparent accuracy of the 536 "starving of cold" entry increases, by implication, the historical credibility of the other mid-sixth-century entries.

3. The year 538 is the most likely date for the mission and the resultant introduction of Buddhism to Japan. It is the date given in three key sources: *Hoo teisets*; a temple manuscript called *The Daianji Shinjo Daitoku ki*, written in the first half of the eighth century; and an early-ninth-century memorial document. The only source that disagrees is the *Nihon shoki*, which gives a date of 552—possibly because, in the Japanese and Chinese sexagenary cycle, 552 was the 1,500th "anniversary" of the Parinirvana of the Buddha, an anniversary that people believed would usher in a new Buddhist era. It would therefore have been appropriate and propitious from a Buddhist religious perspective for the early-eighth-century authors of the *Nihon shoki* to choose 552 as the date for the arrival of Buddhism in Japan. The best analysis of this dating issue—a study that indeed supports the 538 date and to which I am indebted—is by Stanley Weinstein, Yale University Seminar Paper 2, Jordan Lectures in Comparative Religion, 1991.

4. Buddhism was a key issue—but it was probably symbolic of a much wider area of disagreement and conflict, including perhaps access to trade, resources, and power, and the preservation of tradition.

5. Major smallpox epidemics often occur every thirty to fifty years with smaller outbreaks in between, as the size of an outbreak depends on the percentage of the population that has not experienced it before.

6. From the *Nihon shoki*.

7. This murder is described in the *Nihon shoki*, volume 2, xxi, 5 and 6.

8. This was in fact a very rare event, for women seldom sat on the Japanese throne.

CHAPTER 23

1. Much of the survey data was published in *The Basin of Mexico*, by W. Sanders, J. Parsons, and R. Santley, Academic Press, 1979.

2. There is some academic debate as to whether Quetzalcoatl was a full-fledged deity or simply a divine symbol of fertility, immortality, wealth, and power.

3. Quoted on page 90 of *Mexico*, by Michael Coe, Thames and Hudson, 1962.

4. Article by Curtis et al. in the journal *Quaternary Research*, volume 46, pages 37–47.

5. Article by Hodell et al. in *Nature*, volume 375, 1995, pages 391–394.

6. The new Rio-Cisne data has been gathered over the past two years by the tree-ring laboratory in Mendoza, Argentina. The Lenca material was published by A. Lara and R. Villalba in an article on pages 1104–1106 of volume 260 of *Science*.

7. Now renamed the Byrd Polar Research Center.

8. *Bulletin of the Gold Museum*, Bogotá, 1988, article by Plazas et al.

9. *Erdkunde*, volume 46, 1992, pages 252–256, article by T. Van der Hamman and A. M. Cleef.

10. Academics have redated the end of Teotihuacan as a result of recent ceramic studies, supported by some radiocarbon dates (usually plus or minus 50 years or so), and to a much lesser extent by some dates produced by an even less exact system known as obsidian hydration dating. The evidence for the carbon 14 and obsidian hydration dates is published in the journal *Ancient Mesoamerica* (number 7, autumn, 1996) in an article by Linda Manzanilla, Claudia Lopez, and AnnCorinne Freter titled "Dating Results from Excavations in Quarry Tunnels behind the Pyramid of the Sun at Teotihuacan." An American pre-Columbianist, George Cowgill, published data that suggests that the fall of Teotihuacan took place around 600, give or take several decades. The key information is in a chronological chart in an article in *The Annual Review of Anthropology*, 1997.

11. Several dozen different hieroglyphic symbols have been discovered so far at Teotihuacan, but up till now, none of these have ever been found strung together to make sentences. Three is the maximum that have been discovered in a group. The glyphs are always related to religious matters and very briefly describe the qualities of deities or the nature of a particular ritual.

12. The data obtained from these 150 skeletons is published in Rebecca Storey's *Life and Death in the Ancient City of Teotihuacan*, published by the University of Alabama Press, 1992.

13. This was first proposed by Rene Millon in "The Last Years of Teotihuacan," a chapter in *The Collapse of Ancient States and Civilisations*, edited by Norman Yoffe and George Cowgill, 1988. It has by far the best description (to which I am indebted) of the violent end of Teotihuacan. However, although the fall of Teotihuacan was a predominantly drought- and famine-driven internal affair, other peoples in climatically vulnerable parts of Mesoamerica were of course also affected by the drought. Among these other peoples was almost certainly a group of nomads referred to by archaeologists as the Coyatlatelco. They lived in the region 50–100 miles to the north of Teotihuacan and migrated toward the great city, probably as a result of the drought. Although they were not responsible for the fall of Teotihuacan, their presence in the Teotihuacan area no doubt complicated the political and cultural situation and helped in destabilizing the status quo.

14. The excavations were carried out in 1980–82 by the Mexican archaeologists Anna Maria Jaraquin and Enrique Martinez.
15. At Coatlinchan, near the city of Texcoco.
16. The idol now stands in the National Museum of Anthropology in Mexico City.

CHAPTER 24

1. Sky Witness is the name given to the ruler of Calakmul by modern scholars, because his name features the Maya glyphs for "sky" and "eye." Back in the sixth century he may well therefore have been called something like "Sky Eye" or "Watcher of the Sky." Animal Skull is the name given by modern scholars to the puppet ruler Sky Witness put on the throne in Tikal. The hieroglyphic signs making up his name have been only partially translated. One translates as "Great Sun," while the other consists of the head of a reptile. His real name may well therefore have been something like "Great Sun Reptile Head."
2. Double Bird is the name awarded this ruler by modern scholars. Much of his real name is unknown, because the glyph comprising its second part is damaged. However, his name appears to have begun with the words "Great Sun."
3. For guidance regarding Maya dates in this chapter, I am indebted to the British Maya epigrapher Simon Martin.

CHAPTER 26

1. These dates have been deduced by archaeologists by surveying surface pottery types and frequencies, making iconographic comparisons, and utilizing several scientific dating techniques.
2. An idea proposed by the British pre-Columbianist David Browne.
3. David Browne.
4. Described in *Nueva Cronica y Buen Gobierno*, written in c. 1600 by Felipe Guaman Poma de Ayala, and published in 1987 in Madrid in *Historia 16, Cronicas de America*, volume 29.
5. Including David Browne's expedition, 1989.
6. Directed by David Browne.
7. Carried out by the U.S. anthropologist John Verano.

CHAPTER 27

1. Carried out by Steve Bourget, University of East Anglia, England.
2. This "flood-to-sand-dunes" mechanism to explain aspects of Moche decline was first proposed by archaeologist Michael Mosley and is outlined in his book *The Incas and Their Ancestors*, published by Thames and Hudson, 1992.
3. Traditionally, the coastal-plain economy had long been based on irrigation,

agriculture, and fishing—and had involved the construction of urban centers with monumental architecture. This contrasted with the mountainous interior with its predominantly agro-pastoral alpaca- and llama-herding economy.

4. The political fragmentation of the Moche civilization seems to have occurred as a result of the sixth-century climatic crisis. Some time—perhaps many decades—after that fragmentation had started, highland peoples, especially the Huari, seem to have taken advantage of the situation to increase their influence on the coastal plain, thus completing the process of geopolitical change.

5. At some late provincial Moche sites (but not at Moche itself) ceramic art ultimately changed and became far more color-oriented. The iconography changed, too, and began to include a deity holding a staff and wearing a rayed headdress. Settlement patterns shifted and burial practices altered dramatically (from extended to highly flexed, fetal-style positions for corpses). Certainly the more multicolored style of ceramic decoration and the introduction of the staffed deity suggest influence from an Andean highland state called Huari. The burial practice change may also have betrayed Huari influence, or may merely indicate that traditional Moche burial customs were disappearing and being replaced with a tradition that had already been common elsewhere in Peru (including Huari) for many centuries.

6. Galindo and Pampa Grande both appear to have been established during the great sixth-century drought—and their construction was probably the response to it. They were both built on sites with easy access to good water supplies, a fact that suggests that populations were being forced by the drought to move to such locations.

CHAPTER 28

1. Archaeologists are divided as to the nature of the Huari state. Some see it as an empire, or, at the very least, a state exercising political control over a wider area beyond its borders. Others see it as a significant, but smaller, polity that exercised cultural and probably some political influence over that same wider territory.

CHAPTER 29

1. This was its name before the Inca conquest, according to a Spanish cleric, Bernabe Cobo, writing in 1653. Although it means "stone in the center" in the local Aymara language, it is obviously not possible to know for sure what the Tiwanakans themselves called the city because, first, there are no written records and second, it is not known whether they spoke Aymara. The "stone in the center" concept is discussed by Mexican archaeologist Linda Manzanilla in *Akapana: Una Piramide en el Centro del Mundo*, UNAM, Mexico, 1992.

2. San Pedro de Atacama in Chile in c. A.D. 300 and Nino Corin on the eastern slopes of the Andes in the Bolivian province of Charasani in c. 375, according to *Ethnological Studies* 32, Gothenburg, Sweden, 1972.

3. These features are described by Mexican archaeologist Linda Manzanilla in *Akapana: Una Piramide en el Centro del Mundo*, and by Alan Kolata in his book, *Tiwanaku: Portrait of an Andean Civilization*.

4. According to Alan Kolata, *The Tiwanaku*.

5. Article by H. J. Carney et al. in *Nature*, 364-6433, 1993, pages 131–133.

6. D. D. Biesboer's unpublished data are referred to in *Quaternary Research*, 47, 1997, page 237; an article by D. D. Biesboer et al. in *Bio Tropica*, 1998.

7. Doctoral dissertation by Sanchez de Lozada, Cornell University, Ithaca, New York, 1996.

8. Alan Kolata, *The Tiwanaku: Portrait of an Andean Civilization*, page 185.

9. Kolata, *The Tiwanaku*, page 187.

10. Kolata, *The Tiwanaku*, page 194.

11. Kolata, *The Tiwanaku*, pages 189–190.

12. Known today as the Kalasasaya, it is the complex in which the famous great monolithic Gateway of the Sun and the impressive Ponce Stela statue are located.

13. Suggested by Alan Kolata in *The Tiwanaku*.

14. Kolata, *The Tiwanaku*.

15. The valleys of the Tambo, Moquegua, Lucumba, Sama, Caplina, Azapa, Lluta, Camarones, and Loa.

16. Doctoral dissertation by Martin Giesso, University of Chicago, 1999.

17. Fitzroya conifers.

CHAPTER 30

1. Text of John of Ephesus as recorded in the *Chronicle of Michael the Syrian*, 9, 296, translated by Chabot and quoted in an article titled "Volcanic Eruptions in the Mediterranean Before A.D. 630 from Written and Archaeological Sources," by R. B. Stothers and M. R. Rampino, *Journal of Geophysical Research* 88, 1983, pages 6357–6371.

2. Procopius, *Wars, Loeb Classical Library, Harvard*, 4, 14.5 (H. B. Dewing).

3. All the figures in this chapter pertaining to asteroids and comets were calculated specially for this book by the astronomer Alan Fitzsimmons of Queen's University, Belfast.

4. Because of their irregular shape, the half-mile measurement refers to the notional diameter of a spherical object with the same mass and density.

5. The data from this ice-core operation—the Byrd core—is published in "50,000 Years of Recorded Global Volcanism," by C. U. Hammer, H. B. Clausen, and C. C. Langway, in the journal *Climatic Change*, volume 35, 1997.

6. Although a volcanic eruption (or possibly two eruptions) almost certainly triggered the climatic problems of the mid–sixth century, tree-ring and ice-core evidence suggest that there were additional background reasons that made the crisis worse and longer lasting. First, the 535 volcanic event occurred during a longer cold period—at least as far as Northern Hemisphere high latitudes were concerned. Tree-ring evidence from Scandinavia and Russia suggests that at least in these higher latitudes it occurred during the second longest cold spell of the past 2,000 years. Thus the 535 volcanic event seems to have pushed a poor climatic situation into becoming a disastrous one. But not only did a volcanic event transform a potentially normal cold period into a climatic catastrophe, it may also have helped create or at least lengthen the cold spell itself. It is perhaps significant that the two longest-lasting Northern Hemisphere high-latitude cold periods of the past 2,000 years contain within them two of the three most volcanically active periods of the past two millennia. Indeed, the sixth century is the only period of the past 2,000 years for which the GRIP and Dye 3 Greenland ice cores *both* display evidence for record numbers of volcanic eruptions. The GRIP core for the sixth century records four eruptions (yielding 5.8 years' worth of high volcanic acid precipitation). The nearest rival in that core in terms of the number of volcanic events is the seventeenth century with 5.6 years of high acid precipitation. In the Dye 3 core there are five volcanic acid precipitation events (totaling 6.5 years of high acid precipitation). The nearest rival to that, in terms of number of events in that core, is in the fifteenth century (totaling 5.9 years' worth of high acid precipitation). The ice-core information above is derived from data published in an article by H. Clausen et al. in the *Journal of Geophysical Research*, volume 102, no. C12, 1997, pages 26,707–26,723.

CHAPTER 31

1. This manuscript is housed in the Sasana Pustaka Library of the Karaton (Royal Palace) in Surakarta (central Java). The passages quoted in the last few paragraphs were translated from the Javanese into English for this book by an American scholar of Javanese literature, Nancy Florida of the University of Michigan.

2. Translated from the Javanese original by a Dutchman, Mr. C. Baumgarten of Batavia (modern Jakarta), whose account was then quoted in a letter written by Professor Judd of the London-based Royal Society to the scientific journal *Nature* and published in that journal on 15 August 1889.

3. The name Ranggawarsita, loosely translated, means "teacher of senior courtly rank." He lived from 1802 to 1873.

4. Information derived from discussions with volcanologist Ken Wohletz of the University of California, Los Alamos National Laboratory.

CHAPTER 32

1. See page 366 and note below.
2. The remains of just such a massive pyroclastic flow at Krakatoa were examined in early 1999 by the Icelandic volcanologist Professor Haraldur Sigurdsson of the University of Rhode Island. His expedition there was financed by U.K. broadcaster Channel 4 Television in order to gather evidence for the Channel 4 documentary on this book (first broadcast in the U.K. July 27 and August 3, 1999). The calibrated C14 dates and stratigraphic evidence obtained during that expedition combine to suggest a first millenium A.D. date for the eruption that produced that pyroclastic flow. The C14 dates (A.D. 1215–1300 and 6600 B.C. respectively) were obtained from charcoal samples from (a) the strata immediately above and (b) the fifth strata beneath the remains of the pyroclastic flow. Although theoretically this could date the flow at anything betwen 6600 B.C. and A.D. 1300, the stratigraphy (i.e., the five stratae beneath the event) strongly suggests a date much nearer to the thirteenth-century A.D. than to 6600 B.C. The A.D. 1–1200 period is probably the most likely time frame during which this eruption of Krakatoa took place, even if one only takes the C14 and stratigraphic evidence into account. This new data is therefore consistent with the historical and other evidence.
3. Up until now, most geologists have assumed that the seaway between Java and Sumatra, the Sunda Straits, had been formed exclusively by tectonic action—i.e, by very gradual changes in land level over millions of years. However, research for this book carried out by volcanologist Alain Gourgaud of the University of Blaise Pascal, Clermont Ferrand, France, has revealed that it is at least theoretically possible that the straits were fully or partially created by a massive volcanic caldera collapse. Mr. Gourgaud, who has studied the remnants of the 1883 Krakatoa eruption in the field and the underwater (bathemetric) charts of the straits, has concluded that there have been massive caldera collapses there in the past. He proposes three possible sites in the straits for ancient calderas, with approximate diameters of around 35 miles, 20 miles, and 30 miles, respectively.

CHAPTER 34

1. Centered in Pozzuoli near Naples.
2. Quite apart from the massive eruptions that will most certainly occur at some stage in the future at each of these locations, smaller eruptions will also take place—but much more frequently.
3. The latter calibrated age is derived from a new series of high-precision dates obtained from radiocarbon tests carried out at Queen's University, Belfast, but not yet published.
4. Includes repeat attempts.

5. In its recent publication, *World Disasters Report 1999*, the International Federation of Red Cross and Red Crescent Societies suggests that current climate change may be responsible for an increase in the frequency of extreme weather events. Global warming may now be "responsible for harsher and more frequent El Niño/La Niña phenomena" and for "more hurricanes, more droughts and more floods," says the report.

"While climate change is regarded as a gradual phenomenon, it will largely manifest itself in the changing frequency of extreme meteorological events—unexpected droughts and floods, record heat waves and snowstorms—that will trigger human disasters."

The report suggests that El Niños have become "more intense and frequent in the past twenty years" and that there is "some evidence to suggest that this may be a consequence" of current climate change.

The sixth-century data (see pages 218–219 of this book) certainly confirms that acute climate change seems to trigger increased El Niño frequency.

El Niños and other extreme weather events have been affecting much of the world.

The year 1998 was a record year for recorded climate disasters. Nine typhoons killed 500 and affected 5 million in the Philippines, floods killed 4,150 and affected 180 million people in China; killed 400 and affected almost 200,000 in Korea; killed 1,000 and affected 25,000 in Pakistan; killed 1,400 and affected almost 340,000 in India; killed 25 and affected 12,000 in Romania; killed 55 and affected 11,000 in Slovakia; killed 20 and affected 360,000 in Argentina. Monsoon rains and tropical cyclones killed 1,300 and affected 31 million in Bangladesh (140,000 had died just seven years earlier). An exceptionally heavy monsoon killed 3,250 and affected 36 million in northern India and Nepal; and two hurricanes killed a total of 14,000 and affected around 7 million people in the Caribbean and Central American region. In late 1997 and 1998, floods made 500,000 people homeless in Peru. Ecuador was also severely hit. Droughts triggered by El Niño caused huge forest fires in Brazil (37,000 square kilometers destroyed), Peru, Florida, Sardinia, Indonesia, China, Kazakhstan, and Australia. Five million hectares burned in Borneo and Sumatra. Air pollution worsened dramatically—and 40,000 Indonesians had to be treated at hospitals for smoke inhalation, says the Red Cross. Overall, 70,000 people were affected. In Tibet hundreds froze to death in the worst snowstorm for half a century. Economic losses due to climate disasters in 1998 were also massive—$16 billion in Central America/Caribbean, $2.5 billion in Argentina, $868 million in Korea, $223 million in Bangladesh, and $150 million in Romania.

Climatic change also triggers disease outbreaks. The Red Cross report says that current climate change is "already extending the range of infectious tropical diseases such as river blindness, malaria, schistosomiasis, dengue and yellow fevers to areas where they are not currently endemic and where the local population has no immunity."

By 2100, 60 percent of the world's population will be living in potential malaria zones, according to the IPCC (Intergovernmental Panel on Climate Change).

Current climatic change, involving hotter and longer heat waves, is massively increasing death rates from heart and lung disease.

Air pollution and mold spore and pollen problems will all get worse. Predictions by Paul Epstein of the Harvard Medical School (referred to in *World Disasters Report 1999*) suggest that total heat-related deaths worldwide are likely to double by 2020.

Other diseases that are likely to spread more rapidly as a result of current climate change include encephalitis (which spread to New York in summer 1999), leishmaniasis, Lyme disease, and rickettsiosis (boutonnense fever). These last three illnesses are spread by mosquitoes, sand flies, and dog fleas respectively.

El Niño–triggered medical problems have hit both South America and Asia.

In Peru's Piura region, malaria contraction rates trebled in 1997/1998 with 30,000 people becoming ill. At the same time 10 percent of Peru's medical infrastructure was adversely affected by the El Niño storms themselves. The Red Cross report says that in Bolivia "cholera reportedly broke out near La Paz, Cochabamba, and Oruro," and that in Ecuador "outbreaks of leptospirosis and cholera were reported near the southern city of Guayaquil."

Climate change is also likely to cause diseases to jump species. Already, in early 1998, when northeast Kenya was hit by unusually heavy rains, a cattle condition called Rift Valley fever spread to humans and killed over 1,000 people.

The IPCC says that climate change "could create a serious [financial] burden for developing countries."

However, the International Federation of Red Cross and Red Crescent Societies says that it's just as likely that "countries will fail to adapt and will pay the price in increasing numbers of 'natural' disasters."

Just as coastal areas are likely to experience greater extreme rainfall events, so continental interiors are likely to experience more droughts. "As some nations succumb to rising waters, others will become parched and increasingly at risk from catastrophic drought and famine," says the Red Cross report.

"Current climate change will cause the hot deserts of continental interiors to expand as evaporation rates increase," it says. Central Africa; South, Southeast, and East Asia; and Latin America will be most affected. Some rivers will run dry or be substantially reduced in size. According to the Red Cross report (quoting the *Journal of Geophysical Research*), the Indus will loose 43 percent of its volume, the Niger 31 percent, and the Nile 11 percent. At some stage there will be a significant danger of military conflicts over water resources.

"There is little doubt that climatic change is a major contributory factor in making natural disasters nightly television news. The rising incidence and increased severity of windstorms, fires, and floods seems to have its roots in disrupted weather patterns," says the United Nations Environment Programme (*Global Environmental Outlook 2000*, September 1999).

Of course, current climate change is also causing sea-level rise (a particular problem that did not occur in the sixth century).

Coastal zones make up a tiny percentage of the Earth's land surface—but three-quarters of the world's population live in them (i.e., around 4.5 billion people). Coastal populations are increasing at twice the global average. The tides have risen 20 centimeters over the past century. Three million people are now made homeless by flooding every year. Ten million people live under constant threat of flood. Forty-six million are threatened by storm surges. By 2080, sea levels will have risen by at least a further 44 centimeters. Indeed, it could easily be a meter or more. Rising sea levels threaten many of the world's largest and most famous cities: Tokyo, Osaka, Shanghai, Hong Kong, Lagos, Alexandria, Recife, Jakarta, Sydney, Bangkok, Saint Petersburg, Hamburg, and Venice.

Nobody actually knows how high sea levels will rise or indeed how quickly. A total meltdown of polar ice, though not the likeliest option, is certainly not an impossibility in the long term and would cause a worldwide sea level rise of 70 meters. It should be remembered that, for at least 90 percent of its history, planet Earth has existed without polar ice caps. In the event of a total meltdown, much of the U.S. eastern seaboard would be inundated— including New York and Washington. Ten percent of South America would be under water. Also inundated would be much of Holland, Denmark, Pakistan, Bangladesh, northeast India, Egypt, Iraq, the Arabian gulf states, Thailand, Cambodia, and Burma as well as large areas of eastern England, Finland, Belgium, northern Germany, northern Poland, northern Italy, north central Siberia, eastern China, and southern Australia.

Displacement of populations due to constant flooding and limited land loss—not to mention much greater territorial losses due to any total meltdown—would cause huge refugee flows and potential conflict.

The sixth-century period of climatic chaos—the worst dose of global climate change of the past 2,000 years, gives us an indication as to the scale of political transformation that climate change and its epidemiological, demographic, and other consequences can trigger. This book is the only case study of a past global climatic catastrophe and the long-term political changes it engendered.

APPENDIX

1. Text of John of Ephesus as recorded in the *Chronicle of Michael the Syrian*. *9.296*. Chabot quoted in an article entitled "Volcanic Eruptions in the Mediterranean Before A.D. 630 from Written and Archaeological Sources" by R. B. Stothers and M. R. Rampino, *Journal of Geophysical Research* 88, pages 6357–6371, 1983.

2. Procopius, *Wars, Loeb Classical Library, Harvard*. 4. 14.5 (H. B. Dewing).

3. *Chronicle of Zachariah of Mitylene*, F. J. Hamilton and E. W. Brooks, London, 1899. Quoted in an article entitled "Volcanic Eruptions in the Mediterranean Before A.D. 630 from Written and Archaeological Sources" by R. B. Stothers and M. R. Rampino, *Journal of Geophysical Research* 88, pages 6357–6371, 1983.

4. *De Ostentis* by John Lydus (John the Lydian), edited by C. Wachsmuth, Leipzig, 1897. Quoted in an article entitled "Volcanic Eruptions in the Mediterranean Before A.D. 630 from Written and Archaeological Sources" by R. B. Stothers and M. R. Rampino, *Journal of Geophysical Research* 88, pages 6357–6371, 1983.

5. The only full account of the surviving works of Cassiodorus Senator was published in Germany in the late nineteenth century as *Cassiodorus, Variae XII*, edited by Mommsen. This passage is quoted from an article entitled "Volcanic Winters" by M. R. Rampino, S. Self, and R. B. Stothers in *Annual Review of Earth Planet Science* 16, pages 73–99, 1988.

6. K. Briffa et al, "Fennoscandian Summers from A.D. 500. Temperature Changes on Short and Long Timescales," *Climatic Dynamics* 7, pages 111–119, 1992.

7. Personal communication to Mike Baillie, Queen's University, Belfast, from Don Graybill, late of the University of Arizona, using data collected by Valmore C. La Marche and Wes Ferguson.

8. L. A. Scuderi, "A 2,000-Year Tree-Ring Record of Annual Temperatures in the Sierra Nevada Mountains," *Science* 259, pages 1433–1436, 1993. Two thousand three hundred miles to the east in the eastern United States, dendrochronologists have obtained a 1,600-year-long chronology from cypress trees and published it in *Science* 240, pages 1517–1519. (North Carolina climate changes reconstructed from tree rings: A.D. 372 to 1985, by D. W. Stahle et al. Their data reveal that North Carolina's worst drought of the sixth century took place between A.D. 539 and A.D. 544.

9. A. Lara and R. Villalba, "A 3,620-Year Temperature Record from *Fitzroya*

cupressoides Tree Rings in Southern South America," *Science* 260, pages 1104–1106, 1993.

10. According to as-yet-unpublished data gathered in 1997 and 1998 in the Rio Cisne area of southern Argentina by dendrochronologists from the Laboratorio de Dendrocronologia in Mendoza, Argentina.

11. Data collected by Ed Cook of Columbia University, New York.

12. Data from Stepan Shiyatov et al of Ekaterinburg Institute of Plant and Animal Ecology, Russia.

13. Information from dendrochronologist Mike Baillie, Queen's University, Belfast. He says that he found in reviewing the mean values for a set of eight filtered oak chronologies, covering the geographical region from Ireland to Poland, that the value for A.D. 540 is one of the three lowest-growth values in 1,500 years. In a selected subset of four of these oak chronologies, the filtered growth value for the year A.D. 539 is the lowest value in 1,500 years.

14. The 540 record cold year is the first of a series of such cold years in southern South America in the mid–sixth century. Two other ultracold years, both among the coldest of the past 1,600 years, were 557 and 561. What is more, twenty-seven out of the forty-three years (62 percent) between 540 and 583 were below average in temperature compared to just fourteen out of forty (35 percent) in the previous four decades. These conclusions are based on the tree-ring data from Lenca in Chile supplied to me by the Laboratorio de Dendrocronologia in Mendoza, Argentina.

15. Plazas et al, *Bulletin of the Gold Museum*, Bogota, 1988.

16. Other information on the Ohio University expedition is provided in Chapter 23. The original 563–594 data and other relevant material were published in "A 1,500 Year Record of Tropical Precipitation Recorded in Ice Cores from the Quelccaya Ice Cap, Peru," which appeared in *Science* 229 (4717), pages 971–973; and "Pre-Incan Agricultural Activity Recorded in Dust Layers in Two Tropical Ice Cores" in *Nature* 336, pages 763–765. Another Andean source also provides dramatic evidence of the sixth-century drought. Work by Alex Chepstow-Lusty et al, published in *Mountain Research and Development* 18/2, 1998, shows that there was a massive and abrupt surge in sedge growth around the margins of Lake Marcacocha in the Peruvian Andes in around the mid–sixth century A.D. The data suggest that as the lake shrank, sedge began to flourish on those parts of the former lake bottom that had been exposed. It was the highest sedge growth peak experienced at the site in the 1,500-year-period A.D. 100 to A.D. 1600.

17. *Fitzroya* conifers.

RECOMMENDED
FURTHER READING

THE LATE-ROMAN WORLD

The Oxford Dictionary of Byzantium, edited by A. P. Kazhdan, Oxford University Press, 1991.

A Biographical Dictionary of the Byzantine Empire by D. M. Nicol, Seaby, London, 1991.

Justinian by J. Moorhead, Longman, London, 1994.

The Early Byzantine Churches of Cilicia and Isauria by S. Hill, Variorum (Ashgate Publishing), Aldershot, UK, 1996.

Die 'Toten Städte', Stadt und Land in Nordsyrien während der Spätantike by C. Strube, Verlag Philipp von Zabern, Mainz am Rheim, 1996.

The Sixth Century, End or Beginning, edited by P. Allen and E. Jeffreys, Australian Association for Byzantine Studies, University of Sydney, 1996.

Procopius. History of the Wars, translated by H. B. Dewing, Harvard University Press, 1914.

Procopius. The Anecdota or Secret History, translated by H. B. Dewing, Harvard University Press, 1935.

The Emperor Maurice and his Historian by Michael Whitby, Oxford University Press, 1988.

Les Hommes et la peste en France et dans les pays européens et méditerranéens (volume 1) by Jean-Noël Biraben, École des Hautes Études en Sciences Sociales, Centre de Recherches Historiques, Mouton, France, 1975.

ARABIA

The Life of Muhammad, a translation of Ibn Ishaq's *Sirat Rasul Allah,* translated by A. Guillaume, Oxford University Press, Karachi, 1967, 1996.

The History of al-Tabari by al-Tabari, volume 7, translated and annotated by W. M. Watt and M. V. McDonald, State University of New York, 1988.

Muhammad at Mecca by W. M. Watt, Oxford University Press, Karachi, 1979 and 1993.

Muhammad: Prophet and Statesman by W. M. Watt, Oxford University Press, 1961.

A Chronology of Islamic History 570–1000 CE by H. U. Rahman, Ta-Ha Publishers, London, 1995.

The Koran, translated by Muhammad Marmaduke Pickthall, and published by HarperCollins.

Meccan Trade and the Rise of Islam by P. Crone, Princeton University Press, 1987.

Hagarism, the Making of the Islamic World by P. Crone and M. Cook, Cambridge University Press, 1977.

Byzantium and the Early Islamic Conquests by W. E. Kaegi, CUP, 1992.

The Early Islamic Conquests by F. M. Donner, Princeton University Press, 1981.

The Prophet and the Age of the Caliphates by H. Kennedy, Longman, London, 1986.

Encyclopedia of Islam (New Edition), published by E. J. Brill, Leiden.

History of the Jews of Arabia from Ancient Times to their Eclipse under Islam by G. D. Newby, University of South Carolina Press, 1988.

AVARS AND TURKS

The Thirteenth Tribe: The Khazar Empire and its Heritage by A. Koestler, Hutchinson, 1976.

Khazarian Hebrew Documents of the 10th Century by Golb and Pritsak, Cornell University Press, 1982.

Geschichte und Kultur eines Volkerwanderungszeitlichen Nomadenvolkes (2 volumes), Klagenfurt, Austria, 1970.

BRITISH ISLES

Civitas to Kingdom: British Political Continuity 300–800 by K. R. Dark, Leicester University Press, 1994.

Lords of Battle: Image and Reality of the Comitatus in Dark-Age Britain by S. S. Evans, Boydell Press, Woodbridge, 1997.

An English Empire: Bede and the Early Anglo-Saxon Kings by N. Higham, Manchester University Press, 1995.

The Anglo-Saxons from the Migration Period to the Eighth Century, edited by J. Hines, Boydell Press, Woodbridge, 1997.

An Age of Tyrants: Britain and the Britons AD 400–600 by C. A. Snyder, Sutton, Stroud, 1998.

Anglo-Saxon England by M. Welch, Batsford, London, 1992.

Wroxeter: The Life and Death of a Roman City by R. White and P. Barker, Tempus, Stroud, 1998.

The Archaeology of Early Medieval Ireland by N. Edwards, Batsford, London, 1990.

The Irish Ringfort by M. Stout, Four Courts Press, Dublin, 1997.

The Annals of Ulster, edited by S. Mac Airt and G. Mac Niocaill, Dublin Institute for Advanced Studies, 1983.

Wales in the Early Middle Ages by W. Davies, Leicester University Press, 1982.

A Biographical Dictionary of Dark Age Britain: England, Scotland and Wales c.500–c.1050 by A. Williams, A. P. Smyth, and D. P. Kirby, Seaby, London, 1991.

The Age of Arthur. A History of the British Isles from 350 to 650 by J. Morris, Phillimore, Chichester, UK, 1977.

Nennius. British History and the Welsh Annals, edited and translated by J. Morris, Phillimore, Chichester, 1980.

The Mabinogion, translated by J. Gantz, Penguin, London, 1976.

The History of the Kings of Britain by Geoffrey of Monmouth, translated by L. Thorpe, Penguin, London, 1966.

A History of the English Church and People, by Bede, translated by L. Sherley-Price, Penguin, London, 1955.

Sources of the Grail: An Anthology, selected and introduced by J. Matthews. Floris Books, Edinburgh, 1996.

Celtic Britain by C. Thomas, Thames and Hudson, London, 1986.

The Origins of Anglo-Saxon Kingdoms, edited by S. Bassett, Leicester University Press, 1989.

EUROPE

The Early Slavs by P. M. Dolukhanov, Longman, London, 1996.

The Merovingian Kingdoms 450–751 by I. Wood, Longman, London, 1994.

The History of the Franks by Gregory of Tours, translated by L. Thorpe, Penguin, London, 1974.

The Goths in Spain by E. A. Thompson, Oxford University Press, 1969.

Law and Society in the Visigothic Kingdom by D. King, Cambridge University Press, 1972.

The New Penguin Atlas of Medieval History by C. McEvedy, Penguin, 1998.

FAR EAST AND SOUTHEAST ASIA

A New History of Korea by Ki-baik Lee, translated by E. W. Wagner with E. J. Shultz, Harvard University Press, 1984.

The Emergence of Japanese Kingship by J. R. Piggott, Stanford University Press, 1997.

Nihongi. Chronicles of Japan from the Earliest Times to AD 697, translated by W. G. Aston, Charles E. Tuttle Company, Rutland, Vermont, and Tokyo, 1972, 1993.

The Sui Dynasty by A. Wright. Alfred A. Knopf, New York, 1978.

The Indianized States of Southeast Asia by G. Coedés, The University Press of Hawaii, 1968.

AMERICAS

Teotihuacan: An Experiment in Living by E. Pasztory, University of Oklahoma Press, 1997.

The Collapse of Ancient States and Civilizations, edited by N. Yoffe and G. L. Cowgill, The University of Arizona Press, 1988.

Life and Death in the Ancient City of Teotihuacan by R. Storey, University of Alabama Press, 1992.

The Maya by M. D. Coe, Thames and Hudson, London, 1987.

Breaking the Maya Code by M. D. Coe, Thames and Hudson, London, 1992.

Ancient North America. The Archaeology of a Continent by B. M. Fagan, Thames and Hudson, 1991.

The Incas and Their Ancestors. The Archaeology of Peru by M. E. Moseley, Thames & Hudson, London, 1992.

The Tiwanaku: Portrait of an Andean Civilization by A. L. Kolata, Blackwell Publishers, Cambridge, USA.

Akapana: Una Piramide en el Centro del Mundo by L. Manzanilla, UNAM, Mexico, 1992.

Huari Administrative Structure: Prehistoric Monumental Architecture and State Government, edited by W. H. Isbell and G. F. McEwan, Dumbarton Oaks, Washington, 1991.

A L'ombre du Cerro Blanco, edited by C. Chapdelaine, Department of Anthropology, University of Montreal, 1997.

The Lines of Nasca, edited by A. Aveni, The American Philosophical Society, Philadelphia, 1990.

Lines to the Mountain Gods: Nazca and the Mysteries of Peru by E. Hadingham, Random House, 1987.

Pathways to the Gods: The Mystery of the Andes Lines by T. Morrison, Paladin Books, 1980.

TREE RINGS, VOLCANOLOGY, AND ARCHAEOLOGICAL SCIENCE

A Slice through Time: Dendrochronology and Precision Dating, by M. G. L. Baillie, Routledge, London, 1995.

Exodus to Arthur: Catastrophic Encounters with Comets by M. G. L. Baillie, Batsford, London, 1999.

The Year Without a Summer: World Climate in 1816, edited by C. R. Harrington, Canadian Museum of Nature, Ottawa, 1992.

Krakatau 1883: The Volcanic Eruption and Its Effects by T. Simkin and R. Fiske, Smithsonian Institution Press, Washington, D.C., 1983.

Krakatau: The Destruction and Reassembly of an Island Ecosystem by I. Thornton, Harvard University Press, 1996.

Volcanoes of the World, second edition, by T. Simkin and L. Siebert, Smithsonian Institution, Washington, D.C., 1994.

Science-based Dating in Archaeology by M. J. Aitken, Longman, London, 1990.

INDEX